TRUE CRIME

Mafia

**BY
THE EDITORS OF
TIME-LIFE BOOKS**
Alexandria, Virginia

Mafia

CORLEONE, SICILY

1

Sicilian Roots

The man standing before the bench in the federal courtroom in Brooklyn was the defendant, yet he was the most commanding presence in the room. For one thing, he looked wealthy. His thick mane of gray and silver hair was deftly barbered, and the dark suit that defined his muscular frame had obviously never hung on a retail rack. Aside from being well turned out, the man was handsome, his sturdy, middle-aged good looks having served him well in a career that had been unusually well photographed and thoroughly documented in the press. Indeed, he was a darling of the tabloid newspapers, which had accorded him such nicknames as the Dapper Don for his tailoring and the Teflon Don for his nimble sidestepping of full legal retribution for his numerous crimes.

But it was not merely looks and clothes that made this man an arresting figure. Something about him—his attitude, his aggressively erect posture, his swaggering walk, his defiant sneer—exuded crude power. Even if one did not know that John Gotti was the boss of the largest Mafia family in America, he was clearly a man to be reckoned with. On this June day in 1992, as Gotti was sentenced to life in prison for murder and various other evildoing, he appeared sublimely unconcerned. These legal proceedings were merely a nuisance, he seemed to suggest, hardly even worthy of his contempt. When the judge had asked him before sentencing whether he had anything to say, Gotti's only answer was a curt shake of the head.

However, his codefendant and one-time underboss, Frank Locascio, did have something to say. "I am guilty of being a good friend of John Gotti," Locascio proclaimed, "and if there was more men like John Gotti on this earth, we would have a better country."

Outside the courthouse, Locascio's sentiments reverberated. A crowd of some 1,000 people had gathered in protest as Gotti was being sentenced, a vocal, angry crowd. "Free John Gotti!" the protesters yelled. "Justice for all means justice for John!" In time the demonstrators turned ugly, surging against lawmen who locked arms to protect the courthouse doors. Unable to storm the building, the crowd overturned a marshal's car and smashed the windshields of three other vehicles before finally going home.

It was not exactly a spontaneous demonstration. Fliers posted in Gotti-friendly neighborhoods in Brooklyn and Queens had touted the event, and buses had ferried many of the protesters to the courthouse—all courtesy of Gotti's public relations apparatus. But if the protest was not wholly from the grass roots, neither was it wholly insincere. If there were hired hoodlums in the crowd, there were also honest people who'd worked hard and obeyed the law all their lives, and they truly revered John Gotti, a man whose criminal record dated back three and a half decades. "We're not going to forget someone who has been part of our community for years," a beauty parlor owner said. "He's like a member of the family."

To millions of Americans watching such comments on the evening news, the crowd's reaction seemed incomprehensible, perhaps even pitiable. Who was Gotti, after all, but another well-upholstered thug who'd finally got what was coming to him? And how could this murderous mobster command such allegiance? The crowd at the courthouse must have been prompted by either fear or ignorance or both, some thought.

But there was another way to view the day's events, a way that was, if not more accurate, at least more comprehensive. From this vantage point, Gotti was merely the latest player in an ancient drama, one whose origins were older than Christianity and whose native soil was an ocean away from Brooklyn. People whose ancestry stretched back to the teeming streets of Naples, as Gotti's did, or to the rugged, gang-infested southern Italian provinces of Campania and Calabria and Basilicata, were able, perhaps, to take this broader view. Almost certainly, Americans with ancestral roots in the parched rock of Sicily felt the age-old undercurrents of loyalty and betrayal and death that eddied about John Gotti and his ilk.

Not that all Italian-Americans admired John Gotti by any means, or that they venerated his position as a Mafia don, or that they failed to equate the words *Mafia* and *crime*. But they probably also understood that concepts such as criminal or legal, sinful or moral, shameful or honorable, can

---

In Palermo in 1983, a small-time mafioso lies dead while his wife *(seated)* and two daughters reenact an ancient Sicilian drama: mourning a victim of vendetta. Violent death is familiar in the Mafia's island birthplace.

A contemporary map shows Sicily's strategic location in the Mediterranean Sea.

depend on the circumstances that shape or surround them. In Sicily, where the Mafia was born, people had understood such things for a long, long time.

Many nations have, in their time, brought forth secret societies outside the rule of law. The Chinese have produced their tongs and triads, the English of the Tudor and Stuart eras their tribes of thieves, with customs and a language of their own, the modern Colombians their drug cartels. But nowhere else is the history of a land and people so inextricably bound up with that of a criminal brotherhood as on the troubled island of Sicily, three miles across the Strait of Messina from Italy's southwestern coast.

On a map it appears that Sicily has just been kicked into the Mediterranean Sea by the toe of the Italian Boot, and the metaphor is apt. For nearly 3,000 years Sicily was kicked around, fair game for a long succession of foreign conquerors. The island's olive groves and grain were enticing, but its greatest value lay in its strategic location at the crossroads of major Mediterranean trade routes. Sicily was commercially and militarily attractive to the Phoenicians and Greeks and Carthaginians who overran it beginning in the eighth century BC, and these invaders were followed in time by Romans, Byzantines, Arabs, Normans, Catalans, Spaniards, Austrians, and French, among others.

Sicilian history thus became a history of foreign occupation and foreign depredation. Century after century, one outside power after another swarmed over the island's stony slopes, swept up the hard-won harvests from its vineyards and olive groves and wheat fields, took the lion's share of its scarce water, and imposed alien rule on a native population whose only enduring birthright was poverty. Most of the time, the center of power was far from the island—in Athens or Rome or Constantinople, or Madrid or Vienna. Sicily's destiny, it seemed, was to languish on the fringes of the empires that claimed her. The empires weren't all the same: Some were more despotic, some more benign. All, however, were foreign, and none had as its prime objective the welfare of Sicily.

The foreigners left their marks on the island, deep or shallow. They intermarried with the locals, influenced the architecture, brought new gods or deposed old ones. But as the alien powers came and went, most of Sicily's common people—townsfolk and peasants—developed a bedrock culture of their own: a way of thinking and living that owed a bitter debt to the hated parade of marauding foreigners.

Understandably enough, the Sicilian mind-set was cynical and profoundly pessimistic. Oppressed for so long, Sicilians became a silent, clannish people, secretive, distrustful, wary of all outsiders, resentful and suspicious of "legitimate" authority. The very notion of legitimate rule eventually became meaningless, not to say a bad joke. Legitimacy was merely tyranny's threadbare cloak, passed from one despot to the next over the years. Law was foreign law—arbitrary, changeable, never sought or sanctioned by the people expected to obey it. There was nothing intrinsically good about law; it was morally irrelevant and thus not deserving of respect. "The law is for the rich, the gallows for the poor, and justice for the fools," says an old Sicilian proverb.

In Sicily's harsh political climate, morality was stern but circumstantial. The moral Sicilian took care of his own. He owed honesty and loyalty to his family—his family by blood or by friendship and blood oath—not to any transient, exploitative ruler who cared nothing for him or his kind. The moral Sicilian had little or no compunction about lying, cheating, stealing, or even killing, as long as his victims were outsiders. And why not? The outsiders were sure to be vicious predators themselves; history had proved that.

In Sicily, the man to be respected and admired was the man who resisted. He was the man who never betrayed his fellows, who guarded his family's secrets as jealously as its goods, who remained silent before strangers at all costs—silent even under torture, silent unto death. The man of honor was the native son who was strong enough and powerful enough to live on his own terms. He defended his own honor; he never looked to any outsider for help. Never mind that his path toward power might be brutal or corrupt: Sicilians were hardly strangers to brutality and corruption. What mattered was that the power belonged to one of their own.

Sicilians in a medieval mountain village, hiding a homegrown bandit from the government constabulary; Italian-Americans on the steps of a federal courthouse in Brooklyn, decrying the injustice done to a man they knew and respected. They are worlds apart in time and distance, but close in spirit.

Largely in response to the ever-present foreigners, criminal secret societies of one sort or another flourished in Sicily from time immemorial.

An 18th-century house fortified against bandit attacks sits on a hill near the town of Gangi in central Sicily, commanding a view of the rocky, sun-baked landscape.

They called themselves by many different names over the centuries, but in spirit and structure they were all pretty much alike: clannish brother-hoods of intense but narrow loyalties, organized in hierarchical fashion with a chieftain, his lieutenants, and their followers. Changing little with time, bandit tribes operated mostly in rural areas, in the rocky, desolate western and central interior of the island. Their trade of choice was cattle rustling.

The cattle being rustled invariably belonged to landowning nobles of foreign extraction, so local folk usually didn't find the crime particularly objectionable. In fact, they often held in high esteem the bandit chieftains who were good at their work, and in due course many of these leaders began to take on a kind of magisterial authority in their various territories, becoming part of a rough, homemade, informal justice system that grew up in Sicily in the absence of a reliable formal one. Governments came and went, but the brotherhoods persisted. Technically, they always operated outside the law. But in a more realistic sense, they *were* the law. Providing continuity and small but accessible pockets of local power, leaders of the secret societies were looked to for settling disputes and keeping order in a hinterland that no "legitimate" government could ever penetrate.

Most of these rural outlaws served themselves first and foremost; but some were a bulwark against oppressive feudal landlords, and romantic legends grew up about them. They were seen as Sicilian Robin Hoods, stinging the rich and championing the downtrodden. Like most legends, however, these tapestries were woven around a fairly slender thread of truth: Violence usually underlay the power of the bandit leaders. Dangerous to anyone who crossed them, they were feared at least as much as they were respected. And, as for protecting the downtrodden, the rural bandits as often as not did just the opposite. One of their most lucrative pursuits was hiring themselves out to rich nobles to keep the peasants in line and to otherwise guarantee the landowners' security and peace of mind. Toughs who specialized in this work would come to be called *campieri*.

By the 19th century, however, the age-old feudal system in rural Sicily was disintegrating—a collapse that was long overdue. Ever since the Romans ruled Sicily in the third and second centuries BC, the island's farmable land had been divided into vast estates owned by powerful aristocrats. Over the centuries, the nobles were for the most part parasites, living off the wealth of the land, putting little or nothing into its improvement, and letting surplus ground lie fallow instead of allowing peasants to farm it for themselves. As the rocky land was played out and the peasants grew more resentful and restless, many nobles decided to leave the sullen poverty of the rural outland and move their households to the capital city of Palermo or some other part of the fertile, fragrant coastal plain. Life in the cities was far more sophisticated, and less dangerous as well.

This migration, resulting in a host of absentee landlords, wrote an important chapter in the making of the Mafia. To protect the interests of the new nonresident nobility, a new class of middlemen—the *gabelloti*—emerged. Originally hired by the aristocrats to run their estates, the gabelloti soon became the real power in the land. These local managers could be benevolent or despotic at will. Some gabelloti

earned praise as shields of the poor, but others used their positions to extort bribes and protection money from both the landlords and the peasants. A peasant on the middleman's bad side might lose all chance of work and see his family starve. But the noble employers could also be made to suffer if they didn't pay enough to protect their crops and livestock. An enterprising gabelloto might not stop at simple extortion. Some of these middlemen actually replaced the landlords they worked for by coercing their employers into selling them their land.

To enforce his power, a gabelloto assembled his own campieri, or henchmen, to supervise day-to-day farming, gather taxes, and keep the peasants docile. Mounted on horseback, the field guards bullied the workers and enforced bloody discipline when their charges stepped out of line. These overseers, demanding obedience, became known as the "men of respect"—a term that would soon come into use among men of the Mafia.

The men of respect merged into the Mafia, as did members of criminal bands called *cosche* who sometimes swelled the campieri and gabelloti ranks. The name cosche—the singular is *cosca*—refers to the artichoke or thistle, whose overlapping leaves protect a central core and are not easily pried apart. The core of the criminal cosca was a boss, protected by tight-knit layers of loyal strong-arm men.

The cosche expanded homegrown crime beyond the traditional cattle rustling. They robbed and murdered wayfarers from time to time, and wielding fear as their most effective weapon, they—like the gabelloti—were efficient extortionists. They charged protection fees to peasants who wanted to ensure that their produce made the trip to market without incident. Along with diversifying their activities, the cosche also expanded the traditional range of Sicilian banditry: They operated not only in the countryside but in the cities, notably in Palermo on the island's north coast. Sophisticated urban cosche sucked protection money from all sorts of legitimate businesses in the city and coopted public officials to gain control of various lucrative contracts.

Sicilian criminality was evolving with the times, but the new brotherhoods shared with older ones a distinct moral code: Members of each cosca policed themselves through rigid rules of conduct. According to tradition, women and children were not to be harmed: Outside the concealing walls of the household—where the patriarch could raise his hand to anyone—violence was something done only by men to other men. Loyalty to the cosca—the term *family* would soon supplant cosca—was paramount. Slights against tribal honor had to be avenged, and vengeance called forth vengeance; vendettas, as the battles among the clans were called, spun out for generations. But betrayal to the police—not only of one's comrades, but even of vendetta targets or rival criminals—was absolutely forbidden. Such was the code of *omertà*.

Omertà was and is a code of silence, of the sealing of lips and the closing of ranks. But it also implies a broader moral philosophy. The word's origins are variously given as a corruption of the Spanish *hombredad*—being a man—or an elaboration on the Italian word for man, *uomo*, or its equivalent in Sicilian dialect, *omu*. In any case, to embrace omertà was to be manly, or to behave like a man. "The man who is really a man," says a peasant proverb, "reveals nothing, not even with a dagger through him."

Ordinary people, living normal lives outside the cosche, usually approved of such sentiments. A hard life on tough terrain ruled by strangers had taught Sicilians that only "he who is deaf, blind, and silent lives a hundred years in peace." Even the most law-abiding peasant or shopkeeper saw no reason to cooperate with the agents of any officially constituted authority. In living memory, what had the state in the person of prince or judge or taxgatherer ever done for him? Besides, princes were usually remote, while the local cosca chieftain was—for good or ill—close by. A peasant or tradesman with an instinct for survival knew that his safest course was to stay on the good side of the nearest gang lord, who could become a deadly enemy or a valuable friend.

Life under the gang chieftains was not, however, especially peaceful, since the various tribes fought constantly among themselves over matters of honor or of turf. That was the state of affairs at the middle of the 19th century, when Sicily's smaller history was swallowed up in a larger one: the birth of an Italian republic.

In May of 1860 the liberator Giuseppe Garibaldi landed with his troops in Sicily, launching a campaign that would oust from their mainland and island Italian territories the Spanish Bourbon dynasty that had ruled for more than a century. Garibaldi was an ardent revolutionary and nationalist who envisioned an Italy united under an Italian monarch. He would achieve his goal, helping to knit together a patchwork of principalities that had belonged to various European royal houses. By 1870, Italy, in its modern configuration, was under the rule of Victor Emmanuel II.

Sicily's bandit bands had helped the flamboyant Garibaldi: He embodied the boldness and independence so dear to the Sicilian soul, and he promised the island an end, at long last, to domination by foreigners. Moreover, he would turn out to be good for business. The men of respect would thrive in the period of chaos that followed the revolution.

Revolutions are the stuff of history; unfortunately, the shadowy course of criminal conquests is not so well chronicled. Thus no one ever recorded exactly when and how Sicily's warring criminal factions managed to eliminate or incorporate one another until finally, one was clearly paramount. But this much is known: By the time there was a united Italy, there was also a Mafia in Sicily. It was diffuse and loosely organized, but its existence was a well-established fact of Sicilian life.

By the 1860s, the words *Mafia* and *mafioso*, as applied to a criminal underground and its members, were familiar to ordinary Sicilians. In 1860 and 1863, two comedies of prison life, entitled *The Mafia* and *The Mafiosi of Vicaria*, packed Palermo theaters. Both were wildly popular and were revived hundreds of times in years to come. They portrayed the comfortable lives of a jailed Mafia elite that virtually ran a prison in collusion with the guards. The central character in the second play was a portrait from life, without even a change of name, of a local underworld boss, Joachino Funciazza. It was apparently Funciazza himself who encouraged the plays' coauthors to dramatize his story and supplied them with authentic details of Mafia life: the penchant for nicknames, the private slang, the all-important adherence to the code of omertà, and the disciplinary methods of the chieftain.

The head of a Mafia band was known as a *capo*—a word that reverberates in modern Mafia lore. In Italian *capo* means "head" or "top"—or "boss." Toward the end of the 19th century, capos, of large gangs and small, were familiar figures in Sicilian society. Capos who amassed unusual power or commanded a large and loyal following or won great respect for their strength or wisdom were accorded, informally, a special title: don. The word derived from the Latin *dominus*—lord—and it implied aristocratic status. All dons were capos, but by no means were all capos dons. One capo who indisputably was a don—indeed, a charis-

matic leader so prominent that he is widely regarded as Sicily's first true Mafia godfather—was the celebrated Don Vito Cascio Ferro.

Born in Palermo in 1862, Cascio Ferro came from traditional tough campiere stock: His father was the henchman of a baron whose holdings included the village of Bisacquino. By the time he was in his early twenties, Vito had chalked up his first criminal charge—for assault—in an official criminal résumé that would encompass murder, arson, kidnapping, and extortion, among other things. He was, however, no run-of-the-mill thug. A good-looking man with big brown eyes and a taste for flowered cravats and well-cut frock coats, he boasted a commanding personality and a taste for both gambling and the company of ladies.

Don Vito applied his considerable intelligence to perfecting and modernizing the underworld trade of extortion. The old-time cosche had often pursued a kind of scorched-earth policy, bleeding their victims dry, expanding only by moving on to new prey. Cascio Ferro found this method wasteful and suggested a new approach. By charging only a very moderate fee for protection, he reasoned, he could ensure that his victims' businesses survived and prospered sufficiently to provide his organization with a reliable and durable flow of profits. In other words, he propounded the notion that the parasite would have a better chance to thrive if it didn't kill its host.

"You have to skim the cream off the milk without breaking the bottle," Don Vito advised his Mafia brethren. "Don't throw people into bankruptcy with ridiculous demands for money. Offer them your protection instead, help them to make their businesses prosperous, and not only will they be happy to pay, but they'll kiss your hands out of gratitude."

This practice—which became known in Sicilian dialect as the *pizzu,* or "wetting the beak"—was soon applied to all areas of economic activity. As Cascio Ferro had predicted, those on the receiving end of this treatment vastly preferred it to the old ways. In some respects, the pizzu made the people paying for protection feel more like partners than victims. Instead of facing unpredictable and outrageous demands by their local extortionist, traders and farmers could anticipate their protection costs and figure them into their budgets as a necessary expense. In addition, they could expect something for their money: They could rely on their hidden protectors when they needed strings pulled and fa-

A Sicilian woman dressed in traditional mourning black weeps on a coffin. Although omertà is a code of manly honor, its basic tenents of clannishness, toughness, and silence also apply to women. Once a sobbing, black-clad woman from the town of Corleone was walking in a funeral procession, following the coffin of the latest victim in a string of Mafia killings in the town. A journalist approached her and asked, "Who was killed?" "Why?" replied the woman through her tears, "Is anyone dead?"

What's in a Name?

Although the term didn't appear in dictionaries until the late 1860s, *Mafia* was a concept long understood by Sicilians. A dialect word from the poorer districts of Palermo, mafia—or the related adjectives, *mafioso* and *mafiosa*—referred to excellence, grace, perfection, beauty. Applied to a man, mafia denoted strength, determination, self-reliance, and honor: A man who was mafioso protected his own interests. He was brave and bold, a man of action, a man not to be taken lightly. More ominously, he was a man prepared to be a law unto himself if necessary.

While the meaning of the word is clear, its origins are less so. Some theories trace its ancestry to the struggle of 13th-century Sicilian nationalists against French rule. "Morte alla Francia, Italia anela!" was their cry ("Death to France, Italy groans!"), forming the acronym MAFIA. Others claim the word derives from the battle cry of rebels who slaughtered thousands of Frenchmen after a French soldier raped a Palermo maiden on her wedding day on Easter Monday 1282. Their slogan echoed the wails of the woman's mother, "Ma fia, ma fia" ("My daughter, my daughter"). Another theory holds that Mafia was the name of a secret sect that followed the patriot Giuseppe Mazzini, ally of Giuseppe Garibaldi, in the 19th-century guerrilla rebellion against the Bourbon monarchy. Again, the word was the acronym for a slogan: "Mazzini autorizza furti, incendi, avvelenamenti" ("Mazzini authorizes theft, arson, poisoning").

Colorful as these explanations may be, the word Mafia is most likely Arabic in origin. Some scholars assert that it comes from the Arabic *mahias,* meaning bold man, or from *Ma afir,* the name of an Arab tribe that ruled Palermo some time between the ninth and 11th centuries. Others believe the word derives from *mu,* safety or strength, and *afah,* meaning to secure or protect—hence an organization that takes care of its members.

Whatever its source, when the term crossed the Atlantic to the United States aboard immigrant ships, it was soon well understood among city dwellers in America: Mafia meant gambling, racketeering, prostitution, extortion, embezzlement, and murder. Mafia meant organized crime.

Vito Cascio Ferro cradles a puppy while a young nephew holds a shotgun in this 1925 photo. The domestic scene with the shotgun as a jarring element reflects two aspects of the legendary Mafia don: gentle man of respect and remorseless killer.

vors granted. Of course, paying the protection money was still not optional, but a client who failed to pay on time had only himself to blame when his premises or products met with an unfortunate accident.

The pizzu was not Don Vito's only contribution to the development of the Mafia. Around the turn of the century he traveled to America to cement the links between the Sicilian Mafia and the emergent criminal brotherhood on the other side of the Atlantic *(page 56).* He stayed only four years or so, but he made his mark, setting up formal channels of communication between the Italian-American Mafia gangs and their Sicilian counterparts that remain open even to this day.

Back home in Sicily, Cascio Ferro found his prestige growing ever greater. He held sway over the Mafia cosche in at least seven country towns and in several parts of Palermo, and his word was honored by the capos of gangs that he didn't officially control. Prominent figures on both sides of the law owed him favors, and rumor had it that he could recover any goods stolen in Sicily if he felt kindly disposed to the victim of the theft. In Palermo the upper classes welcomed him to their balls and salons. His fondness for art, music, and poetry became well known, even though he'd first learned to read and write in adulthood when his wife—a schoolmistress from Bisacquino—took him in hand.

It was largely because of Don Vito's reputation and force of personality that the brotherhood was able to expand its influence, both within Sicily and to the powerful institutions on the Italian mainland: banks, industrial plants, and the political machinery of state. In Rome, Sicilian legislators knew what was expected of them. In exchange for Mafia support that had won them their seats, they made sure that no new laws or inconvenient reforms troubled the still waters of island life. The dons were, after all, Sicily's entrenched power; they were deeply conservative, happiest with the status quo.

At the beginning of the 1920s, however, the Italian climate suddenly turned unhealthy for the Mafia. Cascio Ferro's troubles began with the ascendancy of Fascist dictator Benito Mussolini, who became Italy's premier in 1922. On a visit to Sicily in 1924, Mussolini suffered humiliation at the hands of the Mafia establishment. Arriving in the small town of Piana dei Greci (now called Piana degli Albanesi), surrounded by a phalanx of leather-jacketed motorcycle guards, the dictator was gently chided by the local mafioso

mayor. "There is no need for so many police," the mayor said. "Your Excellency has nothing to fear in this district when you are with me." Mussolini was quick to pick up on the inference that the Mafia, not he, held the whip hand in Sicily. The notion was infuriating to the egomaniacal dictator, who saw room for only one absolute power in Italy.

Within a year, Mussolini had installed as prefect of Palermo—the most powerful police position in Sicily—his loyalist Cesare Mori, who'd been prefect of Bologna before receiving the Palermo post. Mori's task was to purge the government of all corrupt bureaucrats under Mafia control and replace them with Fascists obedient to il Duce.

Mori discovered that the assignment had its difficulties. More than once his new appointees were murdered. Several were cut down in broad daylight on the bustling streets of Palermo, yet somehow no witnesses to these killings could ever be found.

But if Mori had problems, he also caused them; the Mafia was made to suffer greatly. For four years legal rights were suspended, torture was used to extract confessions, and suspected mafiosi were tried and convicted of nonexistent crimes. At the peak of the purge, there were sometimes 100 arrests in a single night. As a Sicilian himself, Mori understood that killings and arrests were not enough to undercut the popularity and power enjoyed by the men of respect. He also understood the uses of pageantry and symbolism: He encouraged noisy ceremonies of welcome when he visited the Mafia-dominated towns in the west of the island and liked to be photographed taking part in arrests, resplendent in an ornate Fascist uniform alongside handcuffed prisoners kneeling in the dust.

As soon as the Fascist purge began, Cascio Ferro sprang into action, organizing a secret escape route for several hundred young mafiosi. Night after night fishing boats set sail, carrying clandestine human cargo to Tunis in North Africa or to the French city of Marseilles. From these ports, they took ship for the New World. Some traveled directly to New York; others used more circuitous routes, via Cuba or Canada, entering the United States through Miami, Tampa, and other southern ports, or crossing the Great Lakes into Buffalo and Detroit. Once landed, they were taken under the protection of Don Vito's transatlantic colleagues. These émigrés included several young men who would become heads of important American Mafia families, among them Carlo Gambino and Joseph Bonanno.

Prefect of Palermo Cesare Mori, shown here in his Fascist uniform, carried out dictator Benito Mussolini's purge of the Sicilian Mafia.

Don Vito Cascio Ferro, however, could not or would not save himself. In the late 1920s he was framed and convicted on a trumped-up charge involving a double murder. When the trial was over, he broke the silence he'd maintained throughout the proceedings to address the court. "Gentlemen," he remarked contemptuously, "since you have been unable to find any evidence for the numerous crimes I did commit, you are reduced to condemning me for the only one I have not." Cascio Ferro died in prison—an ignominious end for the first *capo di tutti capi*—boss of all bosses.

Even before the purges, some mafiosi had seen which way the political wind was blowing and made their own accommodations with the Fascists. This sort of adaptability, more pragmatic than heroic, would become a Mafia hallmark. Foremost among the early-20th-century mafiosi who practiced it was Don Calogero Vizzini of the town of Villalba.

Vizzini had ingratiated himself with Mussolini's party even before its rise to power by making impressive campaign contributions and by protecting an up-and-coming Fascist activist who'd murdered a political enemy. When the killer became an undersecretary of state in Mussolini's government, he was able to return the favor. There was no way that Vizzini could remain untouched by the anti-Mafia purge, but his government friends in high places made sure that his sentence was the merest tap on the wrist: five years' internment in a remote village. And he didn't need to chafe for long under even this mild restriction, for the undersecretary whose skin he'd saved quickly rescinded the order.

Wily and ruthless, Vizzini was the very model of a successful Mafia don. He had been born in 1877 into a modest farming family in a bandit-infested district of west-central Sicily. His parents were not particularly well-off, but they considered themselves superior to their neighbors, for they had relatives in the hierarchy of the Catholic church. Vizzini's maternal uncle and a cousin were priests, and both of them rose quickly to the rank of bishop; two of Calogero's younger brothers followed their kinsmen into the religious life.

Vizzini had far more worldly ambitions. He couldn't read or write, apart from a poorly scrawled attempt at a signature, but by the time he died—of natural causes, remarkably, at the age of 77—he possessed a vast fortune, controlled a sprawling criminal empire, and could count on the loyalty of an invisible army of powerful men who owed him a lifetime of favors.

Vizzini's force of personality surfaced early. At the age of 17 he developed an adolescent crush on a girl whose father owned the town ice-cream parlor in Villalba. She already had an admirer, a magistrate's clerk, and Vizzini decided to warn him off. Swaggering into the ice-cream shop with a gang of friends, he started a brawl and beat up his rival. Vizzini was dragged off to the police station, where his uncle, the priest, pulled the necessary strings to set him free. Understanding realities, the injured clerk dropped all charges—and the girl as well. Whatever young Calogero's intentions toward the girl, marriage had evidently not been part of the plan. But so effectively had Vizzini marked out his territory that no other suitor ever dared approach her. More than half a century later she could still be seen, an elderly spinster, on the dreary streets of her native town.

To serve his criminal apprenticeship, Vizzini fell in with a particularly savage brigand named Gervasi, whose gang preyed upon the local peasantry. Every farmer who carried his wheat from Villalba to the mill, and his flour back again, lived in fear of bandit raids. Young Vizzini offered to free his neighbors from this dangerous task by conveying their wheat to the mill himself. Having come to an understanding with his bandit friends, he was able to guarantee safe passage. In exchange, he exacted a hefty fee, amounting to ransom, for each sack he transported. With the funds he amassed from this racket and other crimes, he was able to acquire land and become a gabelloto—a traditional first step on the path to Mafia power.

The business of extortion was a delicate art, requiring a fine understanding of human nature. By relieving his clients of the need to risk life and livelihood on the lonely road to the mill, Vizzini could count not only on their money but on their gratitude. And once he controlled land and could offer employment, he found fresh opportunities for putting people in his debt. By proffering help and protection to the weak, he would be perceived as a patron instead of a parasite. He had learned the secret shared by many bosses who would climb high in Mafia ranks: Violence was not the only coin that purchased obedience and respect.

By 1915, when Italy entered World War I, Calogero Vizzini—now familiar to all the countryside as Zu Calò—Uncle Calò—controlled his own sizable Mafia network. He was swift to see the chances for profit that the war brought with it and became an energetic black-marketeer. But his greatest coup took place when military commissioners arrived to commandeer horses and mules for the Italian army.

Don Calò conjured up three ways to profit from the army's need. For farmers who didn't want to lose their precious beasts of burden, he would—for a fee—ensure that these animals somehow evaded the draft. For owners of tired old hacks long past their best, he could arrange a handsome purchase price far in excess of the beasts' real worth. A horse's true condition might, with skill, be disguised just long enough to fool an inspector; otherwise, the army's own purchasing agents could be persuaded to look the other way when some worn-out nag shambled into their holding pens. Finally, a good supply of healthy horses could indeed be ensured if Vizzini's men went out and stole them from those who hadn't purchased sufficient protection against this misfortune.

The army soon found itself responsible for every aged and creaky horse or mule in the western interior. In compensation, however, the cavalry also became the proud possessor of more than 80 fine, strong horses whose previous owners had never intended to make such a generous contribution.

Eventually, army authorities woke up to the plot. Don Calò—along with several civilian and highly placed military accomplices—was hauled up before a military court, charged with sabotaging the war effort. But one by one, all the prosecution witnesses stood up in court and retracted their original statements. They may have suddenly recalled the tribal code of omertà, or they may have been quietly convinced by friends of Zu Calò that their own health and that of their families might suffer if they spoke. Either way, no force could now budge them. Nine of the reluctant witnesses were promptly tried and convicted for noncooperation and supplying false testimony, but none felt moved to change his mind. The case against Vizzini and his associates collapsed, like scores of other Mafia trials before and after it, for lack of evidence.

This episode enhanced Don Calò's reputation within the Sicilian brotherhood. So did his successful evasion, on the same terms of witnesses suddenly falling silent, of murder and robbery charges in 1922.

During the purges that followed, while so many other mafiosi fled to America or languished in Mussolini's jails, Don Calò went into business with several Fascist entrepreneurs to mine the rich supplies of sulfur from the Sicilian hills. When his partners discovered that he was mining their pockets even more energetically than he was mining sulfur, they had him arrested and charged with fraud and other crimes. These charges, like so many others, could never be made to stick.

In time, the sulfur scheme and other shifty behavior cost Vizzini his credibility with the Fascist regime. But the loss was more than amply compensated for by his increased prestige among his fellow mafiosi. He built up a network of cosche covering a large chunk of Sicily while making himself and his associates very rich through skillful black-marketeering. And, as Vizzini's formidable luck would have it, his break with the Fascists was opportune: When the Allied forces finally arrived on the island in 1943, Don Calò's anti-Fascist credentials were sufficiently well established for the Allies to regard him as a friendly power in the land.

From the American point of view midway in a desperate war, mafiosi were less underworld chieftains than anti-Fascist community leaders—which, indeed, they were. Vizzini and other capos were quick to see that the fortunes of war were turning against the Fascists, and they gave invaluable aid to the advancing Allies. Once the Occupation was secured and the local Fascist regime removed, the Americans called on their powerful new friends to help maintain civic order.

Throughout most of Sicily, Vizzini became the man to know. He commuted between his home base in the interior and Palermo, where the occupying forces made sure he had a suite at his disposal in the one hotel still standing. He took advantage of unsettled conditions to build up his own connections, embracing politicians of all persuasions, left and right alike, befriending those he judged safe bets for future elevation in the postwar government, doing favors and thereby storing up negotiable goodwill, in the ancient way of the brotherhoods. Meanwhile, as thanks for his efforts on their behalf, the Allied forces made him mayor of his native Villalba.

Together with other important mafiosi—and a number of blameless civilians—Vizzini gave some support after the war to the newly established Sicilian Separatist party. The Mafia had generally managed to buy benign neglect from mainland politicians, but the new postwar world brought a tantalizing prospect of a Sicily that would be completely free from the attentions of any inconveniently reform-minded government in Rome.

In the end, however, Don Calò's natural conservatism prevailed, and he withdrew his support from the separatists. The Mafia prospered best in an atmosphere where nothing changed, where people knew their places, and where the local strongman was the best force for maintaining order. Vizzini gave his allegiance to the mainstream Christian Democratic party and turned his energies against the fledgling socialist movement springing up in his native territory.

Peasants returning from military service with dangerous new ideas about land reform and trade unions had to be taught a lesson. When a socialist rally was held in Villalba's town square, Don Calò arrived with a gang of bodyguards to disrupt the proceedings. The crowd was sparse: Most Villalbans knew their don's view of left-wingers and wisely stayed out of sight, catching what they could of the fiery speeches from behind half-shuttered windows. The speaker, a dedicated activist, launched into an explanation of why the peasants were poor and exploited. At this moment, Don Calò intervened.

A split second later, his henchmen opened fire. At the same time, hand grenades exploded. Eighteen people were badly injured. Vizzini and his lieutenants were charged with attempted massacre, but their friends in the legal system saw that the case wound its way at a snail's pace through the courts, taking 14 years to be resolved. Even those eventually found guilty received a variety of amnesties and pardons, and no one was ever jailed.

Violence of the sort directed at the socialist speaker was not Don Calò's preferred method of operating. For years he projected the image of a benevolent despot in Villalba. Every morning he would emerge from his house on the square and enjoy a promenade in the company of his brother the priest. The timing of the walk, its gentle pace, the don's meditative demeanor as he strolled with hands clasped behind his back, the pause for espresso at his usual table at the café on the square, were rituals that never varied, as fixed as the ringing of the bells for Mass.

This was Vizzini's time for public audiences. Some wished only to pay their respects by kissing his hand or to offer thanks for favors granted. Others had requests. A woman dressed in funereal black might ask the don to trace a missing son. Peasants in scuffed and dusty boots doffed their caps and asked the don's intervention in some dispute over a boundary or a water source. Men wearing expensive city suits emerged from their cars and waited their turn to pursue unspecified matters of business.

All came with an unshakable faith that Don Calò would help them in their time of need. Vizzini smiled on everyone, listened attentively, passed judgment, dispensed advice, or dispatched his waiting followers to deal with a crisis that brooked no delay.

By some accounts, Don Calò's end was almost as idyllic as his daily procession through the piazza. In the summer of 1954, while being driven home to Villalba, the 77-year-old mafioso suffered a heart attack. His friends lifted him carefully from the car and placed him on the grass verge at the roadside, perhaps hoping the fresh mountain air would revive him. "How beautiful life is!" he told his companions, and slipped away.

His funeral was regal. Four black horses, crowned with black plumes, drew the hearse that bore his body. Two important Mafia chieftains were among the pallbearers for their old friend and colleague. Scores of churchmen, prominent politicians, mafiosi of all ranks, and hundreds of peasants in full mourning joined the cortege. The air was heavy with the scent of hundreds of wreaths, each bearing a broad black ribbon displaying its sender's name in gilded letters: Every Sicilian who aspired to prominence in public or commercial life made sure to send his conspicuously labeled floral offering.

In 1897, at the age of 20, conscript Calogero Vizzini, future Mafia don, wears the uniform of an Italian infantryman.

As a mark of honor, local government offices closed for eight days, as did the Villalba branch of the Christian Democratic party. From the window of every public building, flags hung at half-mast. A black-draped sign on the door of his church proclaimed, "He was a man of honor."

There were those who believed that when Don Calò Vizzini died, the old traditions of the Honored Society—as the Mafia liked to call itself—died with him. A new postwar world had dawned, bringing sweeping changes that touched even the somnolent feudal villages of the Sicilian hinterlands. Within the brotherhood, a new generation now came to the fore.

The man destined to lead a new and more cutthroat modern Mafia began life as a frail and miserable starveling. Born in the winter in 1925, Luciano Liggio was the 10th child of a dirt-poor peasant family in the Mafia stronghold of Corleone. At first the boy seemed unlikely to win the unequal struggle for survival. Generations of bad food and living conditions far inferior to those enjoyed by the horses in any Sicilian aristocrat's stables had done their work. Afflicted in childhood by a crippling disease of the spine, young Luciano struggled to walk upright in the grip of a primitive wooden brace. Eyes older and wiser than their years peered out of a broad face, pain-pinched and deathly pale.

Luciano's parents hoped to make a priest of him: It seemed the only path for a boy so obviously unfit for the backbreaking demands of farm labor. But the priesthood required education, and the youngster disliked school and never even mastered reading and writing. Years later, when he decided it was time to learn, he cornered a schoolteacher and got lessons at gunpoint.

His disability did not prevent Luciano from becoming an expert with the *lupara*—the wolf-gun, as Sicilian peasants called the sawed-off shotgun that they so favored. To polish his marksmanship, the youth spent many hours shooting the heads off sheep and goats. At the age of 20 he found his first human target—a guard on the local landlord's fields who'd caught him stealing wheat and turned him in to police. Liggio shot the guard and killed him. The man's wife witnessed the shooting, and one of Liggio's friends confessed his own part in the murder plot. Even so, Liggio was never convicted, even though the case dragged on for almost 20 years. As in so many trials in Mafia country, the courts could not quite bring themselves to believe the widow—said

to be "incoherent" in her testimony. As for the accomplice's confession, it was presumed to have been extorted.

Thus launched on a career that suited him—killing—Luciano Liggio never looked back. Among the hired toughs of Corleone's Mafia clan, he quickly rose to stardom as a ruthless and efficient murderer. But soon he turned against one of his own. A Mafia capo named Barbaccia controlled the lion's share of cattle rustling, the local underworld's most important industry. Liggio decided to muscle in on the action. If Barbaccia imagined that his own formidable reputation, plus a sinister word of warning, would frighten off the young interloper, he soon discovered his mistake. Liggio and some of his friends shouldered their luparas and went hunting in the mountains, methodically picking off Barbaccia's henchmen. Before their boss could take his revenge, he himself turned up missing.

A successful rustler, Liggio realized, needed a place to graze and slaughter his stolen herds. In the time-honored Mafia tradition, therefore, he became a gabelloto, running an absentee landlord's estate. He got the post by murdering his predecessor, then presenting himself to the landowner to offer condolences for the employee's sudden death.

"I will take the place of the dear departed," he announced. So persuasive was Liggio that the landowner fired his farm hands, allowed his wheat fields to be torn up and replanted with fodder, and agreed never again to set foot on his own estate.

With the profits he made from slaughtering his stolen livestock on his expropriated property, Liggio felt ready to acquire an estate of his own. The estate he chose was ideally suited for his purposes—a tract within the shadow of a remote, mountainous wilderness called Rocca Busambra. The incumbent landlord did not realize his property was for sale until Liggio poisoned his dogs, killed his livestock, burned his crops, cut down his lemon groves, and then paid a personal call.

"Your farm doesn't pay," the bandit observed, indicating the burned stubble and animal carcasses. "You want to sell." The landowner didn't pause to haggle over price, and Liggio, in 1946, at the age of 21, became a landlord.

His new farm was an ideal location for dealing in stolen livestock. It was isolated, far from prying eyes, and easily guarded, yet only 34 miles from Palermo's wholesale meat markets. Night after night, convoys of trucks trundled out of his craggy fastness, crammed with bleeding sides of beef

A fatherly don whose nickname was Uncle Calò, Calogero Vizzini is shown at left shortly before he died of natural causes at the ripe old age of 77. At his well-attended and impressive funeral *(above)* in 1954, pallbearers carried his coffin to the grave site after a hearse drawn by plumed horses led his mourners through the streets of Villalba.

and guarded by a troop of Liggio's thugs from Corleone.

Cattle were not all that was slaughtered near Rocca Busambra. One of the many features that Luciano liked about his property was a deep gap in the rock—a fissure barely three feet wide, but with a sheer drop to a deep and unseen floor. The chasm provided a convenient cemetery for inconvenient corpses. Once dropped into the gap, the bodies of those who incurred Liggio's disfavor were quickly gnawed to pieces by a tribe of resident rats.

Among the shards of bone and bits of rag at the bottom of the chasm lay the remains of one of Liggio's most loathed opponents. No mere Mafia rival, Placido Rizzotto had represented a different kind of threat. He was the district's only left-wing activist, and he irritated both the Mafia and the landlords by trying to rouse the cowed and hungry peasants with ideas about labor unions and land reform. He attacked cattle rustlers in general and accused Liggio in particular of diverting the course of a nearby river for his own use.

One fall evening in 1948 Rizzotto left his parents' house to enjoy a drink with friends at a café in Corleone's town square. According to one witness, the activist was walking through the town's dark streets with a companion sometime later when he was accosted by Liggio, who suggested that Rizzotto join him for "a quiet chat." Rizzotto was not seen again until about a year later when police—having extracted information from two of Liggio's underlings—found the chasm. A team from the local fire brigade hoisted up a heap of remains that included a bit of overcoat instantly recognized by Rizzotto's father. There was also a head whose features had been eaten away by time and rodents, but that still bore hanks of the dead man's distinctive chestnut-colored hair.

There had been at least one innocent witness to Rizzotto's murder. A 12-year-old shepherd boy stumbled into his mother's house, babbling about a terrible sight he'd seen in the darkness, near the gorge at Rocca Busambra. He grew so sick with fright that his mother brought him to Dr. Michele Navarra, head of Corleone's hospital. Dr. Navarra listened to the boy's ravings, then gave him an injection that would, he reassured the worried mother, calm her son and help him sleep. Within minutes the boy was dead. The body was buried quickly and without an autopsy.

Michele Navarra was, it seemed, a man of many interests. He was not only the head of the Corleone hospital but also president of the town's Landowners' Association and head of the local branch of the Christian Democratic party. His energetic work on behalf of the community would eventually bring him the Italian government's honorary title Knight of Merit. Navarra's most important affiliation, however, was with the Mafia. The capo of Corleone's Mafia clan, he was also one of the highest-ranking Mafia bosses in all of Sicily. In the underworld hierarchy, Navarra was much senior to Liggio. Even if the hotheaded young killer had acted without orders in slaying Rizzotto, his capo still felt obliged to protect him from the law.

Nevertheless, rumors about Liggio's involvement in the murder spread, and two of his henchmen were arrested as accomplices. They confessed, but Liggio was ultimately acquitted of the murder for lack of evidence. The star witnesses recanted their confessions at the crucial moment, claiming that they'd been forced into telling these fictions under torture.

Michele Navarra may have protected Liggio, but the two men hated each other. The doctor was a mafioso of the old school, whereas the brash Liggio represented a new breed—one whose role models included the flashy, famous mobsters of New York and Chicago.

The old Mafia godfathers such as Vito Cascio Ferro had exported the seeds of their secret society across the Atlantic, but the New World had worked its alchemy. The men of good Sicilian or Neapolitan stock who ran the underworld in the United States may have retained their old traditions and kept in touch with their cousins in the old country, but they also forged a new kind of criminal culture in their adopted land: fast-paced, crass, and highly citified. Areas of activity such as prostitution and drugs, which might have caused old-fashioned rural Sicilian dons to recoil in horror, were the U.S. underworld's stock in trade—if not at the highest echelon, then certainly among the rank and file.

When these gum-chewing, Brooklyn-accented sons of Sicily came back to the old country—whether as American soldiers, tourists, or court-ordered deportees—they brought their new perspectives with them. Not even Corleone, in its rural remoteness, was immune. Indeed, one of the two men arrested as Liggio's accomplices in the Rizzotto murder was an American mafioso who'd been repatriated.

Coming of age during this time of transition, Luciano Liggio nursed grander ambitions than ceremonious obedience to Dr. Navarra. Inevitably, the new breed and the old clashed in a massive vendetta. At night the streets of Cor-

A sometime healer and sometime hit man, Mafia chieftain Dr. Michele Navarra, in his guise as head of the hospital in Corleone, is the picture of middle-class respectability.

leone were full of gunfire, breaking glass, cries of pain, and shrieking auto tires. Finally, both sides ran out of targets: Twenty-nine members of the Navarra faction—including the doctor himself—and 13 of Liggio's had died. Having inflicted the greater death toll, Liggio was the winner and claimed the spoils—control of Corleone.

The victory was satisfying, but insufficient: Luciano Liggio's native village offered too small a canvas for his criminal talents. Although the little town would remain the heart of his empire, he began looking toward Palermo and beyond. Like many of his Mafia contemporaries, he realized that richer pickings could now be found in the cities than in the stagnant countryside. Sicilian mafiosi would never entirely abandon their old rural trades, such as rustling cattle and monopolizing water, but they saw—and seized—new sources of power and profit.

Postwar Palermo was in the throes of a building boom. Thousands of peasants gave up the thankless struggle to live off the land and flocked into the city's teeming slums. The Italian government began pouring money into Sicily's crumbling capital, sponsoring new housing and other public work projects on a massive scale.

The Mafia could hardly miss the opportunities. There were local officials to court, bribe, or threaten, officials who controlled contracts and building permits. The close alliance between the Mafia and the Christian Democrats, whose party faithful were powerful in Palermo, had to be kept in good trim. Trucking and construction firms were among several business enterprises ripe for plucking, either for outright takeover or as sources of protection money. And while corruption flourished on all fronts, whole districts of the lovely old city were flattened and replaced by vast tracts of jerry-built, substandard housing and polluting industrial plants.

Palermo was uniquely beautiful. Founded as a trading outpost by the Phoenicians as early as the eighth century BC, the city had gleaned from many invading cultures something fine in architecture or decorative arts. Those who had known and loved the ancient capital, however ramshackle its faded splendors, observed that the resulting "sack of Palermo" brought little benefit to its ordinary citizens. But the tiny minority who prospered did so on a grand scale: During a four-year stretch in the early 1960s, for instance, Palermo officials awarded 80 percent of the 4,200 building permits that they controlled to only four individual contractors—all Mafia frontmen. Meanwhile, the expanding city's overtaxed infrastructure—from the corner shops to the wholesale produce market, from the banks to the sewage system, from the hotels to the cemeteries, from the power grid to the docks—lay open to exploitation by the strongest Mafia clans.

The city had long had its own branches of the brotherhood. Now the urban bosses—known collectively in Mafia parlance by the blasphemous epithet *Mammasantissima*—holiest mother of God—had to fight for their territory. Luciano Liggio, up from the countryside, was only one of their new competitors. Many of the mafiosi who'd escaped to America during the Fascist purge had come home—voluntarily or otherwise—ready for action. The resulting underworld family reunions were not always happy. During the 1950s, hundreds of mafiosi were slaughtered in intertribal warfare. Eventually the ruling Mafia council, the Cupola, managed to negotiate a precarious peace, and the shooting temporarily stopped.

By the time the guns fell silent, Liggio's faction held the upper hand. Other families had their share of the action, but it appeared that behind the scenes, most cosche danced to the Corleonesi's tune.

Officially, Liggio was a wanted man: Dr. Navarra's slaying and the murder charge dating back to when Liggio was 20 years old were among the crimes that were still officially unresolved. But his legal status as a fugitive from justice didn't cramp Liggio's style. He moved freely through Pa-

lermo, his well-placed spies making sure that he stayed ahead of the law.

When necessary, Liggio slipped into one of his many disguises. Not every monk who trod with downcast eyes along the pavements—nor every gaudy-jacketed, camera-toting American tourist—was what he seemed to be. At other times the fugitive relied on the protection of his friends among Palermo's upper classes. These worthies would often drive him through the city in a small convoy of luxurious cars, to be saluted with great deference by the white-gloved policemen directing traffic or manning roadblocks.

For some of Palermo's society women, friendship with a Mafia capo offered its own special thrill, and Liggio found a welcome in some of the city's most exclusive salons. Meanwhile, highly placed men often had their own reasons for establishing good relations with the ugly little rustic from Corleone. Such men, claimed one high-ranking Palermo policeman, were lured by Liggio into a web "held together with the spittle of gold and blood. He imprisoned thousands of consciences through corruption and fear. He paid to have the most illustrious physicians, the most beautiful women, the ablest killers."

Reaping the rewards for years of ruthless and bloody effort, Liggio now enjoyed the expansive pleasures of the newly rich. He bought himself a villa worthy of the old nobility, smoked huge cigars, and affected handmade suits. The pallor of poverty was gone, and though his spinal disability couldn't be cured, he now took comfort in the best medical care money could buy. He abandoned his awkward wooden brace in favor of a metal one. He scattered his largess widely, bestowing expensive gifts on his nurses, presenting charitable donations, rewarding his lieutenants for loyal service with flashy cars.

For a while, it seemed there would be few impediments to Liggio's pleasant life in Palermo. Since his precocious entry into crime, he'd been tried and acquitted for murder no fewer than 11 times. Sometimes he would spend long stretches in jail awaiting trial. But, given the Mafia's grip on the legal system and Liggio's own ability to cow witnesses, sooner or later he always walked free. In 1970 an old crime caught up with him: An appeals court overturned his acquittal for the murder of Dr. Navarra. But the sentence—life imprisonment—was passed in the defendant's absence: Liggio had slipped the net.

Equipped with a library of different passports under dif-

Dr. Michele Navarra's dead driver slumps behind the wheel of the doctor's bullet-riddled car. Not visible to the camera, Navarra himself is lying on the seat next to the driver. The doctor was killed in 1958 in a war with his ambitious Mafia underling, Luciano Liggio.

ferent aliases, Liggio vanished from Sicily. Up and down the Italian mainland, he left marks of his passage: New clusters of Mafia activity erupted in areas previously uninfected. Eventually, however, police caught up with him in Milan.

By 1974 Luciano Liggio was serving a life sentence that would take him to several prisons. But that didn't mean that his career was over; he'd merely changed his base of operations. The Mafia had as many friends and puppets inside the prison system as it did in government offices and town halls: Liggio's life would be made as comfortable as possible and his channels of communication kept wide open. On the outside, his trusted Corleonesi lieutenants stood ready to receive his commands. Now, of all times, Luciano Liggio did not intend to stop pulling the strings, for the Honored Society had recently expanded and diversified its activities.

In the early 1990s Liggio was still in prison, and there were two very definite, wholly opposite theories about his activities. One school of thought had it that, jailed and aging, the don was still a major behind-the-scenes Mafia power. The other, more plausible, view was that Liggio, watched too closely to exercise power, was but a relic of the past. It is supposed that he took up painting in prison, turning out bold but rigid canvases, mostly landscapes. There was a one-man show of his work in Palermo, and the paintings sold quite well. But even in his art, Liggio was a creature of controversy: There were credible claims that some of his fellow inmates did the paintings, which he merely enriched with his famous name. In the end, the old mafioso was limited by prison authorities to painting for pleasure and bestowing his works as gifts to fellow convicts.

Luciano Liggio was a transitional figure who came up the old way in the Mafia and prospered in the new. He saw the Honored Society grow from cattle rustling in the feudal countryside to world power and unimaginable wealth. For in the middle of the 1950s the Sicilian brotherhood had made a move that changed everything—its

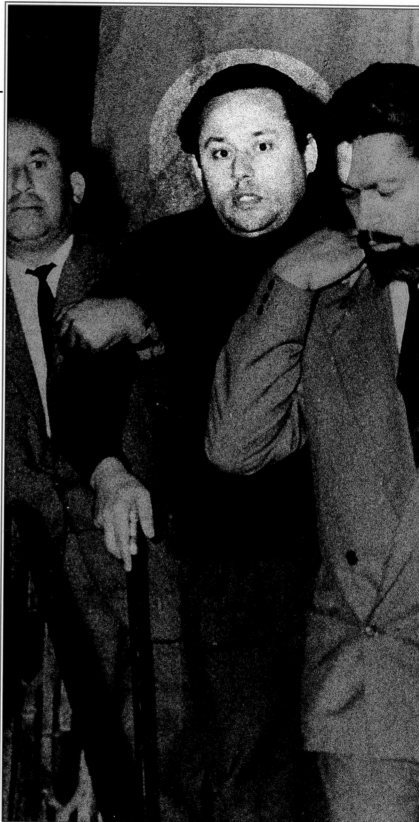

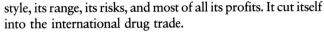

Partially crippled by a spinal defect, Mafia capo Luciano Liggio *(circled)* needs help from authorities to get down a staircase in Corleone during a 1964 arrest. Liggio was acquitted of murder charges 11 times before a legal reversal landed him in jail for life in 1974. In prison he supposedly began producing landscapes such as the Sicilian village street scene below, although critics say he only signed the work of others.

style, its range, its risks, and most of all its profits. It cut itself into the international drug trade.

It began quietly, but explosive secrets can be kept only so long. In 1958, the year that Luciano Liggio took over Corleone from Dr. Navarra, the Mafia's interest in the drug trade came to light purely by chance.

A group of Sicilian fishermen had organized a small maritime police force to combat the use of illegal fishing methods that were depleting the local waters. One night the new motor launch patrolling near Palermo spotted an unidentified fishing boat and bore down for a closer look. Out of the darkness came a blast of machine-gun fire, and the mysterious craft roared away at a speed far beyond the capacity of any fishing boat. The patrol had stumbled on a small link in a hidden chain connecting Sicily with the poppy fields of Asia, the docks of New York, and the back alleys of cities throughout the Western world that were the sites of heroin trafficking.

It was said that deported American mafiosi, notably Charlie Luciano *(chapter 3),* had introduced their Sicilian cousins to the heroin business. Drug running may have been a trade abhorrent to old-line Sicilian mafiosi, but the brotherhood was well set up to handle it: The Mafia had long experience in smuggling cigarettes and other contraband. The secret transport systems were in place, the skills of carriers finely honed. It would be a waste, innovators argued, not to take advantage of drugs as a spectacular source of profits. Why should the traffickers from Turkey, the smugglers of Corsica, and the underworld chemists of Marseilles monopolize this bottomless gold mine?

In October 1957 the most powerful capos on the island, along with some of their American counterparts, came together for a secret summit conference in Palermo. Some accounts suggest that the business was done in the Grand Hotel des Palmes, once the palatial residence of Palermitan nobility; others locate the meeting place at a luxurious seafood restaurant, where the Sicilian men of respect and their transatlantic guests enjoyed a feast of fine wines, pasta, and grilled fish while apparently setting up the organizational systems for their global drug trade.

To ensure its smooth running, the brotherhood established the 12-member commission known as the Cupola, with representatives from those Mafia clans that took an interest in this new international commerce. In its structure and purpose, the Cupola was not unlike a corporate board of directors. It parceled out assignments and responsibilities, with an eye to cost-effectiveness and continued growth. Its most important administrative function, however, would be to prevent members of different branches of the organization from slaughtering one another when conflicts arose.

This last task was not easy. The global drug trade boomed, money rolled in, the stakes grew higher. By the early 1960s, power struggles between two Cupola families—the Grecos and the La Barberas—escalated into all-out war. This time the body count surpassed any in living memory: By June of 1963, on the turf of one cosca or the other, mafiosi were dying at the rate of one per day. The horrors culminated that month in the exclusive Palermo suburb of Ciaculli, site of the well-guarded mansions of several Mafia capos.

An anonymous telephone call to the local police reported an abandoned car with a flat tire in one of Ciaculli's streets. Officers answering the call saw something suspicious in the backseat: A cautious closer look revealed that the object was indeed a bomb, but clearly a false one with a useless fuse. As a matter of routine, one of the relieved officers opened the trunk of the car. The resulting roar shook the whole of Ciaculli, and flames shot 50 feet into the air. The blast gouged a crater out of the roadway, and shock waves crumbled a nearby villa. The only traces of the seven policemen investigating the car were one pistol, one beret, and a single finger wearing a wedding ring.

No one was quite sure who had been the bomb's intended target. It might have been the head of the Cupola, Cichiteddu Greco himself, or even Luciano Liggio—still at large at the time, and on the day of the explosion hiding in a secret chamber in a Ciaculli mansion. But public anger erupted: The public, like the Mafia, had entered the 20th century. To some minds, Mafia dons were as outdated as feudal warlords. To many people weary of gang wars, it didn't matter who was killing whom. They wanted action. And the state, so long ineffectual by accident or design in suppressing the Mafia, was jolted from its torpor.

The Italian government dropped a dragnet over Sicily.

Local police joined with paramilitary *carabinieri*, army troops, helicopters, parachutists, armored cars, and tracker dogs to scour Palermo and its environs. Police combed the streets for everyone with a criminal record, set up roadblocks, searched houses, confiscated an arsenal of lethal weapons, and rounded up nearly 2,000 suspected mafiosi and their associates. Among them were a dozen high-ranking chieftains who were swiftly sent into heavily guarded exile outside Sicily.

As usual, the Mafia responded to the heat pragmatically. A secret meeting of six Cupola members—including Luciano Liggio and Cichiteddu Greco—decided to do what their predecessors had done when Mussolini persecuted the Mafia: They would lie low or flee the country until the crisis cooled. They smuggled themselves out and relocated their operations to Brazil, Venezuela, Canada, Mexico, and the United States, all key points on their specialized commercial map. The corporate headquarters may have temporarily closed down, but the branch offices, with senior management at the helm, flourished as never before.

Now, in 1984, one of the Cupola's founders would step forward to an entirely new kind of notoriety as the Mafia moved into yet another phase, one that would shake to its foundations the old code of omertà. Tommaso Buscetta, known to his underlings as Don Masino, would turn the Sicilian Mafia inside out.

Buscetta was a consummate underworld politician. His early days in the Palermo slums were long behind him; he spoke three languages, read widely, loved the theater, dressed with impeccable taste, and mingled with the Sicilian capital's social and political elite. But while he discussed the merits of some new operatic production or cast a connoisseur's eye over a roomful of society women, his lieutenants were busy supervising the invisible conveyor belt that carried heroin halfway across the world and disposing of anyone who interfered with their profits.

When, after the bomb blast at Ciaculli, Sicily became inhospitable, Buscetta joined the migration across the Atlantic. He spent several years in New York in a cautious collaboration with the American mob, but a brush with the law caused him to move to Rio de Janeiro in 1971.

Behind the gleaming facades of the luxury hotels overlooking Copacabana Beach, Buscetta embarked on a concentrated program of underworld diplomacy. His efforts were critical in establishing an international ring that would supply almost all the heroin to hit the streets of New York City for years to come. And indulging in a brief distraction from business, Buscetta found himself a glamorous Brazilian wife.

But Don Masino had little time to reap the rewards of either marriage or enterprise. Brazilian police arrested him and extradited him to Italy in 1972. In 1968 a court in his native country had sentenced him in absentia to 14 years for criminal conspiracy and multiple murder. When he arrived at Palermo's Ucciardone Prison to begin his sentence, he was celebrated by his Mafia brethren as "the Boss of Two Worlds" and welcomed in the manner of a king returned from exile.

Inside Ucciardone the elite of the Honored Society lived well. Buscetta, clad in designer jeans, received the homage of his fellow inmates, who vied for the privilege of bringing him his morning coffee. Friends outside made sure that all his food was delivered daily from Palermo's choicest restaurants. It was an old story: Prison did nothing to diminish his prestige or power as a Mafia don.

Comfortable as it was, penitentiary life was not the most appealing possible existence, and in 1980 Buscetta left it behind. He'd been transferred from Ucciardone to a less restrictive prison in northern Italy, where, in recognition of his good behavior, he was allowed out on a daily work program for model prisoners. One day he chose not to return. But freedom was not, perhaps, the wisest choice for Buscetta. At least inside prison life was peaceful; outside, another Mafia war was looming.

After bitter battles in the 1960s and still more in the early 1970s, the dons had made a shaky peace. The pressure exerted by the state after the Ciaculli bombing had long since died down, and the Cupola was back in charge. It had allocated specific assignments to all participating clans to be sure that no single cosca could dominate the drug trade. Certain families now concentrated on smuggling in raw materials from Asian sources; others ran the secret refineries in remote districts under Mafia control. Export to the lucrative American markets and elsewhere was the province of other groups, as was the laundering of the money.

The Mafia, according to many veteran observers, no longer had to concern itself with profits. The problem in the 1980s was how to find productive, inflation-proof channels for the unstoppable flood of currency that kept pouring in.

Numbered Swiss bank accounts took care of a fraction of the income; the rest found its way into a variety of legitimate businesses and financial ventures. As well as a good lawyer, a forgiving priest, and a tame politician, the typical Mafia don now also needed a stockbroker.

Even Mafia small fry were rolling in wealth. One cosca dispatched peasant women from its rural base as transatlantic couriers. Grandmothers who'd never in their lives traveled as far as Palermo now became frequent fliers on jumbo jets bound for New York. Under their matronly dresses the women wore corsets that were padded with bags of heroin and saturated with perfume to deflect drug-sniffing dogs. Once the goods had been delivered, the elderly ladies vacationed in Manhattan's luxury hotels. At home, their ancient cottages acquired such untraditional embellishments as pearlescent floors and bathtubs equipped with golden faucets.

Despite the astronomical profits, or perhaps because of them, bad feeling festered once again among the Sicilian clans. Rules that had kept the peace—such as the rigid territorial demarcations setting out exactly where each family was allowed to do its killing—were broken. In the spring of 1981 old alliances disintegrated and new conspiracies emerged. Charges and countercharges—of betrayal, of theft, kidnapping, unauthorized murders, and predatory ambitions flew among the factions.

Bullets flew as well, in the deadliest Mafia feud ever. Instead of limiting their targets to those chieftains directly involved in the power struggle, the combatants attacked rival capos by slaughtering their relatives, trusted associates, and followers of every rank down to the lowliest foot soldier of the clan. At one time, Sicilian dons would have found this sort of behavior unthinkable, a violation of almost everything the old brotherhood claimed to hold sacred. One boss, after a visit to his mistress, was shot to death inside a brand-new car that was supposed to be bulletproof. Another was wiped out on the way home from his own birthday party. Fifteen people—probably all the key personnel in the clan of Don Rosario Riccobono—were thought to have been poisoned at a single family dinner.

If an enemy couldn't be reached because he was in prison or in hiding thousands of miles from the battleground, the next best thing was to leave him in that worst of all possible conditions for a mafioso: alone and friendless. One important boss who himself was untouchable, Don Gaetano Badalamenti, saw 300 of his family members, intimates, and supporters massacred.

The war ended in 1983 with a huge body count—1,000 dead, by some estimates. There were corpses not only in Sicily but as far away as the New Jersey swamps. Dominant among the victors were two bosses from Corleone, Salvatore Riina and Bernardo Provenzano—considered the nominated heirs to the throne of the imprisoned Luciano Liggio—and their ally Michele Greco, nicknamed the Pope. The losers included at least half a dozen Mafia leaders, among them Tommaso Buscetta.

Buscetta watched the war from the comparatively safe vantage point of South America. After his unscheduled departure from prison, he'd made his way back to Brazil to resume control of his operations there. But his pleasant life in the tropical sun didn't last long. In October 1983 he was arrested by Brazilian authorities and held while Italy and the United States dickered over who would try him for helping to establish the flow of heroin and cocaine into the entire Western Hemisphere. Eventually, the Americans decided to support Italy's claim to Don Masino, reasoning that Buscetta would get the harshest treatment from courts in his native country.

When Buscetta heard that he was being extradited to Italy, he tried to poison himself with a secret cache of strychnine. To go back a captive, he knew, would mean humiliation and inevitable death, not only for himself but for everyone loyal to him. The victorious Corleonesi faction had not been merciful to those on the losing side in the bloody tribal war. Buscetta's closest friends—if not already dead—were all marked men. One had been found dead in the yard at the Ucciardone Prison, stabbed 58 times. But Buscetta's suicide attempt failed, and he emerged from his coma with a new resolution: He would turn state's witness and destroy those who had sought to destroy him.

A few mafiosi over the years had talked under

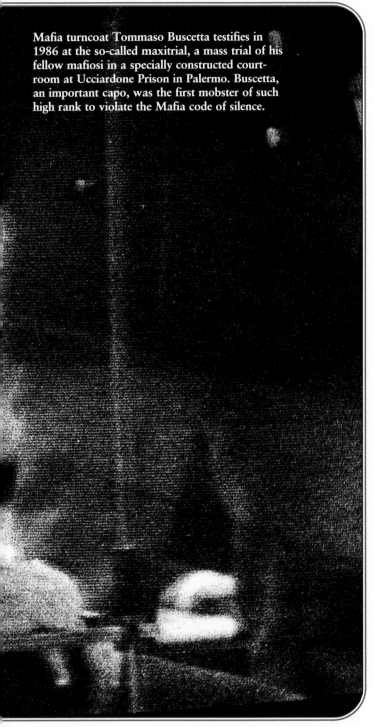

Mafia turncoat Tommaso Buscetta testifies in 1986 at the so-called maxitrial, a mass trial of his fellow mafiosi in a specially constructed courtroom at Ucciardone Prison in Palermo. Buscetta, an important capo, was the first mobster of such high rank to violate the Mafia code of silence.

pressure, but these had almost always been minor figures in the organization. This would be the first time that a mafioso of the first rank chose to violate omertà. At the age of 18, in the ceremony that had transformed him into a "made" member of the Honored Society, Buscetta had sworn on his own spilled blood to keep silence. Now he was about to break that vow.

The floodgates opened, and out poured a torrent of hitherto unknown information about the organizational structure of the Mafia, its rules and tactics, its connections in high places, its complex web of legal and illegal enterprises. And most remarkable of all, Don Masino named names. Taking courage from his actions, perhaps, more than a dozen other members of the brotherhood—representatives, for the most part, of the losing side in the recent war—added their testimony to Buscetta's.

According to Buscetta, this readiness to collaborate with the state was the result of moral outrage on the part of principled men of respect, revolted by the new Mafia's internal corruption and evil ways. "My choice to collaborate with justice," he declared in a letter to one of the investigating judges, "is not dictated by personal advantage. I have reached the conclusion that the Mafia had to be destroyed, and that everyone had the duty to collaborate with the government in this fight."

There were, however, those who suspected Don Masino's newfound moral outrage. It was suggested that his conversion to the cause of law and order was merely an updated version of the time-honored tradition of vendetta. He'd lost not only friends during the bloody Mafia war but blood kin as well: two sons, a brother, a nephew, a cousin, a brother-in-law, and a son-in-law.

Whatever its inspiration, Buscetta's change of heart came at a crucial time. In 1982 Italy had been outraged by the assassination of General Carlo Alberto Dalla Chiesa, a distinguished military commander and newly appointed prefect of Palermo, who'd been sent by Rome to head an all-out campaign against the Mafia. Many ordinary Sicilians were sick of Mafia-induced mayhem and had hoped that Dalla Chiesa would bring it to a halt. On the bloodied pavement where the general, his wife, and their escort had died, someone placed a handmade sign: "Here died the hope of all honest Sicilians."

But some citizens had just begun to fight. A fledgling anti-Mafia movement, spearheaded by a small group of at-

The Pizza Connection

Once famed as the Boss of Two Worlds, renegade mafioso Tommaso Buscetta became the informer of two worlds: at the maxitrial in Palermo, Sicily, and in one of the biggest narcotics cases in North American history, the Pizza Connection.

The case involved a vast smuggling operation that began with the Sicilian Mafia shipping narcotics from Turkey and Thailand to Sicily, then smuggling them in a variety of ways across the Atlantic to such cities as New York, Miami, and Montreal. Once in North America, the drugs—mostly heroin—became the concern of New York's Bonanno crime family—an ironic fact, since family founder Joe Bonanno had liked to trumpet the old-time Mafia line that drug peddling was unmanly. The Bonanno clan sold the drugs through a chain of pizza parlors and other retail outlets in the Northeast and Midwest. The Sicilian Mafia's share of the profits—millions of dollars every year for 10 years—cycled homeward through a complex money-laundering apparatus involving banks in the United States, Bermuda, the Bahamas, and Switzerland.

The pizza pipeline began to collapse when law-enforcement authorities in the United States, Canada, and several European countries—Italy among them—began their own brand of international cooperation. The result was several trials in the United States and in Switzerland, Turkey, Germany, and Brazil. The largest of the trials began in Federal District Court in Manhattan in September 1985 and included in its witness roster Tommaso Buscetta, whose nine days of testimony allowed a fascinating glimpse inside the Mafia.

The most damning testimony in the 17-month trial, however, came from officials who'd painstakingly investigated the Pizza Connection. Their accounts convicted 18 mobsters, American and Sicilian, on a variety of drug-related charges. Among the guilty were Gaetano Badalamenti, former leader of the Sicilian Mafia, and Salvatore "Toto" Catalano, a Bonanno family leader in Brooklyn. Badalamenti was sentenced to 30 years in prison, Catalano to 45.

torneys, churchmen, and reform-minded politicians, dedicated itself to the struggle. For the first time, Palermo elected a mayor—Leoluca Orlando—who ran on an anti-Mafia platform. Orlando worked to get his party, the Christian Democrats, to oust its old guard with its links to the brotherhood. Prosecutors, led by Giovanni Falcone and Paolo Borsellino, began the painstaking and dangerous task of accumulating evidence against mafiosi. Gradually they accumulated a list of more than a thousand witnesses, then summoned them to do what so many had failed to do before: talk in open court.

The result was an extraordinary trial, unlike any other in Italian legal history. It came to be known as the maxitrial. In all, 474 mafiosi or Mafia associates were indicted. Of these, some 200 were already in jail, and upwards of 200 more avoided arrest and were tried in absentia. Nevertheless, so numerous were the defendants when the trial started in February 1986 that a specially constructed maximum-security courtroom was required. It was built onto a wall of Ucciardone Prison, and its accommodations included 30 steel cages situated behind partitions of bulletproof glass. The indictment for those present ran to 8,607 pages. Prosecutors added to this mountain of paper 22 volumes of legal documents.

The scores of defendants spit and jeered at journalists and photographers and bellowed threats and abuse at members of the court. One of the prisoners stapled his lips together to announce to the world that he would not violate omertà. Meanwhile, outside the fortified, bombproof courtroom, more than 2,000 armed officers in bulletproof battle dress stood on patrol.

There was good reason for caution. Public figures standing against the Mafia knew themselves to be marked for death. Assassinations of senior judges and law-enforcement officers were commonplace, as was the slaying of friends and relatives of informants. Not even those innocent of all Mafia links were immune. In a Palermo suburb, the peaceable owner of a pottery factory was gunned down a few yards from his own front door. His only connection with the underworld was the fact that his wife was the sister of Tommaso Buscetta.

"I have five children," she lamented, "and I'm constantly in fear for every one of them. He's not my brother anymore. I wish to God he'd never been born."

The hundreds of defendants in the maxitrial undoubtedly

Mafioso Luciano Liggio sits in a defendant's cage at the maxitrial, brought into court from his prison cell to be both a defendant and a witness. Liggio expressed amazement at allegations that even behind bars, he still directed criminal acts. "I've always been a tranquil man," he protested. He was acquitted on all counts, but was returned to prison to continue his earlier life sentence.

A woman peeks out from behind a shutter *(above)* at a tank-mounted paramilitary policeman, one of some 2,000 officers who patrolled streets outside Palermo's Ucciardone Prison during the maxitrial. Inside the courtroom *(below),* tight security included a heavy police presence. To the rear of the room were 30 defendants' cages, topped by a spectators' gallery.

shared the widow's sentiments. In all, after appeal 254 convictions resulted from the trial (including convictions in absentia), carrying sentences that totaled 1,576 years in prison. The most important victory of the maxitrial prosecutors was the 12 life sentences that were secured against members of the Cupola.

Buscetta himself did not back down from his new role as avenging witness. "It is not possible," he wrote, "to force me to be silent again." With good reason. Don Masino's bargain with the state included arrangements for his own long-term safety. As well as testifying in the Palermo maxitrial, he had already been secretly conveyed to the United States to act as a witness for the prosecution in cases against American and Sicilian Mafia drug barons (page 32). Having thus made his contribution to law enforcement on both sides of the Atlantic, he was spirited away—along with his wife and children—to receive a new identity, a new appearance, and a new life in some unknown place under the U.S. Witness Protection Program.

Back in Sicily, the Mafia entered yet another phase in its history. For something was stirring, on the streets of Palermo and even in the hill towns of the hinterlands. Ordinary citizens who for generations had been unwilling or afraid to raise their voices against the Mafia's secret empire now began to challenge its power. The longtime leader of Palermo, one-time mayor Vito Ciancimino, was tried and convicted in 1992 on Mafia-linked corruption charges and sentenced to 10 years in prison. Priests spoke out from their pulpits. Shopkeepers and businessmen joined antiextortion associations to support one another's refusals to pay the time-honored pizzu. A new anti-Mafia party, pledged to rid the body politic of the old machine politicians, gained thousands of new members.

The old myths were crumbling: The romantic notion of the homegrown bandit-hero protecting his downtrodden fellow Sicilians from the hated foreigners had at last worn thin. So had the myth of the brotherhood's invincibility—and its honor. Too much greed and too much bloodshed had argued against honor.

Still, the Mafia's hold on Sicily was old and strong, and challenging it took courage. An organization that survived by buying off, intimidating, or killing anyone who stood in its way was not going to be easily undermined. And leaving aside Mafia ruthlessness, there remained the matter of Ma-fia wealth. As the 20th century neared its end, the ancient brotherhood once confined to the Sicilian countryside had extended its reach throughout Europe and to Asia and the Americas. Its profits defied accurate computation, but certainly they ranged in the tens of billions of dollars annually. Some estimates put the number at more than $120 billion, about a fourth of it from drugs.

With so much at stake, the leading anti-Mafia activists knew themselves to be at risk. Prosecuting attorney Giovanni Falcone, reflecting on his role in the maxitrial and its aftermath, acknowledged that "I have opened an account with the Mafia which can only be closed with my death—natural or otherwise."

In May 1992 that account was closed. Despite round-the-clock guards and a shroud of secrecy over all his movements, Falcone could not escape his enemies. Driving along a stretch of coastal highway near Palermo's airport, the prosecutor—together with his wife and three bodyguards—was killed by a bomb containing a ton of dynamite. Someone, briefed by an informer, knew the precise time and place to trigger the blast.

Enraged, thousands of Sicilians took to the streets, marching through Palermo with banners demanding an end to the Mafia and all its works. The government promised a harsh new crackdown on the brotherhood.

Falcone's veteran, knowledgeable colleague, Paolo Borsellino, had also been a prosecutor in the investigation that led to the maxitrial. Borsellino warned that the battle lines were not so easily drawn. "The Mafia," he told an interviewer two months after Falcone's murder, "is inside and outside the state." A few days later, he too was blown to pieces, as he rang the doorbell at his mother's apartment building in Palermo.

The brotherhood had given notice once again that it wouldn't readily give up its power. Not that Sicilians ever expected it to. "The Mafia," sighed an anonymous Palermo civilian who'd grown up in its shadow, "is like a serpent. It just keeps changing its skin." He might have said just as aptly that the Mafia was like the Hydra of Greek legend—a many-headed monster that could grow a new head for every one that its enemies lopped off. On the island that had spawned the Mafia monster, one head was under attack. But the monster had grown huge since its birth on Sicily, and its many heads existed in many places.

In the United States, for instance.

Detectives, reporters, and photographers swarm over the site where a dynamite bomb killed anti-Mafia prosecutor Giovanni Falcone and four other people in May 1992. The front was blown off Falcone's car, shown in the center of the picture. Inset below are Falcone and two victims of separate incidents of Mafia violence—Falcone's fellow prosecutor Paolo Borsellino and General Carlo Alberto Dalla Chiesa, police prefect of Palermo.

GIOVANNI FALCONE

PAOLO BORSELLINO

CARLO ALBERTO DALLA CHIESA

2

Coming to America

Giuseppe Esposito was, in a sense, the stuff of which America was made—an immigrant from the Old World seeking a fresh start and new opportunities in the vast, rich United States. He was like millions of others in that regard, so his arrival in New York in November of 1878 went unremarked. Even so, it was a milestone for crime in America. Giuseppe Esposito was hardly the first mafioso to venture abroad, but he was the most prominent by far—a leader, a pure representative of the breed, commanding the Mafia version of respect to the highest degree.

Esposito was a well-known thief and killer in his native Sicily, but his greatest renown stemmed from his role as second-in-command in a kidnapping engineered by bandit chieftain Antonino Leone. In 1876, Leone, Esposito, and two other men had snatched a 22-year-old British banker named John Forester Rose near a rural railway station 20 miles south of Palermo. Rose, the scion of a prominent family, had the misfortune to be in Sicily to inspect some sulfur mines owned by his family. His kidnappers soon contacted the Roses by mail, demanding a ransom payment of £5,000. Soon after came a second letter, threatening to cut off one of Rose's ears if the money wasn't forthcoming.

Instead of paying, the family asked British Prime Minister Benjamin Disraeli to send troops to the rescue. Not long afterward, John Rose's wife received a small package from Sicily. Inside was one of her husband's ears. This was followed by a package containing the other ear. Frantic, unable to persuade the family to pay the ransom, she took her story to the press. As the newspapers splashed the gruesome details of the kidnapping across their front pages, the British public cried out for satisfaction. Disraeli resisted the calls for a military expedition, but he exerted heavy diplomatic pressure on Italian authorities.

Another package arrived, this one holding a slice of John Rose's nose, along with a letter promising to deliver the rest of his body piece by piece if the ransom was not paid. By this time Mrs. Rose's plight had drawn contributions of £2,600. She wired the money to Sicily, explaining that she had no more. The kidnappers, reasonable men in their way, decided that it was an acceptable profit. They sent John Rose home, his head heavily bandaged.

The affair was not over, however. Disraeli told the Italian government that unless the kidnappers were captured and punished, British soldiers would land in Sicily to do the job for them. This threat brought immediate action. The government rounded up a number of mafiosi and summarily executed them. For more than a year, Leone, Esposito, and 160 of their fellow brigands eluded the Italian army, but eventually the location of their secret hilltop headquarters in the countryside was discovered. Several thousand soldiers closed in and overran the hill after a long and bloody battle.

Italy's government resolved to make examples of the 14 surviving outlaws. After parading them through Palermo, police laid elaborate plans to transport them to Rome for public trial. The men were loaded into two heavily guarded horse-drawn vans. The occupants of one, including Antonino Leone, made it to Rome, and the prisoners all wound up in jail. But the other van mysteriously disgorged its passengers en route. Esposito was among the escapees.

Despite the heat caused by the Rose kidnapping, Esposito won widespread admiration for the audacity of the deed, and the hilltop battle and his getaway enhanced his reputation even more. Over the next year he continued to burnish his legend in murderous Mafia fashion, personally killing 11 wealthy landowners and two city officials. But after a second brush with capture, he decided that it was time to quit his homeland and take his skills abroad. His departure was a sign of the Mafia's future. Like a cancer, the Sicilian approach to crime was metastasizing, sending out its aberrant cells to colonize social tissues elsewhere, especially in the United States.

During the 19th and early 20th centuries, immigrants poured into the United States in huge numbers and from almost every corner of the earth. In the motley multitude were Irish families propelled by famine at home, Chi-

Between 1880 and 1920, more than four million Italians—most of them from the south, the Mezzogiorno region—came to America, among them this mother and trio of children, shown arriving at New York's Ellis Island in 1905.

nese recruited as cheap labor to build railroads, Jews fleeing oppression in eastern Europe, Scandinavians and Germans responding to word of available farmland in the American West. But Italy provided the most immigrants of all—fully 4.7 million between 1820 and 1930. Northern Italians made up the majority of the firstcomers, but after 1870, when the flood of immigration began to crest, the main source was the Mezzogiorno—the southern part of the country, including Sicily. Poverty motivated most of them; they were largely drawn from Italy's lowest socioeconomic strata—the struggling ranks of peasants, day laborers, village artisans. Many couldn't read or write. Many came without their families, planning to return to Italy as soon as they made enough money to improve their lot back home.

For a good number of these new arrivals, however, nostalgia was mixed with bitterness when they thought of their homeland. Sicilians, particularly, had expected great changes when Giuseppe Garibaldi's revolution ousted the Spanish Bourbons from the island and from the southern mainland—territories that the Bourbons had called collectively the Kingdom of the Two Sicilies. But the dream of equality under a unified Italy was short-lived. After the dust of the revolution had settled, the government in Rome, dominated by northern Italy, heaped contempt on the less sophisticated south. The northerners scorned the southerners as backward "Africans" and treated them with no more respect than had the long succession of foreign conquerors.

Disillusioned as they were with their native land, the Ital-

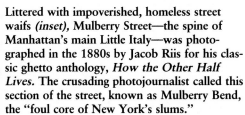

left behind found almost undiminished expression in the urban ghettos of America.

Yet if people clung to the comfort of the familiar, it was about the only comfort they had. The tenements and streets of most of the Little Italys were a chaos of overcrowded humanity. "It is impossible to depict the degradation, the dirt, the squalor, the stinking muck, the rubble, the disorder of the neighborhood," wrote an Italian playwright after a visit to New York's Lower East Side. A New York police commissioner looked at the district through the lens of the law; the Lower East Side, he said, "represents an insoluble problem for the police. The density of the population in some areas verges on the unbelievable. It is simply impossible to pack human beings into these honeycombs towering over the narrow canyons of streets and then propose to turn them into citizens who respect and obey the laws."

The commissioner probably failed to understand that even if conditions had been more humane, respect for the law would have come hard to these newcomers, who brought with them their age-old distrust of authority. In traditional fashion, they dealt with their own problems as best they could—which meant that the brutal found it easy to prey on the weak. Crime, largely committed by Italians against Italians, took forms that had prevailed back home. One all-too-familiar plague was extortion, a major source of criminal profits in the old country.

The usual method was to mail a letter to the target individual, demanding money as the price of avoiding bodily harm. The signature on these notes was a standardized symbol of terror: a black hand. (Evidently the image was invented by a revolutionary group in Spain in the 1830s and had such a sinister effect that criminals elsewhere adopted it.) If the payment was not delivered, more letters would follow, spelling out how the person or his wife or children would be maimed or killed or how his place of business might be dynamited; the menace in the words was reinforced by drawings of knives, pistols, bombs, skulls and crossbones, and other such threatening imagery. Generally, the extortionists meant business; many murders in the Italian ghettos of American cities were traced to the fulfillment of such threats.

When the Italian government cracked down on criminal brotherhoods in the 1870s and prompted some transgres-

ian immigrants still sought comfort in reminders of it. For the most part they congregated in Little Italys—ethnic enclaves in big cities. New York and New Orleans drew the greatest Italian influx, but large settlements also sprang up in Chicago, Boston, Philadelphia, Detroit, Buffalo, Milwaukee, Kansas City, Denver, and San Francisco, among others. Surrounded by people like themselves, the Italians replicated their old way of life with remarkable fidelity, re-creating the flavor of cities like Naples or Palermo or any one of scores of little villages scattered across the Mezzogiorno. The deep attachment to family and friends, the Old World pleasures of food and wine and music and gossip, the superstitions and conservatism, the wariness of officialdom— all the cultural apparatus of the world the immigrants had

A typical signature for Black Hand extortion notes, this one warns, "la mano nera colpira"—"the black hand will strike."

sors to seek refuge abroad, Black Hand activities—as these extortion tactics came to be called—showed a marked upswing in the United States, and they continued to cast their shadow over Italian communities for decades. The press often speculated about a Black Hand society, a secret criminal organization that specialized in this form of crime. There was, in fact, no such society; some transplanted Italian criminals undoubtedly practiced extortion, but they worked as individuals—not under the umbrella of a single huge and malignant organization.

Throughout the 19th century, in fact, there was no single brotherhood that could be said to monopolize Italian-American crime. Along with the Sicilian Mafia, criminal societies rooted in the southern provinces of Calabria and Basilicata in the old country were represented in some degree in America's Little Italys. And from Naples and the surrounding province of Campania came members of the Camorra, a criminal organization that once easily rivaled the Mafia in power.

The Camorra—the name is a Spanish word for "dispute" or "fight"—took shape in the 1820s as a self-protection society for inmates of Neapolitan prisons. Outside of jail, camorristas organized themselves into gangs that practiced several felonies but specialized in extortion. In the United States, Camorra and Mafia factions often warred for supremacy in various arenas, particularly in New York City and New Orleans. The camorristas were much more structured than the mafiosi. Back in Naples there had been precisely 12 Camorra families, each supervised by a boss, and each subdivided into groups called *paranze* whose capos designated specific tasks to the membership: extortion, robbery, blackmail, murder, loansharking, or kidnapping. The

Camorra would eventually be subsumed within the Mafia, but it would leave its distinctive stamp on the larger brotherhood, especially in the areas of structure and ritual.

Not only the Mafia and the Camorra, but all the various Italian-American criminal groups in the United States—however contentious at times—would learn to cooperate. There was, after all, much common ground: a disdain for every form of governmental authority, a family-like structure, an emphasis on the notions of honor and respect, and an unwritten law of silence. Even at times of conflict, their dark roads to power ran in parallel, and it was probably inevitable that—in a country whose very nature was to meld disparate peoples—those roads would converge.

Giuseppe Esposito's personal path in America wound through New York fairly quickly: He spent only six months in the city. Perhaps he found the horizons too limiting. At that time, criminal activities beyond the bounds of Little Italy were dominated by Irish and Jewish gangs whose political influence made them difficult to challenge. Perhaps he simply disliked New York's cold winters.

New Orleans was his next stop, and it was more to his taste. The climate was warmer, and the large Italian population was heavily Sicilian. New Orleans had its Little Italy, centered in the city's fabled French Quarter. But social mobility abounded for ambitious men who worked hard, and many Sicilians found that they could, if they wished, move to almost any part of town that they found agreeable. Several immigrants had prospered in New Orleans in thoroughly legitimate pursuits. And, for those who preferred illegality, local politicians were by no means incorruptible, and a flourishing seaport was ripe for rackets. So it was when Giuseppe Esposito arrived.

Esposito's high rank among the mafiosi back in Sicily was known in New Orleans, and he was regarded from the outset as a daring and dangerous man, one to be treated with great respect. Although he'd taken an alias, calling himself Vincenzo Rebello, he made no secret of his status as an international fugitive. In the city streets he cut a commanding figure, carrying himself with the air of royalty in exile. He wore expensive clothes, dined in the best restaurants, and even bought himself a yacht, flying from the masthead what he claimed was the flag of the Sicilian Mafia. (There was, of course, no such flag.) Despite this ersatz bit of advertisement, he was—as everyone recognized—the real thing, the ferocious embodiment of the secret brotherhoods that held much of Sicily in their grip. Inevitably, the reins of criminal power in New Orleans fell into his hands. But irony would intervene to undo Giuseppe Esposito, tangling his fate with that of a woman and a policeman in ways that would eventually deal a brutal blow not only to the immigrant don but to all the Mafia in New Orleans.

Not long after his arrival in the city, Esposito married a young Sicilian woman, and a year later she gave birth to a son. As it happened, however, Esposito already had a wife and five children back in Sicily. In January of 1881 the Italian consul in New Orleans paid a call on the city's chief of police to present a sealed dossier that had been dispatched from Rome in a diplomatic pouch. Inside was a photograph of a man identified by the consul as Giuseppe Esposito, Italy's foremost fugitive from justice. The gangster's Sicilian wife, it seemed, had not responded well to the news of her husband's American marriage, and she'd taken her revenge by telling the Italian authorities where he was. Amazingly, a man with innumerable murders and kidnappings in his résumé was about to be felled by bigamy.

The New Orleans police chief handed the case to a young patrolman named David C. Hennessey, a tough Irish cop who came from a family of policemen (his father had been killed in the line of duty). Initially Hennessey's efforts in the Esposito case focused on a hood named Tony Labruzzo, who had a weakness that the policeman could exploit. Labruzzo had recently brought his mother over from Palermo, and Hennessey threatened to have her deported unless Labruzzo agreed to become an informant. Reluctantly, Labruzzo began to sing. Soon Hennessey realized that Es-

posito was the leader of the local Italian criminal element, yet he felt that he needed to accumulate more evidence than Labruzzo's whisperings. But his probe was cut short as mounting pressure from the Italian government resulted in orders from Hennessey's superiors for him to forget the fine points: He was to do anything necessary to arrest Esposito. If his methods weren't altogether proper, he was given to understand, the authorities would look the other way.

On the morning of July 5, 1881, Hennessey arrived at New Orleans's St. Louis Cathedral in the back of a curtained carriage. Taking up a position across the street from the lovely old French Quarter church, he settled in to wait. At 11 a.m. Esposito arrived for his daily devotions. As always, the mafioso was splendidly attired, this day in a suit of fawn and gray, topped with his trademark Panama hat. When Esposito started up the cathedral steps, Hennessey approached from behind and jammed a pistol into his back. Before the surprised gangster could react, Hennessey hustled him into the carriage, where he stripped him of a knife and two pistols. The following morning, the young cop slipped the renowned mafioso onto a steamer bound for New York. Having been told of the Sicilian's talent for escape, Hennessey weighted his prisoner down with 40 pounds of chains and padlocks before turning him over to the two New York detectives who'd been dispatched to guard Esposito during the boat trip. In New York an Italian warship stood ready to carry the fugitive back to Italy.

Esposito's followers found out about the abduction the day after it happened, but by then their capo was embarked on a 12-day boat ride to New York. The news of his arrest panicked his underlings, and several fled New Orleans, three of them aboard the Mafia yacht. The rest went into hiding in the city. The whole Sicilian community was stunned. "What agitated them and surprised them most," reported the city's *Daily Picayune* in its customary florid prose, "was the quiet manner in which the brigand had been captured. How so famous a bravo, so blood-thirsty a criminal and desperate a fugitive could be captured at all, filled them with consternation, and only one reasonable theory presented itself to their minds: Esposito had been betrayed."

For many New Orleans Sicilians, the betrayal was worse than anything Esposito may have done, a profoundly dishonorable act, and they began looking for the traitor. Suspicions quickly came to rest on Tony Labruzzo, who vehemently denied having been involved in any way.

Conscious that denials were not enough, he joined a group known as Tiro el Bersaglio, meaning "shoot the target." The committee, which met regularly in the upstairs rooms of a boardinghouse, had been formed solely to ferret out the man who betrayed Giuseppe Esposito. On the night of July 16, 1881, the meeting grew particularly heated. After several complaints from the landlady about the noise, the group broke up and filed out into the street. Labruzzo was one of the last to leave, and he didn't get far. His fellow committee members had concealed themselves in doorways on either side of the street. As he stepped into view, a dozen men jumped from their hiding places with guns blazing. Labruzzo fell dead in the street.

In New York, meanwhile, Esposito busily prepared a defense for his extradition hearing. He planned to present himself as a victim of mistaken identity. To bolster his case, a number of Sicilian businessmen testified that the accused was, in fact, a respected merchant named Vincenzo Rebello. In what was to become a hallmark of the American Mafia, mobsters in both New York and New Orleans worked in close harmony to provide seamless testimony.

David Hennessey's role in the matter had not been forgotten. In New Orleans, Joseph Macheca—the city's chief criminal luminary before Esposito's arrival—generously tried to save his successor by offering Hennessey $50,000 to get Esposito off the hook. All the policeman had to do was travel to New York and claim that a switch had been made and that the accused was not the man he'd arrested. When Hennessey refused, Macheca flexed his political muscle and had the police department reorganized, resulting in Hennessey's demotion. Within a year he was off the force.

By then, however, the effort to rescue Esposito had failed. Further identification from Rome soon established that Vincenzo Rebello and Giuseppe Esposito were one and the same. On September 21, 1881, authorities in New York placed the mafioso aboard the ship that would take him back to Italy. In Rome he was convicted of six murders during his career in Sicily. The mob boss would spend the rest of his life in prison, in chains. Authorities remembered his talent for escapes.

Esposito's departure threw the New Orleans underworld into turmoil. His former colleagues literally knocked down Esposito's house looking for a hoard of gold said to be hidden inside. The money, if it existed at all, was never found. Esposito's young wife was left destitute. She aban-

doned the city for Louisville, Kentucky, where she eked out a living as a laundress. But her income wasn't enough to support a child. Eventually, the son of Giuseppe Esposito, Mafia kingpin, was placed in an orphanage.

Joseph Macheca, a big-time fruit importer whose original power rested with his control of the New Orleans docks, tried to reclaim his old position atop the local underworld. But his stature was not enough to maintain peace among the Sicilians. In the power vacuum created by Esposito's capture, two Sicilian-born crime bosses fought for dominance. One was Charles Matranga, who ran a gambling den and dance hall and controlled a gang of stevedores. The other was Joe Provenzano, who'd made his reputation enforcing the edicts of Giuseppe Esposito. The two men became bitter foes after Provenzano lost out to Matranga in competition for a contract granting exclusive rights to unload fruit boats at the Port of New Orleans. Enmity between the two eventually boiled over into violence. A shooting war broke out, and Macheca sided with Matranga.

After losing a number of foot soldiers, Macheca devised a strategy that was to become a Mafia tradition: He replenished his dwindling ranks with reinforcements brought directly from Sicily—more than 300 of them. Outnumbered, Provenzano sent a lieutenant named Vincenzo Ottumvo to negotiate a peaceful settlement to the dispute. Ottumvo was to meet Matranga's chief enforcer, Rocco Geraci, over a friendly game of cards and, if possible, work out an agreement for the two factions to split the work on the waterfront. It was not possible. While Ottumvo sat studying his cards, a Matranga assassin crept up from behind and stabbed him. Provenzano soon retaliated by killing a leader of Matranga's imported Sicilian henchmen.

As the belligerents edged toward all-out vendetta, an old adversary stepped into the fray: David Hennessey, the policeman who had put Giuseppe Esposito behind bars. Hennessey was not only back on the force, thanks to reformist politicians, but he'd been named chief of the New Orleans Police Department the previous year. Making up for lost time, he compiled a fat dossier on killings in the Sicilian community. His efforts didn't go unnoticed. By the end of his first year in office, he received an anonymous warning that the Sicilian gangsters had sworn an oath to eliminate him. But Hennessey was undeterred. As the Matranga-Provenzano war threatened to get out of hand, he rounded up Macheca, Matranga, and Provenzano and issued them

Mob-busting New Orleans police chief David C. Hennessey is shown in the engraving used by *Harper's Weekly* magazine when it reported his murder by Mafia gunmen.

an ultimatum: If the violence didn't stop, they would go to prison. Having said his piece, Hennessey pulled out a bottle and poured drinks all around. Matranga and Provenzano shook hands, and it appeared that the hostilities were over.

A warning from a cop couldn't stop a blood feud, however. Shortly after midnight on May 6, 1890, as a wagonload of Matranga's workers made their way home from the docks, a team of Provenzano's gunmen ambushed them. Tony Matranga, the gang leader's younger brother, was badly wounded and lost a leg as a result.

By dawn Hennessey had rounded up the Provenzanos and thrown them in jail. He was worried about his ability to keep them there, expecting that witnesses would be stifled by omertà. To his great surprise, however, the Matrangas did an unheard-of thing for members of a criminal society: They filed into the police station and swore out formal complaints against the Provenzano brothers and four of their lieutenants.

Two months later, the six men went on trial for attempted murder. As the case unfolded, it was clear this was not to be the police department's finest hour. A total of 24 policemen, ranking from captain to patrolman, took the stand to offer alibis for the Provenzanos. Everyone in the courtroom, including the jurors, realized that the officers had been bought off. The Matrangas gave a consistent and compelling account of the ambush, and the jury found the Provenzanos guilty. They had, however, an ace in the hole—the presiding judge. Ruling that no positive identification had been made, he overturned the jury verdict and ordered a new trial. The Provenzanos, meanwhile, were to remain in custody.

With so many of Hennessey's officers perjuring themselves on behalf of the Provenzanos, people began to wonder about the police chief himself. Indeed, over the years he had forged a curious alliance with Joe Provenzano, who had the reputation of being a reasonable man, willing to cooperate with the police on occasion. Perhaps Hennessey reasoned that Provenzano was the lesser of two evils. In any event, he and Provenzano had formed a kind of cautious friendship, and the police chief had even sponsored Provenzano for membership in one of the city's exclusive clubs.

Hennessey was generally deemed to be too upright to take bribes, but he had obviously sided with the Provenzanos at the trial, and he kept working to help their cause. Hoping to turn up something on Charles Matranga's criminal background, Hennessey wrote to the chief of police in Rome for dossiers on known mafiosi wanted in Italy. The Italian official wrote back to say that he would gather the files immediately. Before he could do so, however, he was murdered. Hennessey then made a similar request of the Italian consul in New Orleans. Soon afterward, the consul got an invitation to dine at the home of Matranga's powerful ally, Joseph Macheca. The meal made the diplomat so violently ill that he suspected he'd been poisoned.

Clearly, Macheca and Matranga intended to shut down the investigation, but Hennessey refused to back off, even though he probably knew that he himself was under constant surveillance by his enemies. Macheca's men had rented a small room in a shack near the house that Hennessey shared with his elderly mother, and they kept a careful record of the police chief's comings and goings.

On October 15, 1890, nineteen members of the Matranga gang congregated in the shack, ready to take action. Shortly after 11 o'clock that night, Hennessey started walking home after a police board meeting. A close friend, police captain William O'Connor, escorted him most of the way but parted company with him as Hennessey neared his house. As the chief walked the final block, a teenage boy ran past and gave a long, trilling whistle.

At the sound, two men standing across the street opened fire with sawed-off shotguns. Several other gunmen fired from Macheca's rented shack. Hennessey, wounded, man-

As David Hennessey walked toward his New Orleans home at 275 Girod Street *(above),* mafiosi hiding in a low shed *(below, between the two larger buildings)* opened fire from within and from the sidewalk. The three red circles indicate where the doomed police chief's return fire struck.

aged to draw his revolver and return fire. Then, gushing blood, he collapsed and tried to crawl away. The gunmen fired several more rounds at him, then slipped into the night.

Captain O'Connor heard the gunfire and ran back to his friend. Kneeling beside the fallen man, O'Connor saw that the chief was still alive. "Who gave it to you, Dave?" O'Connor asked. There are several versions of how Hennessey replied, some holding that he merely shook his head to imply that he didn't know who his antagonists were. But the story that passed into legend goes this way: In a choked, barely audible voice, the chief said, "The dagos did it."

Hennessey, who'd suffered six gunshot wounds, died the next morning at New Orleans's Charity Hospital. His murder sparked outrage not just in New Orleans but all across the United States. Protesters took to the street in anti-Italian demonstrations in New York, Chicago, Cleveland, St. Louis, and San Francisco — all cities whose Italian communities were hotbeds of crime. New Orleans Mayor Joseph A. Shakespeare, who'd appointed Hennessey police chief two years earlier, gave a fierce speech to the city council, promising to "teach these people a lesson they will not forget for all time." The mayor put the entire police force on duty and instructed the men to go to the Italian district and find the killers. "Scour the whole neighborhood. Arrest every Italian you come across, if necessary," he told them. In short order, more than 100 people had been thrown in jail, and bigotry had clearly overtaken righteous indignation at Hennessey's death. One of the city's newspapers fanned the flames of hate by writing of "Sicilians whose low, receding foreheads, repulsive countenances and slovenly attire proclaimed their brutal natures."

Only the Provenzanos, who'd been friendly with Hennessey, seemed above suspicion. They remained safely tucked away in the Orleans Parish Prison, where the chief himself had put them. It seemed as good a place as any to ride out the wrath against Italians. The mobsters were lodged in a comfortable section of the jail. Gourmet meals and fine wines were brought in regularly, along with fresh linen three times a week. The mafiosi wore their usual expensive suits rather than prison stripes, and they enjoyed the free run of an entire wing of the building. Once, when a reporter visited the prison, they stayed in their cells for the sake of appearances.

Not so elegantly housed at the jail were several members of the Matranga gang, who'd been tossed into the prison as part of the roundup ordered by the mayor. But as it turned out, the worst part of jailhouse life for the Matranga contingent had less to do with the accommodations than with an undercover Pinkerton detective named Frank Dimaio, who insinuated himself among them. Playing the role of a sophisticated out-of-town counterfeiter who scorned the lowly New Orleans foot soldiers, Dimaio soon had the locals vying with one another to impress him with boasts of their derring-do. Inevitably, as the weeks wore on, they confided the secret of their most impressive deed—the Hennessey murder.

One hoodlum in particular, Joe Polizi, waxed lavishly loose-lipped when Dimaio convinced him that his fellow mafiosi were trying to poison him in order to keep him quiet. When Polizi started refusing his food, Dimaio offered to share his own meals. Grateful, Polizi began babbling details. He named Charles Matranga and Joe Macheca as the masterminds of the Hennessey killing. He described in detail the drawing of straws to select the triggermen. Dimaio took notes on a small slip of paper and then had Polizi—who was illiterate—mark at the bottom.

The confession led to grand jury indictments that resulted in the trial of Macheca, Matranga, and seven other men for conspiracy to commit murder. The trial began in February of 1891 and was marred from the outset by back-room dealing and maneuvering. Matranga defenders urged Italians across the country to contribute two dollars apiece to the defense fund, and the inflowing cash was used to hire a prestigious team of lawyers and to distribute a number of healthy bribes. The prosecutors produced 67 witnesses supporting their case, but the defense countered with a similarly impressive number offering alibis for the accused. The turning point came when Polizi's confession was ruled inadmissible. The ruling may have resulted from Matranga machinations, but it could also be that the judge truly believed that Polizi—who repeatedly jumped up at the trial to shout new and unsolicited confessions, and who once tried to

New Orleans Mafia leader Charles Matranga, seen in an *Illustrated American* sketch, escaped the lynch mob out to avenge Hennessey by hiding under a discarded mattress in the prison yard.

leap out a window—was crazy. On Friday, March 13, the jury filed into the courtroom and handed over its verdict. The judge stared at the slip of paper in disbelief for a full minute before ordering it read. Six of the defendants were acquitted, including Macheca and Matranga. The other three—including Polizi—were granted a mistrial.

None of the defendants walked free. All nine were returned to the parish prison to await another trial: They and 10 other men faced an ambush charge stemming from the Hennessey killing. Even so, the not-guilty verdict in the original trial sent a shock wave through New Orleans. Everywhere citizens gathered to vent their anger. Rumors flew that the jury had been bought off or intimidated. The morning after the verdict, a crowd gathered outside City Hall to hear a series of speeches by prominent citizens. Peaceful at first, the crowd grew more and more agitated, the speeches more and more inflammatory. Eventually, the throng headed for the parish prison. Many people in the mob were armed.

At the jail's main gate a dozen policemen who tried to block the crowd were quickly pushed aside. The mob leaders tried to batter down the iron gate with rifle butts, but the doors held. At the side of the prison was a smaller door, heavily barred. This was smashed open with paving stones and timber beams. Sixty armed men streamed through. A heavy door reinforced with iron blocked the passage to the lockup area of the prison. They knocked it off its hinges.

The deputy sheriff on duty at the prison could see that a lynching was in the offing, so he let Matranga and the others out of their cells. The terrified prisoners fanned out through the prison, crouching in stairwells, fighting one another for the best concealment. Some, too frightened to hide, simply dropped to their knees and prayed. As the vigilantes reached the prison's main wing, the sound of gunfire began to echo through the building. Non-Italian inmates helped the hunters, pointing out the mobsters' hiding places.

Enraged by the acquittal of police chief David Hennessey's killers, New Orleanians gather by the statue of Henry Clay that once stood on Canal Street. "Hang the murderers!" was their call to arms.

Joe Macheca and two other Sicilians were trapped when they ran into a gallery for condemned prisoners and a grate clanged shut behind them. Vigilantes aimed their guns through the grate and shot the three men dead.

Elsewhere in the jail, Joe Polizi was squatting under a staircase, babbling to himself, when the mob found him and dragged him outside into the street. There, in full view of the approving crowd, he was beaten with clubs. As he lay half-senseless on the ground, a noose was fitted around his neck, and the other end of the rope was looped over the crossbar of a lamppost and pulled fast. When his feet left the ground, Polizi reached above his head and grabbed the rope, pulling himself up hand over hand until he reached the lamppost's crossbar. As he clung to the bar, his legs dangling above the heads of the crowd, a man scrambled up the post and hit him in the face until his fingers loosened. The gangster fell but once again managed to grab the rope above his head. Then the vigilantes tied his hands behind his back, hoisted him up, and let him drop. Polizi's legs kicked furiously for a moment. Then he was still, dangling limply. But the vigilantes weren't finished. Raising their rifles, they fired round after round into his body. The crowd roared approval.

Inside the prison, six more prisoners had been flushed out of hiding and rounded up in an open courtyard. Many were wounded. Others, half-mad with terror, begged for mercy. Backed against a bare stone wall, the prisoners watched as a large, makeshift firing squad formed at the far end of the courtyard. The six men fell in a hail of bullets.

Something stirred in the pile of bodies. An elderly man, somehow missed by the storm of bullets, struggled to his feet. He was a cobbler named Monasterio, who'd lived in the shack that served as the Mafia's lookout post. The old man rose unsteadily and faced the line of gunmen. His gray hair and prison clothing were matted with blood. He raised a trembling hand, pleading for his life. A voice called across the courtyard: "Give him another load." A revolver shot caught him in the chest. Monasterio fell dead on the pile.

As the slaughter drew to a close, anger and bloodlust gave way to glee. A series of long, trilling whistles ran through the crowd, mocking the signal that had alerted the Sicilian assassins to the approach of Chief Hennessey. The crowd also derided the accents of the Italians. "Who killa da chief?" they called over the prison walls. "Who killa da chief?"

In all, the assault on the prison lasted less than one hour.

In news sketches of the largest lynching in U.S. history, vigilantes storm the Orleans Parish Prison, trapping and shooting three Sicilian men *(inset)* caught against a metal grate, and cornering six others *(bottom)* whom they executed in the prison yard. Before the violence ended, 16 Sicilians had died for the murder of David Hennessey.

Eleven men were left dead, and five were mortally wounded. None of the vigilantes was ever prosecuted; indeed, the leaders of the mob became folk heroes in the community. To the Italian government, however, they were murderers. In the wake of the vigilante action, Italy recalled its ambassador and threatened to break off diplomatic relations with the United States unless the ringleaders were punished. It was rumored — falsely — that Italian warships were headed for the American coast. Tensions eased only after President Benjamin Harrison offered to pay an indemnity of $25,000 to the family of each victim.

Three Sicilians had escaped the lynch mob at the prison. Ironically, one of them was Charles Matranga, a chief author of the plot to kill Hennessey. Matranga had spent the long hour of the bloodbath huddled under some rubbish in a corner of the prison yard with a crucifix pressed to his lips. Subsequently, the ambush charge against him was dropped, and within weeks Matranga had resumed control of rackets throughout the city. He no longer faced any competition from the Provenzanos. The brothers and their lieutenants had been acquitted in their second trial for the attempted murder of Tony Matranga. But, fleeing the new anti-Sicilian sentiment in New Orleans, they moved their operations to a suburban parish across the Mississippi River.

In time, things settled down to business as usual again for the evolving Mafia in New Orleans. But the memory of what had happened at the parish prison was slow to fade. For years, the trilling of the Sicilian signal whistle haunted the city. It issued not from Matranga's hoods, but from the lips of local schoolboys. Italian vendors and shopkeepers would hear the sound as their young tormentors raced past; then, a moment later, a mocking cry would drift back: "Who killa da chief?"

The New Orleans lynchings may have chilled the millions of honest Italian immigrants who'd hoped for an equality in the United States that they'd never enjoyed back home. But, in the long run, the incident made scarcely a ripple in the transplanted Mafia's gathering tide. The mafiosi of that era lived by violence, and they knew the odds were good that they might die by it. At the same time, the strongest among them found that the rewards were worth the risk, and they could thrive in the New World on mayhem. For men of cunning and ruthlessness, economic opportunities abounded.

In New Orleans, New York, and other port cities, the most prized of cash cows were the docks. Whoever controlled the stevedores could demand under-the-table payments for loading or unloading ships; the waterfront was also prime territory for pilfering and, even more profitable, smuggling. From the wharves, the Mafia and the other criminal brotherhoods generally branched out into gambling, loansharking—and corrupt politics. The Italian underworld won an important role in the political machines that ruled many cities: Crime bosses oversaw the trading of jobs and other favors in return for votes, and they were useful to politicians in rougher ways, deterring challengers by intimidation, mayhem, or murder.

New York, whose Italian population eventually exceeded that of Naples, was a near-perfect breeding ground for organized crime. Toward the end of the 19th century, tens of thousands of Italians were packed into several ghettos, each known as Little Italy, in Manhattan and Brooklyn. Italians victimizing Italians in these neighborhoods had nothing to fear in the way of official reprisals, since the city's police force, heavily Irish, avoided the areas. At a time when roughly a quarter of New York City's population spoke Italian, only 11 city policemen understood the language. This situation reflected not just neglect by the city government but actual strategy—an approach whose author was New York's chief of detectives, Thomas Byrnes.

Exhibiting a profound cynicism coupled with remarkable administrative talent, Byrnes had forged informal treaties with the city's criminal elements. Under his rules, local thieves agreed to limit themselves to certain poor and middle-class neighborhoods. Out-of-town felons were informed that New York was off-limits, except as a hideout. Byrnes thus guaranteed the protection of the wealthy and powerful and thereby ensured his own job. His detectives, who were quick with their fists and night sticks, came down hard on anyone who dared violate the guidelines.

This tidy state of affairs was threatened, however, by Italian gangs whose growing power disrupted the delicate equilibrium, and Byrnes was quick to act on the problem. When a stabbing murder of a Sicilian immigrant came to trial early in 1889, the chief of detectives testified that the homicide had been ordered by the Mafia as part of an ongoing feud over the extradition of Giuseppe Esposito

In Bandit's Roost, as this squalid alley off New York's Mulberry Street was called in the 1890s, the camera of photojournalist Jacob Riis caught a gauntlet of the young Italian toughs who gave the place its name.

Called Lupo the Wolf by the press, ruthless mafioso Ignazio Saietta poses for a police photographer after being booked on a charge of counterfeiting in 1909.

more than seven years earlier. If the crime went unpunished, he warned, the underworld killings would undoubtedly continue. But Byrnes's scary testimony failed to convince the jurors, who may have been reluctant to believe his story about the existence of a criminal Italian secret society. The trial ended in acquittal. The chief of detectives threw up his hands in disgust and declared that Little Italy outlaws could "go ahead and kill each other." The implication was that he wouldn't intervene, so long as the violence didn't spill beyond the Italian ghettos.

In washing his hands of the matter, Byrnes unofficially sanctioned one of the longest and bloodiest gangland feuds in history. In New York, battles between Manhattan mafiosi and Brooklyn-based camorristas would rage for nearly three decades, claiming more than 1,400 lives. A favorite tactic of the combatants was to throw bombs into one another's homes and businesses. New York's authorities recorded more than 2,300 such incidents. As the death toll rose, both sides brought in reinforcements from Italy. These recruits not only restored the dwindling ranks, they also reinforced the discipline and resolve—and the ferocity—characteristic of old country vendettas. The war would go on until 1916, when, after the murder of Mafia boss Nicholas Morello, the top leaders of the Camorra would be convicted of the killing and jailed for life, breaking the back of the Neapolitan organization.

One casualty of the conflict was Thomas Byrnes, who lost his job in 1895 at the height of the battle between the Mafia and Camorra factions. Theodore Roosevelt, then New York's commissioner of police, demanded the detective chief's resignation. The future president was dismayed not just by gangland violence and Byrnes's tacit condoning of it, but by the corruption that was rife in the police department.

Long and bloody as it was, the Mafia-Camorra war wasn't the only mob-related violence drawing attention from the New York press around the turn of the century. Two killings that were known as "barrel murders" drew huge headlines; even by gang standards, they were partic-

ularly gruesome. The first, in 1902, involved a large, unmarked barrel that turned up at a swimming hole in Brooklyn. Inside the barrel was Mafia underboss Joe Catania, whose throat had been cut. A second barrel was found in 1903 on a sidewalk on 11th Street in Manhattan. This cask contained another mafioso, Benedetto Madonia. He'd been stabbed to death, and his genitals had been sliced off and stuffed into his mouth.

The grisly barrel crimes appeared to be the work of the Morello family, who'd arrived in the United States in 1895. Originating in Corleone, the deadly Sicilian clan was led by Antonio Morello, older brother of the ill-fated Nicholas, whose death would end the war with the camorristas a few years hence. Antonio Morello claimed credit for some 30 murders in New York in the 1890s. He and other Morellos—brothers, half-brothers, cousins, and in-laws—would dominate the New York Mafia for years to come.

Perhaps the most notorious member of the Morello gang was Ignazio Saietta, who came to be known as Lupo—the Wolf—to his fellow Italians. The press, closely following Saietta's career, called him, redundantly, "Lupo the Wolf." Saietta was a Black Hand extortionist and a professional killer. Together with his brother-in-law Ciro Terranova, a half-brother of Antonio Morello, he ran an establishment known as the Murder Stable, on East 107th Street in Italian Harlem. There many of the city's mob slayings were contracted and carried out. Eventually the U.S. Secret Service would find the remains of more than 60 murder victims on the premises. Almost certainly, countless more were disposed of without a trace.

Saietta had been so feared in his native Sicily that people who strayed across his path would often cross themselves as an antidote to his evil. In New York he trolled the streets in a white carriage, looking for enemies of the Morellos or for extortion targets who'd failed to pay up. The carriage was drawn by a horse that Lupo had trained for terror. When its master flicked the reins in a particular way, the animal would rear up, give a fearsome neigh, and kick its front

Police lieutenant Joseph Petrosino, a native of southern Italy, headed New York City's Italian squad and was the first policeman to take on the Mafia and the Camorra.

hoofs over the head of Saietta's target. Faced with this inspiration, the mark would usually cave in quickly to Lupo's demands, whatever they might be.

Unlike many mobsters, Saietta cared little for fancy clothes, fine food, and other luxuries. He liked making money for its own sake, and he had many money-making enterprises. Along with extortion, the Wolf had a hand in robbery, counterfeiting, illegal lotteries, and drug sales. "Business is like cherries," he once remarked, explaining his liking for diversity in business. "You yank one off a tree, but it doesn't satisfy you, so you yank another, and then another, one after the other." Violence was, of course, an essential business tool. Among Saietta's foot soldiers were bomb-throwing experts, sharpshooters, knife artists, and various other specialists in death. Many were trained by Saietta himself, who had a complete set of killing skills.

With Thomas Byrnes out of office, Saietta and the rest of the Morello family began to draw more attention from the police force than they were used to. Much of it came from a young patrolman named Giuseppe Michele Pasquale Petrosino—Joe or Joseph to his friends—who was working on the barrel-murders case. A short, thickset, extremely strong man, Petrosino had emigrated to New York from Salerno, Italy, at the age of 19. After working as a tailor, a clerk, and a garbage man, he joined the police force in 1883 and quickly made his mark. He was rough, even brutal. Rather than arrest a criminal and risk losing him to a fast-talking lawyer, Petrosino tended to drag his suspects into an alley and beat confessions out of them. "This way," he would tell them, "you'll remember who Petrosino is." But he had brains as well as brawn. He made a careful study of the latest techniques of scientific police work, and he maintained an extensive library of reference works, newspaper clippings, and intelligence reports. It was information resulting from Petrosino's work on the barrel murders that would eventually lead authorities to the Murder Stable.

Petrosino rose quickly through the police department's ranks, partly because of his talent and diligence, and partly because of his ethnicity—Italians being extremely scarce on the force. Moreover, Theodore Roosevelt took a personal interest in moving his career along. Following Petrosino's promotion to detective in 1895, he traded in his patrolman's uniform for a wardrobe of dark suits and overcoats, double-soled shoes to make himself look taller, and a trademark derby hat. Soon, journalists took notice of "the detective in

THE WORLD: THURSDAY EVENING, APRIL 23, 1903.

DETECTIVE PETROSINO AND SEVENTEEN DESPERATE CRIMINALS
WHOM HE HAS RUN DOWN, CONVICTED AND SENT TO PRISON.

In 1903 the New York *World* portrayed Joseph Petrosino encircled by pictures of 17 assorted con men, robbers, and killers brought to justice in his one-man campaign against organized crime.

the derby." "He lacks refinement and seems rather slow of comprehension," one reporter wrote. "His face is expressionless, and he could move through a crowd without attracting anyone's attention. But it is precisely this that is the detective's strength. He is a master in the art of feigning a timid naivete. But more than one robber and killer have learned to their cost how quick is his mind and how nimble is his arm."

Petrosino would cut through the Italian gangs like a one-man army. He proved particularly effective against the Camorra, but he didn't neglect the Sicilians. Altogether, he arrested at least 60 mafiosi and camorristas and gathered enough evidence to have them all deported. Most of the arrests were carried out in dramatic style. After quietly stalking a Camorra boss named Enrico Alfano, for instance, Petrosino calmly strolled into a Harlem apartment house and waited in the hallway outside one of the rooms until he was certain his quarry was inside. He then kicked his way in, bashing the door with such force that it bowled over three armed men standing on the other side. Grabbing Alfano by the collar, Petrosino dragged him all the way to the police station.

Such deeds made the detective famous in Italy as well as in America, and he became a hero of fiction: Italian pulp novelists published almost 50 books about him, reporting—and much embellishing—his adventures. Petrosino became "the Italian Sherlock Holmes"—a legend in his own time. But the policeman was about to meet another legend, and he wouldn't survive the experience.

Around the turn of the century, there arrived in New York City that most powerful of Sicilian dons, Vito Cascio Ferro *(chapter 1)*. The elegant capo di tutti capi from the old country had several reasons for coming to America. For one thing, he wanted to visit his sister, Francesca, who kept a shop on 103rd Street in Manhattan. Another consideration was his legal situation in Sicily: A period of particularly annoying heat from the authorities made it convenient for him to go abroad. It is also said that Don Vito might have made the trip to deal personally with detective Joseph Petrosino.

But beyond all that, there was more to the visit. Don Vito was not just a criminal, he was a statesman of crime. He was a visionary and missionary of crime. It seems that he viewed from afar the contentious and bloody doings of the immigrant Italian gangs and managed to see in their petty, parochial viciousness something grand—an organized, efficient American Mafia with prospects as boundless as the new land. He came to America in pursuit of his vision. He was 38 years old at the time.

In New York Cascio Ferro was warmly greeted by Ignazio Saietta and other members of the Morello family, and with them he shared his professional wisdom, mainly the pizzu, his revised, less vicious version of the protection racket. His American cousins noted admiringly that Don Vito had a particular genius for calculating extortion payments, determining the largest amount possible without driving a shopkeeper or workingman out of business.

Cascio Ferro stayed in New York for more than two years, establishing relationships between Italian-American gangsters and the Sicilian Mafia. But the New York climate got unhealthy for him about the time of the second barrel murder, when the ensuing police investigation led in Don Vito's direction. He fled to New Orleans, where he found a haven among the criminal brotherhood there. After about six months in the Crescent City, the don embarked for Sicily. But when he left, he carried with him a photograph of Joe Petrosino. The detective was a marked man.

Five years after the don's departure, events in New York conspired to arrange Cascio Ferro's eventual showdown with Petrosino. The city's reform-minded police commissioner, Theodore Bingham, was considering a plan devised by an Italian law professor to decimate the Italian underworld by a prosecutorial masterstroke. The scheme involved dispatching an American detective to Italy to gather up police dossiers on all fugitives from Italian justice. These files would then be carried to America and checked against the files of suspects living in New York. Those wanted in Italy would promptly be deported.

The idea seemed promising: In one stroke, Italian authorities would close the files on numerous crimes, and their New York counterparts would be rid of a sizable portion of their city's criminal class. As fate would have it, the American agent tapped for the overseas mission was Joe Petrosino, who volunteered for the job. He confidently anticipated dealing a death blow to the mob. Of course he was also aware that his assignment might end up the other way around, and he set sail for Italy in February of 1909 amid security so tight that not even his wife was allowed to see him off.

In Rome the detective was greeted warmly by the chief of police, who gave him a suitcase full of photographs and documents. It seemed a good start, but Petrosino was growing ever more wary. He'd been under surveillance from the moment he left New York. He knew it. A glance over his shoulder almost invariably revealed some stranger watching him. One of the men he spotted tailing him was a mafioso he'd arrested in New York the previous year. As the investigator left Rome for Sicily, the American ambassador urged him to watch his step. In Sicily, the ambassador warned, there were "perhaps a thousand criminals who know you." It was no exaggeration.

Petrosino arrived in Palermo on February 28, 1909, and set off on a tour of small, Mafia-infested towns, perhaps to

Mafia chief Vito Cascio Ferro appears on a Palermo police document that describes him as a big man with bronze skin and chestnut eyes and hair. Legend has it that Cascio Ferro was behind detective Petrosino's murder, and that he may even have shot him personally.

On March 20, 1909, Joseph Petrosino's mile-long funeral procession winds through Palermo, where schools, offices, and shops closed in his honor. A second spectacular funeral followed when the popular policeman's remains arrived in New York less than a month later.

study the origins of his adversaries. He was particularly intrigued with the village of Bisacquino, birthplace and residence of Vito Cascio Ferro.

Petrosino returned to Palermo on Friday, March 12, and that evening he dined alone at a restaurant called the Café Oreto. He sat at a corner table with his back to the wall, enjoying pasta, fish, potatoes, cheese, fruit, and a half-liter of wine. As he was finishing his meal, two men approached his table and spoke to him briefly. Petrosino dismissed them with a wave. Soon after they departed, he paid his bill and left the restaurant.

A few blocks away, Don Vito Cascio Ferro was dining at the home of a deputy to the Italian parliament. Midway through the meal he excused himself. Borrowing his host's carriage, he drove to the Piazza Marina and waited.

One of Palermo's busiest centers, the Piazza Marina was normally bustling with activity and patrolled by at least six policemen. That night, however, the crowds had all but disappeared, and not a single policeman was to be seen. About 9 p.m., Petrosino walked into the open plaza. Two gunmen stepped from behind a tree and fired four times, hitting him in the right cheek, the right shoulder, and the throat. As though an act of will could keep death at bay, Petrosino refused to fall, holding himself upright for a time by clinging to the iron window grate on a house abutting the plaza. Nevertheless, he eventually dropped to the pavement, dead. According to Mafia legend, one of the assassins was Don Vito Cascio Ferro himself.

There would be a cursory investigation and a handful of arrests, but no one was ever brought to trial for Petrosino's murder. Don Vito, a prime suspect, had taken great care with his alibi. His dinner-party host testified that the don had never left the house on the night of the killing. Privately, Cascio Ferro made no secret of his role in the affair. "My action," he claimed, "was a disinterested one and in response to a challenge I could not afford to ignore."

In both New York and Italy, underworld leaders rejoiced at the killing, but the mob hadn't completed its revenge. Petrosino's death was meant to serve as a warning to anyone who might dare mount a challenge in the future. To add to its effect, the Morellos took aim at the detective's widow: Pulling strings at City Hall, they managed to deprive Mrs. Petrosino of her husband's pension. The murdered detective's friends tried to stage a benefit concert to recoup the loss, but this, too, was quashed by the mob.

In their vendetta against Petrosino, however, the gangsters had overstepped somewhat. Together with the Secret Service, the New York City police, in a mood of retaliation, launched a new offensive against organized crime, concentrating their efforts on the most visible target—the Morello family. Ignazio Saietta and Antonio Morello were both nailed for counterfeiting. Morello was sentenced to 25 years in prison, Saietta to 30 years. The presiding judge later explained that the sentences were unusually stiff because of the two mobsters' suspected connection to the Petrosino killing and because their defense fund was apparently the result of "extortions throughout the country as far south as New Orleans."

If Petrosino's death was a mixed blessing in New York, it was nevertheless unalloyed gold for Vito Cascio Ferro in Sicily. It enhanced his fame and power at home and at the same time affirmed his ties with grateful mobsters in the United States. As he went on to consolidate and expand his influence at home, the ambitious don continued to dream of a united transatlantic Mafia, to be led by him or one of his minions. Farseeing as he was, however, Don Vito miscalculated the course of the Mafia in America.

In the United States, the mob and the nation were taking shape at the same time, and the young, raw country saw the birth of a disorganized, bloody, combative, and freewheeling mob—the mob of Esposito and Saietta, of the Morellos and Matrangas and Provenzanos. But America was growing up, poised on the verge of becoming the most powerful nation in the world. And the Mafia would adapt. In the new brotherhood, organization would be the key to success, and bloodshed would be scorned as bad for business.

Don Vito would never realize his dream of being capo di tutti capi in Old World and New. He would, ignominiously, die in prison. At the height of his power, however, when the dream was still intact, he dispatched one of his lieutenants to America to help pave his way by organizing the New York underworld. The protégé was Salvatore Maranzano, who arrived in the United States in 1927. Maranzano had something of the flair and the cunning of his old boss, and he, too, envisioned himself as capo di tutti capi.

Maranzano would come closer to the dream than Don Vito had, but the two men had the same flawed vision. Don Salvatore, too, would fail to sense which way the winds of change were blowing in America. Other men—younger men—would not fail. ◆

I told them we was in a business that had to keep moving without explosions every two minutes.

CHARLIE "LUCKY" LUCIANO

3

Chairman of the Board

Salvatore Maranzano had prepared his coronation with the greatest pleasure and care. His ascent to the throne had taken him half a dozen difficult, dangerous years. He had arrived in the United States from Castellammare del Golfo, Sicily, in 1925, already a renowned mafioso at the age of 40. Ruthless, avidly ambitious, far better educated than most (he was fond of quoting Julius Caesar), Maranzano had killed and connived his way to supremacy over one rival after another. Now, in the summer of 1931, he'd emerged victorious from a ferocious gangland war and was about to crown himself capo di tutti capi—boss of all bosses—ruler of every racketeering enterprise in America.

The ceremony took place in an immense banquet hall on the Grand Concourse in the Bronx, New York. The place resembled the interior of some fantastic cathedral, for the 46-year-old Maranzano made a fetish of his Roman Catholicism and had ordered the hall decorated with dozens upon dozens of crucifixes, portraits of saints, and statues of the Virgin Mary.

Invitations—commands, actually—had gone out to 500 of the top Mafia people in New York and around the country. No one ignored the summons; if for any reason a man could not attend, he hastened to send a deputy. The minions were seated in prearranged order of rank, as determined by Maranzano. On the dais, facing his subjects, the overlord sat on a huge thronelike chair rented from a theatrical supply house. To either side ranged the subordinates Maranzano had accepted as his princes and barons, chiefs of the various Mafia families.

The don rose and began to speak in Italian, occasionally shifting to Sicilian dialect, here and there injecting Latin quotations that baffled most of his audience. Yet there was no mistaking the import of his speech—if anyone was ever in doubt. Maranzano announced to the assembled mafiosi that henceforth they all belonged to him, minds and bodies, fists, knives, and pistols. No longer would there be a loose affiliation of more or less independent families; now all would be joined in one empire under one rule—his. And as he explained the division of territories and who would report to whom, Maranzano raised his arms as might the pope in bestowing a benediction.

When he finished speaking, the moment arrived for tribute. Maranzano resumed his seat on his throne and with a nod of his head summoned his vassals to the dais, one by one. As each man approached, he laid a cash-filled envelope on a large table positioned for the purpose. When the bills were counted later, Salvatore Maranzano's take for the evening came, by some accounts, to well over $1 million.

But the don of dons would not have long to savor his reign. Within a month he would be dead, coolly swept aside by a new breed of farseeing and highly intelligent leaders who saw him as an outdated obstacle to progress. Foremost among the newcomers would be Charlie "Lucky" Luciano, 34, whom the unsuspecting Maranzano had placed at his right hand that night of the coronation. Luciano had contributed a princely $50,000 to Maranzano's treasure chest. He could afford to be generous; he fully expected that he'd soon get it all back—and a lot more.

By then, Luciano and his colleagues were already firm in their vision of what the Mafia must become. Instead of a semifeudal, exclusively Sicilian association, the Mafia must be Americanized to reflect the diverse character and lush opportunities of the adopted land. It must grow more flexible, more cooperative, and above all more businesslike—more like a giant American corporation.

That was how Luciano had modeled his own gang in New York over the past dozen years. Starting from a springboard of Prohibition bootlegging, he and his men had moved into big-time theft, loansharking, labor racketeering, and gambling of every description. To his distaste, yet with his compliance, some of his lieutenants had also involved themselves in narcotics and prostitution. The millions were rolling in. But the old dons, the Maranzanos of the Mafia with their medieval horizons, Sicilian wariness of outsiders, incessant vendettas, and lust for personal power, stood in the way of untold billions. Once the greaseballs and mustache Petes, as the younger men scathingly called them, had been eliminated, the Mafia could move ahead to a level of nationwide power and profitability that the old-timers couldn't even have dreamed of. And Lucky Luciano would be the man to take it to the heights—not as the king that Maranzano would have been but as chairman of the board.

It was clear from the start that the boy christened Salvatore Lucania was marked for something other than a Sicilian immigrant's life of labor in New York City's teeming Little Italy. Lucania had arrived as a nine-year-old with his parents and siblings in April 1906, the family escaping from the mean little hillside village of Lercara Friddi. The boy's main memory of the place was the stink of the nearby sulfur mines. "It was the smell of no money, the smell of being hungry all the time," he would recall.

His father, Antonio, became a day laborer at a handsome wage by Sicilian standards, but the money was barely enough to sustain existence in America. The children went to public school, where Salvatore, the oldest pupil in his class but one who spoke no English, swiftly concluded that formal education was a miserable waste of time. He took to the streets and joined other truants preying on Jewish youngsters passing through the neighborhood on their way to and from school. The Jews either shelled out a penny or two for protection or they got beaten and robbed. Except for one.

Salvatore accosted this victim expecting easy money. The Jewish boy was about eight years old—five years younger than the strapping Sicilian—and he was about a head shorter. But when Salvatore demanded money, the runty little kid merely snarled a brief but pointed obscenity. Salvatore started to laugh. He admired guts.

"O.K.," he said, "you got protection for free."

The smaller boy offered a suggestion as to what his tormentor could do with his protection. The two stared at each other, and some wordless recognition passed between them. In that moment, one of the great partnerships of crime was born. Future organizational wizard Lucky Luciano had just met future financial genius Meyer Lansky. "We both had a kind of instant understanding," Luciano later explained. "It was something that never left us."

But it would be a while before the partnership could take effect. Lansky stayed in school and was a whiz at it, greedily soaking up knowledge, a near prodigy at math. Meanwhile,

Salvatore Lucania was about to serve his first sentence—committed as a chronic truant to four months at the Brooklyn Truant School. All it taught him, outside of hating Brooklyn, was how to be a better thief and pickpocket.

He also emerged with eyes newly opened to the broader spectrum of criminal possibilities. "I found out that kids wasn't the only crooks," he would later tell Martin Gosch, a writer who was working on a book about him called *The Last Testament of Lucky Luciano*. "We was surrounded by crooks." Landlords, shopkeepers, the cop on the beat, everybody seemed to be stealing from somebody. Then there were what Lucania called "the real pros," the Mafia dons from the old country with their black suits and big black cars. People feared them. They had power and wealth, and to young Lucania, big money and notoriety was everything. "We knew they was rich," he said, "and rich was what counted, because the rich got away with anything."

Lucania himself was something of a celebrity, having served time at such a young age. And with his natural flair for leadership, he and a dozen or so Sicilian friends soon were marauding through the Lower East Side, robbing merchants and mugging lone pedestrians. Even then Lucania was a crafty, careful organizer whose watchword was unity. All loot was put into a common pot to be shared equally; everybody had to have some sort of job as a front to explain his unusual wealth, and the new clothes and other possessions bought with that wealth had to be acquired gradually so as not to arouse suspicion.

Dozens of such teenage gangs roamed the Lower East Side, getting in one another's way and battling for whatever escaped the clutches of the older Mafia mobsters. Lucania began to look north, to Midtown, where the real money was. Other bands, including a number from East Harlem, had the same idea, and from time to time, uneasy alliances sprang up in the interests of pooling manpower and knowledge. One that endured for Lucania was with the leader of the 104th Street Gang, Francesco Castiglia, soon to be renowned as Frank Costello.

That Castiglia was not Sicilian, but from Calabria on the toe of the Italian Boot, bothered Lucania not in the slightest. The man was a couple of years older, tough, practiced, and with a fertile brain to go with his experience. Castiglia's intellect came as a mild surprise to Lucania, who had credited Jews with a monopoly on superintelligence. But here was an Italian who was as clever and perceptive as anyone else around. The two became immediate friends and colleagues in a relationship that would remain steadfast until the last days of Lucania's life.

By now it was 1916. Europe was at war and the United States edging toward the conflict. Lucania had turned 19 and was making crime pay well enough. But for one of the few times in his life, he allowed greed to get the better of his own high intelligence. While working as a delivery boy for a ladies' hat manufacturer, he started running drugs. Some weeks he made as much as $100 from the local pusher. But he grew careless; the police noticed him going in and out of a poolroom frequented by addicts. Salvatore Lucania was arrested, convicted of selling narcotics, and sentenced to one year at Hampton Farms Penitentiary.

He was out within six months for good behavior. No longer did he use the name Salvatore; the other cons had started calling him Charlie, and he liked it because it sounded better in English than the slightly feminine nicknames Sal or Sally. Gone, too, was any recklessness remaining in his character. "I made up my mind I was never going to get caught again," he swore. "I'd kill myself before they'd ever put me away again." He came very close to making good on his vow. Twenty years would pass before the law could snare him once more.

The first thing Lucania did once he was free was get back together with Frank Castiglia, who'd been serving his own one-year sentence on a gun possession rap. Meyer Lansky—only 15 and still a runt, but prodigious in a fight and awesomely knowledgeable—had quit school by now, and he joined Lucania's gang. Lansky brought with him another Jewish youth, Benjamin Siegel, scarcely 11 but big and strong for his age, and so wildly fearless that his friends called him Bugsy.

So there they were, four young hoodlums in search of some big scores. "We was the best team that ever got put together," said Lucania. "We knew our jobs better than any other guys on the street." For a joke, Charlie started calling Castiglia by the Irish name of Costello; the moniker not only stuck but proved useful later when they got deeply into New York City's Irish-dominated politics.

The Mafia dons, with their cult of Sicily, would have been scandalized. But before long, those same dons would begin to notice something about this odd hybrid gang: how brilliantly it was succeeding.

Within a couple of years, Lucania's outfit numbered more than 20 members and was operating over the whole of Manhattan. Each job was carefully planned and executed. The gang hit small banks, warehouses, stores, pawnshops, loan companies—wherever there was cash or merchandise that could be fenced. The profits rolled in so fast that the boys considered banking some of it. But when Costello went to take a look at the bank, he returned with a better idea. The place employed only one aged guard. A couple of weeks later, instead of making a deposit, Lucania's gang took the bank for an $8,000 withdrawal. "If that's the way they're going to protect our dough, the hell with them," said Lansky.

Besides, there were other ways to put the money to work, ways that would soon make the bank heists and store robberies look penny-ante by comparison.

Everybody gambled, and offtrack betting on the horse races was just starting to become a major business. Lucania and his friends bought into a number of established midtown Manhattan bookmaking operations, taking a share of the profits in return for an infusion of capital. Though making book on the horses and other athletic events was illegal, society winked at bookmaking as a victimless crime. Charlie Lucania quickly learned what kind of money could be made with little risk.

And he absorbed another important lesson: that even small risks could be virtually eliminated by buying protection from police and other officials. With $5,000 he established what he called the gang's "Buy-Money Bank" and turned it over to the suave and clever Costello. Frank started cautiously, putting out the money where it would do the most immediate good—into the hands of the precinct cops and the ward heelers in neighborhoods where the gang had bookmaking interests. In less than a decade, the Buy-Money Bank would have virtually unlimited funds, literally millions to spread around.

Lucania's contact with the Mafia dons in these early years seems to have been minimal. As his gang began to make its presence felt, some of the older mobsters approached him with offers to join their outfits. From time to time he went out on jobs with them, yet he always kept his distance. Charlie Lucania regarded himself as a leader, not a follower, and his fledgling gang was as different from the transplanted Sicilian mobs as New York City was from Palermo.

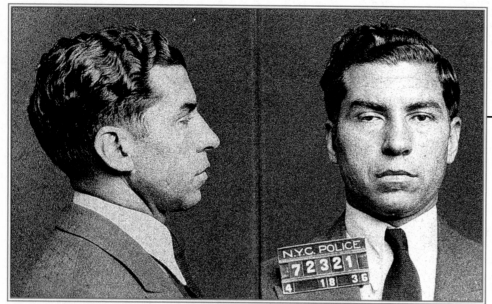

Four young knights of the mob exude confidence for New York City police photographers: Charlie Luciano (top left) and his three most trusted associates, Meyer Lansky (bottom left), Frank Costello (opposite, top), and Ben Siegel (opposite, bottom).

York's Little Italy. The gangsters operated a lottery and took their cut from every little poker game. They loaned money at usurious rates, imported and distributed narcotics, and held monopolies on vital foodstuffs: olive oil, cheese, anchovies, the tasty little artichokes so dear to the heart of every south Italian. A grocer either bought from the Mafia supplier at inflated prices or he found his store wrecked; himself beaten; his wife and daughters harassed, perhaps assaulted, possibly mutilated. Every merchant paid a dollar or two a week as protection money, right down to the pushcart peddlers, whose carts would be smashed and merchandise scattered if they withheld so much as a dime. Murder was so casual that robbery victims frequently gave up their lives as well as their possessions.

In this rapacious criminal society the mantle of leadership rested on uneasy shoulders. For all the Mafia's vaunted brotherhood, the bands fought violently among themselves, and killing was a way of life even within the so-called families. One building on Manhattan's East 107th Street became known as the Murder Stable; according to police, no fewer than 23 unruly, treasonous, or overly ambitious mob members were executed there between 1900 and 1917.

The Mafia's homicidal nature would never change. And in 1919 a momentous event occurred that would increase the stakes in the deadly mob competitions even as it opened vast new horizons for organized crime. On January 16 the Eighteenth Amendment to the United States Constitution was ratified. It forbade the manufacture, sale, import, or export of intoxicating beverages. Ten months later, on October 27, Congress passed the Volstead Act to enforce the amendment. It defined an intoxicant as any beverage containing more than one-half of one percent alcohol by volume. The act also authorized federal agents to prosecute all violations and mandated stiff penalties for those convicted

Organized crime was epidemic in New York in the first decades of the 20th century. But there was no real citywide operation such as Lucania even then was building. The ethnic mobs—the Irish owning the West Side of Manhattan and the Brooklyn waterfront, the Jews and Italians laying claim to the rest of Brooklyn, Harlem, and the Lower East Side—remained largely within their own slum neighborhoods, terrorizing the masses of immigrants jammed into the festering tenements. Now and again ethnic struggles erupted, particularly along the waterfront, where there were warehouses to be looted. But mainly the gangs guarded their turf and preyed on their own kind.

With its ingrained clannishness, loathing for the law, brutality, and talent for organization, the Mafia ruled New

of trading in booze. America was going dry—and dying for a drink.

The Volstead Act went into effect on January 16, 1920. Literally overnight, hundreds of millions of dollars that ordinarily flowed through the channels of legitimate commerce became available to anyone with brains and muscle. Virtually every gangster in New York and elsewhere—all the Irish, Jewish, Italian, and Sicilian mobs, all the Young Turks like those led by Charlie Lucania—scrambled after the bonanza. In the blink of an eye, the ethnic bands—and the well-organized Mafia in particular—were catapulted out of the immigrant slums and into the mainstream of American business.

On one level, Prohibition was the triumph of the Women's Christian Temperance Union in its long campaign against dissipation among the menfolk of the nation. But the struggle went deeper than that. It found roots in the distaste that was felt by conservative rural America toward the ascendancy of big-city America. The sprawling cities were where much of the liquor came from, where factories belched smoke and immigrant hordes infested tenements, where killers roamed freely and every evil reigned.

But Prohibition was not without its supporters within those troubled cities. Urban reformers, aghast at the chaos and corruption of the cities, linked the saloon to the plight of the poor. Abolish liquor, these social theorists said, and the workingman would become more responsible, efficient, and, presumably, happier.

The problem was, it wasn't only the poor and the working class who enjoyed a tipple. Almost everyone did, and the upper and middle classes pitched in and did their share to make a mockery of the Eighteenth Amendment. It was not illegal to drink, but simply to supply booze, and bootlegging became another of those victimless crimes condoned and even encouraged by the public.

In the Little Italys of New York, Boston, Philadelphia, Pittsburgh, Cleveland, Detroit, and Chicago, virtually every household produced homemade wine and had its own little still for making a bit of brandy now and again. Put into steady production and multiplied by the hundreds of thousands, these tiny distilleries poured out a torrent of alcohol for the Mafia gangs to distribute. And that was just the beginning.

Vast stocks of liquor were on hand in warehouses everywhere when the Volstead Act went into effect. These were immediately burglarized, and their contents were distributed at handsome prices to thirsty Americans. Under the law, production of denatured alcohol was still permitted for medicinal purposes and for the preparation of photographic film, smokeless gunpowder, and a hundred other items.

A speakeasy patron stands for a peephole inspection by a cautious doorman on the lookout for federal prohibition agents. Curiously, the law forbade supplying intoxicants but not drinking them.

Output in 1920 was 28 million gallons—and shot up to 180 million gallons annually by the end of the decade. About one-third, 60 million gallons, found its way into the illicit liquor industry, and each gallon of denatured alcohol was treated to make three gallons of bogus Scotch or gin "fresh off the boat," as the bootleggers assured their customers.

The booze actually coming off the boat never approached the quantity produced domestically. But there was plenty of it, and being "the good stuff," it commanded both the highest prices and the greatest prestige. Bootleggers from the United States and abroad established numerous bases outside the country: on the island of Saint Pierre and Miquelon, just south of Newfoundland; in the Bahamas, British Honduras, Mexico; and even at Papeete, Tahiti, where freighters would load the cases and carry them to market in America. Canadians, in particular, leaped at the new business opportunities. At one point something like 80 percent of all Canadian whiskey production found its way overland or by sea into the United States—to say nothing of the genuine Highland Scotch that flowed across the border.

Onto this vast stage in 1920 strode Charlie Lucania and his partners. Lucania was only 23; Frank Costello had turned 25, but Meyer Lansky and Bugsy Siegel were still in their teens. It is not known whether they had tested the waters with any of the home-distilled alcohol coming out of Little Italy. But when the opportunity came for big money, with quality merchandise, they eagerly reached for it.

A new man had entered the picture by now: Giuseppe Antonio Doto, an 18-year-old Neapolitan who'd changed his name to Joseph A. Adonis to emphasize his movie-star looks. He was tough, shrewd, and ambitious. Lucania liked him. They were eating spumone one day in a local ice-cream store when Adonis suddenly blurted out a request for a $10,000 loan. He explained that he'd been in Philadelphia the night before and had struck up a friendship with a powerful bootlegger named Waxey Gordon. Gordon had offered him a carload of 100-proof bottled-in-bond rye whiskey for $35,000. An advance of $10,000, Adonis said, would entitle Lucania's gang to half the profits on the deal.

Without hesitation, Lucania told Adonis to keep his money; the gang would put up the whole stake, and Adonis would have partners. Costello, Lansky, and Siegel concurred, and Charlie and his friends were in the liquor business in a big way.

The success was due in no small part to a shrewd decision

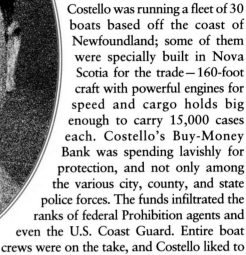

that Lucania and his colleagues had made at the outset. Most bootleggers believed in quantity, not quality, and the temptations were great to follow that course. The boys could reap a huge profit by diluting and otherwise adulterating their whiskey until it was rotgut fit only for cheap speakeasies. Or they could start out, at least, by selling the spirits pure, still realize a massive profit, and win for themselves the cream of the clients in midtown Manhattan. It was an easy decision. They sold their whiskey straight.

Soon Gordon offered 3,000 cases of premium, uncut Scotch. Before Prohibition, distilleries in the Scottish Highlands had charged $17 for a 12-bottle case. In 1920 the price shot up to $26 a case. Considering transportation expenses and Gordon's markup, those 3,000 cases might have cost Lucania & Co. as much as $150,000. But with good Scotch going for at least $30 a bottle—and the best 12-year-old brands fetching upward of $175 a bottle—those 3,000 cases were worth well over $1 million on the street.

The gang sold every drop it could lay its hands on. The market was insatiable, not just in the hotels and clubs and among New York's wealthy, but particularly in the huge midtown Garment Center, where manufacturers wooed out-of-town buyers with booze. Good Scotch was number one on most lists.

Lucania made arrangements with Waxey Gordon to take all the liquor the Philadelphian could import. But there never was enough, and it didn't take Charlie and his people long to conclude that they would have to start cutting their liquor. It had to be done right, naturally. With class. The bottles and labels had to be identical and the quality high. Yet with some pure alcohol and a little caramel coloring, one bottle of first-rate Scotch or Canadian whiskey could be blended into three bottles of pretty good stuff that most customers would accept for the real thing.

With Gordon as a partner, Lucania, Costello, Lansky, and the others built a bootlegging empire. At one point

The vain Giuseppe Doto, shown above in a 1937 New York police mug shot, changed his name to Joe Adonis around 1920, when he spearheaded the Lucania gang's drive into bootlegging.

Costello was running a fleet of 30 boats based off the coast of Newfoundland; some of them were specially built in Nova Scotia for the trade—160-foot craft with powerful engines for speed and cargo holds big enough to carry 15,000 cases each. Costello's Buy-Money Bank was spending lavishly for protection, and not only among the various city, county, and state police forces. The funds infiltrated the ranks of federal Prohibition agents and even the U.S. Coast Guard. Entire boat crews were on the take, and Costello liked to brag that Coast Guard cutters occasionally ran whiskey in to the beach from freighters lying just outside territorial waters.

Lucania's mobsters bought into—or otherwise subverted—legitimate producers of domestic alcohol, thus assuring themselves ample supplies. They established plants for blending whiskey, went into the bottling and labeling business, acquired enormous warehouses and massive fleets of trucks. Once in a while the gang lost a truckload, or an entire shipment, to federal agents or to hijackers. But mostly the business ticked along with the precision of an immense Swiss watch. "I'll bet when me and my guys got our whiskey business together, we had a bigger company than Henry Ford," Lucania boasted.

Charlie and his crew kept a sharp eye out for useful recruits and new alliances, as usual paying no attention to birthplace or ethnic background. Into the gang came Vito Genovese, a short, muscular Neapolitan who was merciless in a fight; Carlo Gambino, a tough, businesslike character with a certain quiet courtliness; Albert Anastasia, brother of a notorious waterfront racketeer, himself a violent man just released from Sing Sing's death row when a murder conviction was overturned on appeal. Intensely loyal to Lucania, Anastasia would become one of the gang's most effective enforcers.

Lansky opened communications with Louis Buchalter, better known as Louis Lepke, a fellow Jew who was beginning to make his weight felt selling protection in the Garment District. But Lepke was going about it the wrong way, the Lucania gang thought, haphazardly tossing a bottle of acid here, setting a fire there, dispatching goons here and there without any real plan. They made him one: Concentrate first on the smaller, weaker outfits and then, with them in line, go after the top manufacturers. Lepke was grateful. He joined the gang and would provide the beachhead for its invasion of the garment business.

Costello courted another Jew, Arthur Flegenheimer, who'd taken the name Dutch Schultz and was carving out a bootleg barony of his own in the Bronx. Lucania forged a mutually profitable alliance with Schultz that endured long after Prohibition.

By the mid-1920s Charlie Lucania, not yet 30 years old, was close to the pinnacle of his universe—indeed of the whole New York scene. Tall, darkly good-looking, impeccably dressed, affable, even charming when he chose to be, he was entertained at elegant Long Island estates and counted Wall Street mogul Jules Bache among his friends. He developed a passion for golf and earned himself a respectably low handicap at the most exclusive suburban country clubs. Showmen Florenz Ziegfeld and George White enjoyed his company, and Charlie reciprocated by backing their Broadway extravaganzas. Women flocked to his side; show girls and debutantes alike found him irresistible.

Everyone from the mayor to the police commissioner and city councilmen, from judges and state legislators to United States senators and congressmen, paid his respects to Charlie Lucania. Why not? It sometimes seemed as if half the world was on his payroll—or in his debt. The great sporting event of 1923 was the fight between heavyweight champion Jack Dempsey and the huge Argentine challenger Luis Angel Firpo: the Manassa Mauler versus the Bull of the Pampas. Tickets to the match at New York's Polo Grounds were impossible to buy. But Lucania, through renowned sportswriter Bill Corum, paid $25,000 for 200 ringside seats ordinarily reserved for the press and gave them away to his friends and colleagues. Few recipients of such generosity ever forgot it.

The money meant nothing to Lucania. In 1925 the profits from his bootleg business alone amounted to at least $12 million. The gang had about 100 men steadily employed in the liquor trade, drawing $200 a week at a time when a hard-working clerk was lucky to make $25. That meant a payroll amounting to $1 million a year. Of the remaining $11 million, a mind-boggling $5 million in bribe money went to police, politicians, and various other officials. The cost of liquor and other operational expenses was $2 million more, which left $4 million to be split among Lucania and his partners. They kept virtually all of it, for they paid taxes only on what they reported from such modest jobs as chauffeur or salesman, which they used as fronts.

The peak for liquor was still to come, and now a number of other enterprises were showing promise. At first, the gang's gambling interests focused on the casinos and horse parlors favored by the relatively well-to-do. But one night Lucania and Lansky were in Covington, Kentucky, a wide-open town just across the border from Ohio, for the opening of a casino called the Beverly Club. Lansky took in the scene, noting all the rich who'd come from everywhere to gamble, and pondered out loud: "What about the little guy who can't even bet two bucks on a horse? Isn't he entitled to some of this pleasure, even if he can only bet a couple of pennies?"

Lansky wanted Lucania & Co. to establish a numbers game among the poor. If enough people bet their pennies every day, the gang could make the odds and the payoff attractive enough so that players would imagine they could strike it rich any day of the week. For city slum dwellers, that was a powerful lure.

Lucania and Lansky hurried to Cleveland and stayed up all night, fortified by a bottle of rye, working out the details of what would become the policy game. The daily number, from 000 to 999, would be based on an unfixable and well-publicized figure, such as the last three digits of the New York Stock Exchange volume. The winner would get a huge payoff of 600 to 1. But the real odds were 1,000 to 1, thus assuring the operators immense profits.

Frank Costello tested the idea first in Harlem. It proved a stunning success—among New York's poor and then in cities and towns all across the country. "So much money was coming in from policy that we had to have meetings all the time to figure out what to do with the dough," recalled Lucania. The solution seemed a natural one: The gang expanded into the loan business.

Lucania was no innocent about usury. The Mafia dons ruling Little Italy traditionally applied themselves to that old and dishonorable practice, lending out money to immigrants at such high rates that the borrowers were for-

The capture of this rum-running boat and its 700-case cargo gave the overworked U.S. Coast Guard a rare victory in May of 1932, just 18 months before the prohibition amendment was repealed.

ever in debt. The techniques of such loansharking were known to all, and where better to put them to use than in Manhattan's Garment District, where Louis Lepke, assisted by a Lucania lieutenant named Tommy Lucchese, was making considerable progress shaking down the nation's dress manufacturers?

One of the perils of the dress business was that styles changed at least yearly and frequently more often. Each change meant new patterns, new materials, sometimes new machines—all requiring short-term capital at high risk. The hazards were unattractive to banks, so garment makers fell into the maws of the loan sharks. In short order, Lucania's crew muscled aside the competition and got a lock on the business, supplying whatever cash was needed at rates ranging from 100 percent to 1,000 percent, depending on the length of the loan. A common rate was 20 percent a week; in four months that added up to more than 300 percent, in a year to better than 1,000 percent.

There was no excuse for failure to pay, and debt collection could be painful for the borrower. However, there were times when an alternative arrangement might suggest itself. As Lucania said, "if the guy had what looked like a good business then we would become his partner." That's how he and his mob gained a foothold in legitimate enterprises.

The gang worked both sides of the industrial street for even greater profits. Those were the days when the International Ladies' Garment Workers and other unions were struggling to organize the Garment District. Lucania gave the organizers a hand, assuring them of members and seeing that dues were paid. In return, the gang got control of a number of unions' locals. As a result, manufacturers who came to terms could count on reasonable wage demands and no strikes. It was a sweet business all around, and Lucania acted the benevolent godfather to the whole district.

What smoothed the way for everything was that $5 mil-

lion in bootleg protection money. In late 1925 Lucania's gang practically owned every police precinct in New York City—by virtue of the fact that the mob not only paid off the line cops and their officers but also funneled huge sums to the police commissioner himself. The graft started at $10,000 a week and within a couple of years doubled. At noon on the appointed day each week, a red-haired, freckle-faced Irishman named Joe Cooney would walk into City Hall dressed as a maintenance worker and deliver a brown bag filled with cash to the commissioner's office. If and when there had to be a token raid, a police commander would call or visit Lucania personally to work out the details and minimize damage.

With business booming, Lucania made some adjustments to his image and personal life. One involved his name. Just as Salvatore seemed unacceptable in America, so his family name had nettled him for years. No one except an Italian seemed able to pronounce it correctly, with the accent on the next-to-last syllable. His swank friends, his women, his Jewish and Irish pals, the cops and politicians, all managed to mangle it. From time to time, Charlie had used the alias Luciano, and he noticed that hardly anybody had trouble with that. Luciano it would be from now on.

That matter settled, Luciano set about revising his lifestyle. For some years he'd lived in a tastefully furnished apartment in the respectable Murray Hill district of Manhattan's East Side—not quite Park Avenue, but reasonably classy. But with his social calen-

South of Times Square, delivery trucks crowd the streets of New York's Garment District, where the high risk and capital demands of fashion drove manufacturers into the embrace of organized crime's loan sharks.

dar full to bursting, Luciano found the apartment inadequate. Deciding to live in a hotel, he moved to the Barbizon Plaza, to a lofty suite with a nice view of Central Park.

Even without the uptown address, Luciano was attracting serious attention in Mafia circles. Older dons had already made a number of alliance-seeking passes at their powerful young compatriot, and with good reason: Whoever landed Luciano would not only eliminate a strong competitor but might also gain enough money and muscle to rule the entire Mafia in New York, perhaps in America.

Foremost in the bidding for Luciano's favor were two dons, about equal in strength, each determined to destroy the other. As early as 1923, Salvatore Maranzano, whose band was composed almost exclusively of Sicilians from his hometown of Castellammare del Golfo, had offered Luciano the position of chief lieutenant. He called Charlie "the young Caesar" and said that he, Maranzano, would treat him like his own son. More important, he would put Luciano in charge of their enormous pooled liquor operations. Luciano would be the undisputed whiskey king

of New York and share in all the other spoils of Maranzano's enterprises as well.

Luciano called a meeting of Costello, Lansky, Siegel, Adonis, and Genovese—"my board of directors, you might say"—and they decided to turn down Maranzano. Instinctively, Luciano knew that "sooner or later Maranzano would have to go." Shortly thereafter, Luciano, Lansky, Siegel, and Adonis made up a shortage of whiskey in their operation by personally hijacking two truckloads of Maranzano's liquor en route to New York from the Jersey beaches. One of Maranzano's men was killed and another wounded in the resulting shootout. But there was no retaliation, possibly because Luciano and his men wore masks, possibly because Maranzano still entertained hopes of winning them over.

The other suitor was Giuseppe Masseria, a loathsome, piggish creature who styled himself "Joe the Boss." Masseria had arrived in the United States from Palermo around 1903. He was 16 years old and already had a reputation as one of Sicily's foremost triggermen. Masseria soon achieved legendary status in the skirmishing among Mafia mobs. The

70

man seemed to lead a charmed life. No matter how many times his enemies came after him with guns blazing, the legend went, fat little Joe the Boss managed to elude harm.

But his aura of invulnerability didn't do much for his disposition. Masseria was mean, petty, and nauseatingly uncouth: His gluttony and swinish table manners managed to arouse disgust even among colleagues who were normally tolerant of casual dining. Nevertheless, he eventually came to command a family of some 500 men. Despite Joe the Boss's power and his reputation for having more lives than a cat, Luciano targeted him for elimination along with Maranzano: "To me, the whole thing was like organizing a business," said the pragmatic young don. "For them, it was the pride that came first. Who was going to be the Boss of Bosses."

Before he could rid himself of the old dons, however, Luciano needed time to consolidate his own position and make his plans. He deftly delayed committing himself to either side until 1927, when the pressure from Masseria became so intense that Charlie capitulated—at least temporarily. The deal made Luciano second-in-command of Joe the Boss's mob, with a slice of all Masseria's rackets, robberies, and other business. In turn, Luciano contributed to the pot the proceeds from everything that he and his gang did—except, as he told Masseria, profits from the liquor.

Masseria became outraged, screaming and hurling lamps and bric-a-brac around the room. But eventually he agreed. Though he lusted after Luciano's bootleg empire, there was more at stake: With Charlie at his side, Masseria would be far more powerful than Maranzano.

Masseria also was smart enough to let Luciano modernize the mob's operations. The newcomer already had more than 200 men reporting to him; with Masseria's troops, there would be an additional 500. Luciano set about

Known as Joe the Boss to his underlings and as Joe the Glutton to nearly everyone else, Giuseppe Masseria *(above)* was New York's most powerful don until challenged by Salvatore Maranzano.

streamlining the organization. Among other things, he merged Masseria's loansharking with that of Lepke and Lucchese in the Garment District, thereby achieving economies of scale. And he threw his enormous Buy-Money Bank protection umbrella over Mafia activities, particularly the robberies that Masseria's men were always committing in midtown Manhattan.

To Luciano, planning held the key to everything, whether for a simple warehouse job or monopolizing markets in olive oil and cheese. When schemes were brought to him, he would listen, eyes closed sometimes, then ask questions. How well had the place been cased or the market researched? What kind of security or enemy strength was involved? Had the planners included enough muscle of their own? What about protection? Usually he found things to correct or improve.

Like any sensible businessman, Luciano took care to establish connections with noncompeting mobsters: Al Capone in Chicago, Moe Dalitz in Cleveland, the Purple Gang in Detroit, Nig Rosen, who'd risen to power alongside Waxey Gordon in Philadelphia. For their own bootlegging account, Luciano's gang and the Philadelphians joined in cooperative supply and distribution ventures with Boston's Charles "King" Solomon and Atlantic City's Nucky Johnson, who ruled all of southern New Jersey with its long stretches of isolated beach. By the end of 1928 this core group had bootlegging ties to no fewer than 22 mobs from Maine to Florida. And Charlie Luciano, scarcely 31, was the cartel's unofficial chief executive.

East Coast bootlegging had developed severe problems by late 1928. Chaotic competition throughout the country sharply limited supplies and drove up prices. Gangs were going to war over a few boatloads of liquor. Obviously, the way to halt this foolishness was to organize bootlegging on a national scale.

These six associates of gangster Bugs Moran were murdered in a Chicago garage by Al Capone's gunmen on Valentine's Day, 1929. The St. Valentine's Day Massacre, as it came to be called, rattled Mafia bosses, who feared such carnage would expose gang violence and alienate the public.

Lansky put out feelers, the gang leaders agreed to meet, and in May of 1929 the greatest underworld conference ever known got under way in Atlantic City.

They came in long, black limousines: Al Capone and his retinue from Chicago, and gang leaders from Philadelphia, Boston, Cleveland, Detroit, Long Island, and northern New Jersey. The biggest contingent came from New York: Luciano, Costello, Lansky, Lepke, Adonis, Anastasia, Schultz, and a number of others. Conspicuously absent were the Mafia's Masseria and Maranzano. Neither of the old dons had been invited. Luciano regarded New York bootlegging as his province.

Nucky Johnson, representing South Jersey, hosted the conference with lavish hospitality. He put everybody up in suites at the finest hotels. He supplied the best food and liquor, the prettiest women. If a mobster had brought his wife or his girlfriend, Johnson gave the lady an expensive fur cape. Nothing much got done during the first few days of parties. Then the serious conversations began.

One morning, after breakfast, the delegates strolled out onto the Boardwalk and stepped into the resort's famed two-person promenade chairs. They chatted about anything but business while attendants sedately pushed the canopied chairs to the end of the Boardwalk. There they alighted, took off their shoes, rolled up their trousers, and walked out on the beach to the water's edge. There, beyond earshot, they sauntered in small groups discussing mutual plans and problems. At the end, everybody came together in a large conference room at the President Hotel to formalize and ratify a general agreement.

Henceforth, the cutthroat bidding for imported liquor would end, as would the killings and the hijackings. Instead of competing, the gang lords would work to form a cooperative national commission, representing everyone, that would establish equitable allocations and territories. Peace would reign. Prices would drop. Everybody would win. The Atlantic City conferees did not establish a specific mechanism to achieve their aims; that was left for another day. And they didn't suddenly stop warring. But at least they'd made a start toward forming an organization of cooperating equals.

One issue did bring concrete results. Al Capone, with the blood of perhaps 100 men already on his hands, was giving organized crime a very bad name in Chicago. Three months earlier, on St. Valentine's Day, Capone gunmen had trapped seven members of the rival North Side mob in a garage and mowed them down with submachine guns. Grisly photos of the massacre, splashed across newspapers from coast to coast, had horrified the country—and energized normally

dormant law enforcement officials. To make matters worse, just before traveling to Atlantic City, Capone and some of his goons had beaten to death three allegedly disloyal members of his own gang.

More bloodletting obviously was in store when Capone returned to Chicago. To take the heat off everybody, the conferees ruled that Capone would be arrested for carrying a gun and serve a year in prison. Faced with unanimity among his peers, the ferocious Scarface Al did as he was told and took the fall.

But if gangland battles were about to simmer down in Chicago, violence would shortly start boiling in New York. Joe the Boss Masseria and Salvatore Maranzano were about to clash in a fight to the finish. Known as the Castellammarese War, the struggle would last for more than a year and claim, by some accounts, close to 60 lives. For Charlie Luciano, maneuvering deftly between the lines, the conflict would be his road to the top.

The war began with an important hit, an assassination that could not be ignored. The two dons had been skirmishing for years, hijacking each other's trucks and sending their musketeers, as they called them, to ambush the enemy. But early in 1930, Masseria decided to up the ante by gunning down Gaspar Milazzo, the Mafia capo in Detroit, a Castellammare native and a close ally of Maran-

zano. A second Castellammarese, also close to Maranzano, died with Milazzo. Shortly thereafter, a third Castellammarese, Vito Bonventre, a wealthy bootlegger, was slain outside his Brooklyn home.

Hostilities had started out badly for the Castellammare forces, and there was word that Joe the Boss meant to "eat those people like a sandwich." But Masseria was about to provoke his chief lieutenant, and that in due course would prove unhealthy.

Charlie Luciano had been steaming for months over Masseria's old-fashioned bloodlettings and dictatorial ways, especially after Atlantic City. The older man made impossible demands on his lieutenant's time and violently resented the attention Luciano gave his bootlegging business. When Charlie went to the Jersey shore one night in the summer of 1929 to supervise the landing of a million-dollar Scotch shipment, Masseria lost all control. He started screaming that he would have Luciano ripped apart, his eyes gouged out, his tongue torn from his head. "From now on, you work for me 24 hours a day," he shrieked, "and everything you get goes into the pot."

"Joe, we got a deal. We shook hands. You're not in the whiskey business," replied Luciano.

"The whiskey belongs to me," shouted Masseria. "I break the handshake." Within half an hour, Luciano was confer-

ring with his colleagues. They started thinking hard about ways to weaken both Masseria and Maranzano.

On October 17 Luciano met Maranzano in the cavernous shed of a Staten Island shipping pier. Maranzano chided him about going in with Masseria and repeated his offer to make Luciano his own top man. But there was now one important condition: "You, personally, are going to kill Giuseppe Masseria," Maranzano ordered.

Luciano instantly saw the trap. By ironclad Mafia tradition, no one could personally assassinate a leader and then succeed him. The most the killer could expect would be a secondary role; more likely, he would be slain in revenge. Maranzano wanted no young lions around him.

"You're crazy," snapped Luciano.

Suddenly a blackjack crashed down on Luciano's head. When he came to, Maranzano's goons went to work on him, half a dozen men with belts and clubs and glowing cigarettes. They hung him by his hands and pounded him senseless, revived him, and started in again. From time to time Maranzano would repeat his demand. "Charlie, this is so stupid," he would chide gently. "You can end this now if you will just agree."

At one point Luciano kicked out and caught Maranzano in the groin. Gasping for breath, the old don grabbed a knife and slashed Luciano across the face, severing muscles that would give his right eyelid a permanent droop. Another slash opened a huge gash in Luciano's chest. His assailants then cut him down and dumped him on a dark street, where a cruising police car found him lying in a pool of blood. At the hospital, it took 55 stitches to close his wounds.

Luciano never made public what had happened to him. There were all sorts of rumors—he'd been kidnapped by rival bootleggers, federal agents had tortured him, he'd been assaulted by an outraged cop whose daughter he'd made pregnant. On one thing everyone agreed: Hardly anybody had ever survived being taken for a ride. They started to call him Charlie Lucky and Lucky Luciano.

While he was recuperating, Luciano puzzled over why Maranzano had let him live. He finally concluded that the don believed that Charlie would in fact eventually eliminate Masseria, if not personally, then by surrogate. Maranzano had several times sent hit men to assassinate Joe the Boss. They never got near the target; Masseria was too well guarded. It had to be someone close. And Luciano was still close, if in serious disfavor.

Luciano decided to accommodate Maranzano—in his own fashion. But first, there needed to be some serious attrition to weaken both destructive, vendetta-bent dons.

Charlie knew that in the shifting allegiances of the New York underworld, a Bronx capo named Tom Reina was contemplating a switch in loyalty from Masseria to Maranzano. Masseria sensed treachery, yet so far lacked evidence and had done nothing. With consummate guile, Luciano arranged for Reina's murder. Vito Genovese blew the man's head off with a shotgun, after which word was passed to Maranzano that it was a Masseria job. What followed was precisely what Luciano intended.

Masseria appointed one Joseph Pinzolo to take charge of the dead Reina's family interests. If anything, Pinzolo was even more disgusting and dictatorial than Joe the Boss. Within seven months, one of Reina's loyally grieving lieutenants blew Pinzolo away with two shots to the face.

In the meantime, Luciano had been busy igniting further deadly fires. Masseria's constant bodyguard and confidant was a veteran gunman named Pietro Morello; among the mobs, he was known as the Clutching Hand for his deformed, clawlike right hand. But the infirmity did not diminish his effectiveness, and it was clear to Luciano that Morello had to go before anybody could get to Masseria.

This assignment went to the ever-eager Albert Anastasia, who, Luciano remembered later, grabbed him in a bearhug and kissed him on both cheeks. "Charlie," Anastasia said, "I been waiting for this day for at least eight years. You're going to be on top if I have to kill everybody for you. That's the only way we can have any peace and make the real money."

On August 15 Anastasia and a companion trapped Morello in his East Harlem loansharking office and riddled him with bullets. There was a tidy little dividend for the killers: $30,000 in cash that Morello was counting at the time.

Again, Luciano put out false word—that Maranzano was behind the Morello hit. This time, Masseria retaliated in Chicago, where his ally Al Capone machine-gunned a Maranzano capo named Joe Aiello. Don Salvatore retaliated in November, when Masseria himself was spotted entering a Bronx apartment house with two top aides. Maranzano musketeers blasted the aides with 12-gauge shotguns when they emerged. But Masseria escaped, his life and the legend of his charmed existence intact.

A few months later, Luciano finally sent word to Maranzano that he would do the don's bidding. They met in front of the Lion House at the Bronx Zoo. Luciano promised to kill Masseria, and Maranzano agreed to accept the non-Sicilians in Luciano's gang and not to interfere with any of their businesses. Then he pointed to Charlie Lucky's scarred face and said how sorry he was he'd been provoked to inflict such a wound. Luciano told him to forget it.

Spring smiled on New York the morning of April 15, 1931. Luciano and Joe the Boss had apparently patched up their differences and were together in Masseria's downtown Manhattan offices. The fat old mafioso listened eagerly as Luciano went over plans for the slaying of 20 top Maranzano men—the final victory. Masseria danced a little jig at the thought of it. Around noon Luciano suggested that the two of them go out for a nice lunch at a restaurant called Nuova Villa Tammaro. Masseria stuffed himself with antipasto, pasta, lobster with tomato sauce, Chianti wine, rich pastries, and strong Italian espresso. By now it was 3 p.m. and they had the place to themselves. The two companions started to play cards. Then Luciano excused himself to go to the lavatory.

As soon as he left, the door to the restaurant burst open. In rushed Vito Genovese, Joe Adonis, Albert Anastasia, and Bugsy Siegel, all of them firing pistols at the astonished Masseria. More than 20 shots exploded and whined around the room. Six of them slammed into Joe the Boss. He wasn't invulnerable after all.

During the great celebration marking his victory in the Castellammarese War, Don Salvatore Maranzano made a contribution to the Mafia in New York that would endure to this day. In assuming control over all Mafia activities in the city, he affirmed the basic structure of the five-family New York organization. Luciano would head one family that would include his own gang's enterprises and the Masseria interests; four other Maranzano chieftains would head similar families.

Charlie would supervise and coordinate the five families as Maranzano's deputy, but in each family the capos would have direct access to Maranzano and be ultimately responsible only to him. Beneath the capos would rank an underboss, then two, three, or more lieutenants, and finally the ordinary soldiers in *decinas,* or groups of 10, exactly as in Julius Caesar's legions. Discipline would be rigidly enforced, and the family would be bound by a set of inflexible rules:

Every man would observe the Sicilian creed of omertà, or manly behavior and silence about family affairs; all orders would be instantly obeyed, no man would ever strike another family member, all earlier grievances would be forgotten, and finally, no man would covet another's business or his wife. This was the traditional code of the old Mafia, and Maranzano meant to graft it onto all his operations in America.

Predictably, perhaps, the graft didn't take. Don Salvatore's love of old Sicilian values might not have been a critical problem for the younger men, but his imposition of imperial control and unquestioning obedience definitely was. There was a new breed, cast in Charlie Luciano's mold, and these men prized debate, flexibility, resiliency. What is more, a number of the important figures in the Maranzano regime, even including some family subcapos appointed by the new capo di tutti capi, were longtime allies of Charlie Lucky. Luciano's own second-in-command was Vito Genovese. Tommy Lucchese and Albert Anastasia were named underbosses of other families. Lepke, Schultz, Lansky, and Siegel all remained loyal. And not for an instant had Charlie Lucky forgotten the scar on his face or how he came to acquire his new nickname.

The plot to eliminate Maranzano began to take shape almost immediately after the coronation. With Lansky, Luciano drove to Pittsburgh to confer with Salvatore Calderone, Mafia boss of western Pennsylvania; Calderone had been at the Grand Concourse affair and had come away dismayed by Maranzano's imperial airs. Luciano and Lansky drove on to Cleveland to meet with Ohio leaders who were also disenchanted with Maranzano. Another Mafia boss came up from Florida; Al Capone sent an emissary from Chicago. All agreed that Maranzano had to go.

Back in New York, Luciano informed Maranzano that he hadn't personally pulled the trigger on Joe the Boss after all. That was a mistake. While Maranzano seemed to shrug it off, he instantly perceived a new danger from Luciano. He drew up a list of names. Charlie Lucky was to be executed, as were Frank Costello, Vito Genovese, Joe Adonis, and Dutch Schultz. Maranzano apparently didn't regard Lansky and Siegel as much of a threat; their names weren't on the list. And he failed to realize the true loyalties of Lucchese and Anastasia. The first executions were contracted out to a freelance killer named Vincent "Mad Dog" Coll. As an advance, Maranzano gave him $25,000.

Meanwhile, Luciano was laying his own plans. Since it would be suicide for anyone who was familiar to attack the boss, four Jewish gunmen were assigned to the job. The idea was for them to pose as federal tax agents, thus gaining them at least a few seconds' edge on Maranzano's bodyguards. Lansky rented a house in the Bronx and for the next couple of weeks coached the killers; he taught them to look and act like feds, had them study pictures of Maranzano, walked them through diagrams of Maranzano's office suite in Park Avenue's Grand Central Building. Lansky took his time. It had to be right, and Luciano later said that the cost of the hit overall came to more than $80,000.

At the end of August, Luciano learned of Maranzano's contract with Mad Dog Coll. The plan, it seemed, was for the don to ask Charlie Lucky and another intended victim to meet in his office, where Coll would put them away. The phone call came on September 9. There was business to discuss, said Maranzano. He wanted Luciano and Vito Genovese in his office at 2 o'clock the next afternoon.

Sometime before 2 p.m. on September 10, Don Salvatore was waiting for Coll in the office reception room with his secretary and five bodyguards. The door swung open. In marched the four gunmen. They identified themselves as tax agents, lined the Maranzano people up against the wall, frisked them, and removed their weapons. Then two of the "agents" ordered Maranzano into his office for questioning.

Once inside, the two pulled out knives and started slashing and stabbing. The execution was to be silent. Had detachment been possible, Maranzano might have appreciated how similar his own death was to Caesar's. As it was, however, he fought furiously, and the slaying got messy. In a panic, the killers yanked out their pistols and started shooting. Don Salvatore Maranzano, capo di tutti capi, fell dead with four bullets in his head and body, his throat cut, and six stab wounds in the chest.

For weeks afterward, the press reverberated with stories that Maranzano's murder had signaled a mass extermination of old-style Mafia leaders. "The night of Sicilian Vespers," writers called it, and reported that 40 or 50 murders were secretly carried out across the United States on September 10. Luciano conceded much later that there had been a second phase designed to eliminate Maranzano partisans around the country. But he vigorously denied that it had been put into effect. He and his allies had called off the hits because, in the end, they agreed that it wasn't necessary. With Maranzano gone, the young leaders had done enough to secure their command of the American Mafia.

Nevertheless, Luciano made haste to consolidate the victory and Americanize the mob. With characteristic tact, instead of summoning the family heads to New York, he went to them by calling a conference in Chicago. Al Capone hosted the event and outdid even Nucky Johnson in Atlantic City two years before. Capone took over the luxurious Congress Hotel on Michigan Avenue and part of the Blackstone. Floors were assigned to the various city groups, with large suites for the family heads. Capone's troops and a number of Chicago cops on the mob's payroll ringed the hotels to ensure the conferees' privacy.

"I knew that they wanted to hear from me direct, face-to-face, not in a big auditorium," said Luciano. So he held a series of private meetings in which he told each group the same thing: The wars were over. No more fighting and senseless competition. No more scrambles to be capo di tutti capi. From now on, things would proceed on a basis of consent, cooperation, consensus, as they would in a well-run corporation. "I told them we was in a business that had to keep moving without explosions every two minutes," said Luciano. "Knocking guys off just because they come from a different part of Sicily, that kind of crap, was giving us a bad name."

Luciano proceeded to the details. On the national level, power would rest with a commission on which would sit as permanent members the heads of the six biggest and most powerful families: four from New York—foremost among them Luciano's—and one each from Buffalo and Detroit. Other families would have representation on the Commission on an ad hoc basis as their interests warranted. The Commission would function like a board of directors, setting policy, defining territories, and adjudicating disputes. For example, no one could strike at a member of another mob unless the hit was first sanctioned by the Commission. If it gave approval, the Commission would most likely direct the killing itself.

To keep families from ambitious recruiting races aimed at outmanning their rivals, there would be a freeze on admitting new members until further notice. Novices already proposed for membership would be allowed to complete their apprenticeship, but that would be it. Thenceforth, the core Mafia would be fixed at about 5,000 soldiers nationwide; with allies, employees, and part-timers, total manpower might come to 15,000, only about 15 percent of the estimated 100,000 mobsters in the United States. But the Mafia's disciplined cohesion, its ruthlessness and intelligent direction, would make it, for a long time, the nation's supreme union of crime.

By virtue of his power and leadership, Charlie Luciano would sit as the Commission's chairman of the board. But he would simply be first among equals, with one vote like everyone else. To underscore the point, he firmly refused the ritual envelopes of cash pressed on him as tribute by the Chicago conferees. "I don't need the money," he said, adding, "We're all equals." Al Capone thought he was crazy.

Beneath the six permanent commission members would be 24 families recognized across the country, ranging in size from a few score members in some southern regions to the 800 or so soldiers in the bigger cities. The chiefs of these families would be free to run their businesses as they saw fit within the general guidelines—so long as they didn't run them into the ground. A family head could remain a family head, even if he was in prison.

One innovation the Commission decreed for all families was an addition to the family hierarchy—a consigliere, or counselor. The consigliere was an adviser to the don, but an even more important function was as a sort of labor arbitrator, an intermediary between the don and the ordinary soldiers. Traditionally, the soldiers had been too frightened to confront the boss on matters that affected them; now they would have a voice—whose safety was guaranteed—in the highest councils.

Not everybody cheered everything Luciano proposed, or his attitude, for that matter. Joe Bonanno, a fervent Castellammarese who assumed the leadership of Maranzano's personal family, swiftly decided to cooperate with Luciano. But he was distressed at the lack of emphasis on such revered Sicilian values as trust, honor, and respect. It also pained him to observe the power wielded behind the scenes by non-Sicilians—even though, at that time, all the dons on the Commission were Sicilian—and to see families in businesses that many of the old Sicilians deplored, such as narcotics and prostitution.

"Luciano," Bonanno wrote in his autobiography, "had never 'lived' the Tradition and therefore never truly understood it. Charley Lucky was a true American in that he was free of tradition." All that really mattered to such men, he believed, was making money. Bonanno and others like him would see to it that there would be a tempering, a "mixing of the waters" between the old school and the new. Yet the old-timers could thank their stars that Luciano's sort had come to power. America was in the grip of the Great Depression, and gangland, like any other institution, needed all the business acumen it could muster.

Virtually every facet of the Mafia's business was hit by the stock market crash of 1929, bootlegging among the hardest. High-stakes gambling—on the roulette wheel, on dice and cards, on the horses—plummeted. Slot machines went down, then picked up again. Only the policy game showed no softness at all, churning out a steady torrent of small change; a man might be selling apples on the street, but he still wanted to put a few pennies each day on a number.

Luciano was as generous with his friends as his own fortunes would allow. He loaned money to the Wall Street and Social Register crowd at bank interest rates of two to three percent, and he forgave some loans altogether if the borrower was particularly hard up. Not so, however, in the Garment District and other venues of mob usury. With everybody desperate for money, the organization put its bootleg millions to work loansharking. And with companies failing by the hundreds, it soon found itself the proprietor of dress-manufacturing companies, meat packers, trucking firms, and other legitimate businesses.

Despite his eminence, Luciano's lifestyle changed very little. He did move from the Barbizon Plaza into an elegant six-room apartment atop Park Avenue's Waldorf Towers, where he was registered as Mr. Ross. It was his habit to rise around noon, have breakfast, then confer with Costello, Lansky, Genovese, and whoever else among his close associates wanted to talk. Later he might go out to his box at Belmont Park racetrack or call Polly Adler, the city's foremost madam, to send over an afternoon's companion. Luciano never tipped the prostitute more than $5 over the standard $25 fee. "Why spoil it for everybody?" he said.

Dinner would be with associates and friends such as Jimmy Durante, Frank Fay, Bobby Clark, Ed Wynn—Luciano liked comedians—at some favorite Italian restaurant, after which would commence the business of the evening. He had rented an unmarked, sparsely furnished, two-room office in a building at Broadway and 51st Street, and to this place came supplicants wishing an audience with the great man. They might want permission to operate slot machines or

Police arrive at Salvatore Maranzano's Park Avenue office on September 10, 1931, to find the Boss of all Bosses dead on the floor, his white shirt stained with blood from multiple knife and gunshot wounds *(below)*. At right, friends and family of the fallen Castellammarese leader bear his remains to a New York cemetery, where they buried along with him much of the Old World Mafia tradition that Maranzano had embodied.

In 1934 New York's antigambling mayor Fiorello La Guardia bludgeons confiscated slot machines while city officials and reporters watch. After this largely symbolic pounding, the slots were dumped into New York harbor. Pressure from the reform mayor helped persuade Frank Costello to move his gambling operations to New Orleans.

jukeboxes, to open a policy game or run a handbook on the horses, to start a loansharking operation, or simply to have the maestro check plans for an important heist. To this office also came the weekly financial reports of Luciano's manifold interests. The money itself was cached in safe places; all the messengers did was recite the numbers. Luciano prided himself on knowing with some exactitude what they should be in any given week. If a subordinate reported in short, he needed to have a good reason.

By now it was 1933. Prohibition died a natural death on December 5, with the ratification of the Twenty-First Amendment, which repealed the so-called Noble Experiment. Mobsters—along with a few die-hard drys—sincerely mourned its passing. But only fools were unprepared, and their number definitely did not include Charlie Luciano and his board of directors.

The liquor business was now legal, but there remained ample opportunities for goodwill and profit in booze. The gangs still had an enormous investment in vast stocks of domestically produced and imported liquor warehoused around the country. Luciano liked to say that his people gave away most of their merchandise to churches and synagogues, which gratefully sold it. Some small portion may have gone to charity, but it's virtually certain that the bulk of it went to make as much money as possible.

Imported liquor was no problem. The ex-bootleggers were transformed into legitimate businessmen with distribution franchises from the overseas distilleries. Frank Costello, for example, set up Alliance Distributors as exclusive agent for Scotland's Whitely Company, makers of King's Ransom Scotch, among other brands. The domestic industry was more of a problem. Anyone with a prison record was barred from controlling an American distillery, brewery, or vineyard. But with legal liquor, beer, and wine heavily taxed by both federal and state governments, a thriving market for illegal untaxed alcoholic beverages continued. When federal agents finally raided one major operation in Zanesville, Ohio, in January 1935, they found that it turned out 36,000 gallons of beer and 5,000 gallons of 190-proof alcohol every 24 hours, seven days a week.

Even so, gangland's annual take from liquor declined to a modest fraction of the estimated $3 billion that it had generated before Repeal. Now gambling was the big thing, with the mobs running every kind of game and house from penny-ante policy to slots, high-stakes poker, horse and dog tracks, bookie parlors, and casinos. The gambling joints were particularly profitable, and they blossomed wherever enough police and politicians could be bought to create what the gangs called an "open" city, town, or county. Mafia-connected casinos boomed in New Orleans; in Florida's Palm Beach and other rich Dade and Broward county resorts; in Hot Springs, Arkansas; in half a dozen Kentucky towns; and along the New Jersey Palisades across the Hudson River from New York City. Luciano's colleagues made a new pact with Atlantic City's Nucky Johnson to open up all of South Jersey; Johnson got 25 percent of the take, while the organization supplied equipment and capital.

In the spring of 1933, the ever-alert Meyer Lansky had reported that Havana, just 90 miles from Miami, was enjoying a tourist boom. It could be a gold mine, and Lansky guaranteed a cordial reception from Cuban strongman Fulgencio Batista, a rum-running friend since the start of Prohibition. But the Cuban connection would be expensive. Luciano convened a meeting of the Commission at the Waldorf Towers and laid it on the line: Cuba would cost them each $500,000 for openers. There was a lot of groaning, but they all anted up. Batista received $3 million, deposited in a Swiss account, in exchange for Havana's gambling rights, with a guarantee of at least another $3 million a year.

Eventually, extraterritorial operations expanded to Nassau in the Bahamas and then throughout the Caribbean. How much wealth organized crime's gambling empire brought in from enterprises offshore and domestic during the 1930s has never been calculated. But some idea may be had from the fact that in 1935, the numbers racket alone accounted for at least $100 million in just one American city, New York.

Meanwhile, the Mafia was applying its persuasive techniques to an ever-expanding roster of legitimate businesses. Prohibition had taught Luciano & Co. practically everything there was to know about trucking. "So we looked over the market and decided to put a little squeeze here and there on companies that should be happy to have our experience," he related. "For example, milk spoils pretty fast and so does bread and fresh vegetables. In no time at all, we had a lock on three or four of the biggest fresh food businesses in America, and took in as much as half a cent on a loaf of bread." The same applied to meat and fresh fish; New York City owned the mammoth Fulton Fish Market,

By the early 1930s Charlie Luciano was on top of the world, surveying the city from a spacious suite on the 39th floor of the Waldorf Towers *(right),* where he was registered under the inconspicuous alias Charles Ross. There, shunning publicity, he entertained his longtime mistress, Russian-born show girl Gay Orlova *(below),* and women selected especially for him by famed madam Polly Adler. Presenting himself not as a criminal but as a highly successful man of business, the impeccably attired Luciano was the toast of the New York social scene—often literally. At left, he modestly accepts a toast at a house party given in his honor.

but the Mafia ran it and collected around $20 million a year in tribute from the market's vendors, big and small.

Charlie Luciano estimated that even after Prohibition, his scores of enterprises, legitimate and otherwise, grossed about $2 billion a year. That was very big business anytime. In the Depression mid-1930s, it staggered the imagination. But a strong, gusty wind was beginning to howl around the Mafia bastions.

Despite all their political clout, despite all the millions of dollars in payoffs they spread around, Lucky Luciano and the Commission never managed to subvert the United States government at very high levels. By and large, federal prosecutors were immune from mob influence, and in the early 1930s these prosecutors were having some success with a new tactic: Instead of trying to convict Mafia leaders for their worst crimes—an often frustrating experience—the government was going after the mobsters for income-tax evasion.

In May of 1932 the bloodthirsty Al Capone was sentenced to 11 years in a federal penitentiary, not for murder but for tax evasion. Nineteen months later, a tough U.S. Attorney named Thomas E. Dewey put away Waxey Gordon for 10 years on a similar charge. Dewey then fixed his sights on Dutch Schultz, the Luciano ally who raked in $20 million a year from policy alone in the Bronx. Dewey indicted Schultz for failure to pay $92,103.34 in taxes between 1929 and 1931. The amount was ridiculously low; Schultz owed millions. Still, the charge was no joke. If convicted, Dutch faced up to 43 years in prison.

Schultz managed to evade the law for a year, then he gave himself up and stood trial in Syracuse, New York. Dewey had him cold, but Schultz's lawyers were clever, and the jury, incredibly, deadlocked at seven-to-five for conviction. A second trial, in the tiny upstate town of Malone, ended in a farcical acquittal; Schultz had arrived several weeks early and seeded the town with money, a fact that just might have influenced the happy outcome of his case. But Tom Dewey was a bulldog. He went after Schultz again in 1935, this time as a New York State special prosecutor charged with cleaning up New York City. The new attack focused on Schultz's restaurant-protection racket—and this time the charges included murder.

Luciano and the other mob commissioners were seriously concerned about their colleague. So sure had everyone been of Schultz's impending conviction on the federal tax charge that Luciano had parceled out his old ally's rackets for safekeeping among the faithful. But when Schultz returned to reclaim them, he suspected betrayal—and reacted by killing his chief lieutenant with his bare hands, a witness said.

Dutch's edgy nerves were one thing, but Luciano's real worry was that in the face of the murder trial, Schultz might try to make a deal with Dewey: his freedom in exchange for everything he knew about organized crime in New York. In fact, Schultz took a quite different tack. Increasingly anxious about his chances in court, he decided to murder Tom Dewey. He offered the contract to Albert Anastasia at any price. Anastasia immediately informed Luciano.

From then on, Schultz's fate was merely a matter of following Commission procedures. In the new Mafia, high-profile hits against prominent opponents like Dewey were strictly out of bounds—and certainly not to be contemplated without the unanimous consent of the Commission. Luciano called a conference. After six hours of discussion, everyone agreed that Dutch Schultz was out of control and had to be eliminated. The contract was carried out by one of Luciano's bodyguards on October 23, 1935, while Schultz and three associates were dining in a Newark, New Jersey, chophouse. The gunman walked in and cut them all down in a storm of bullets.

With Schultz gone, however, Dewey needed a fresh target, and he soon took aim at Charlie Luciano. In less than six months the prosecutor got his man. On April 1, 1936, Dewey proclaimed Luciano Public Enemy Number One, and a blue-ribbon grand jury returned a criminal indictment against him that carried a maximum penalty of 1,950 years in prison. The charges didn't involve murder, or gambling of any sort, or tax evasion, grand larceny, illicit liquor, protection shakedowns, loansharking, or union racketeering. Luciano was manifestly guilty of all of those, but he was also too well covered. With profound irony, the 90 counts—later reduced to 62—involved only compulsory prostitution, the one thing that Charlie Lucky always maintained he abhorred and would have nothing to do with.

But some of his colleagues were engaged in that line of work, and Luciano had made the sort of mistake that can undo a chief executive: He'd allowed his subordinates too much latitude.

Of all Dewey's investigations, the only one that showed promise of involving Luciano personally focused on pros-

Uncharacteristically mixing business and pleasure in 1937, Meyer Lansky brought his family, including sons Paul *(left)* and Buddy, on vacation to Havana, where, at the invitation of dictator Fulgencio Batista, he assumed control of several failing Cuban casinos.

Appointed special prosecutor of New York State in 1935, Thomas E. Dewey soon built a reputation for tenacity and incorruptibility in the pursuit of racketeers.

titution in New York. Evidence accumulated of a vice ring that included perhaps 200 brothels with 1,000 prostitutes whose bosses were known to be members—if small-timers—of Luciano's organization. It seemed impossible for the ring to operate without Charlie Lucky's full knowledge and participation. At least that was the logic of it. Arrests were made, and prostitutes, pimps, and other principals were questioned. A number of them decided to cooperate and were carefully coached. Then, on May 13, 1936, Dewey brought to trial 11 of the ringleaders, plus Charlie Luciano.

At first, Luciano and his friends thought the whole thing ridiculous. "Organized prostitution?" snorted Costello. "They were about as organized as a flea circus." Luciano was confident, even when his lawyers suggested that Dewey might have a case. "You mean to tell me Dewey expects to put me away because some crummy two-dollar whore says I was her boss?" he snapped at his lead attorney.

But that was precisely the intent of a procession of hard-used and bedraggled women, some of them longtime drug addicts. "I'm going to organize the cathouses like the A&P," one hooker quoted Charlie as saying. "We could syndicate the places on a large scale, same as a chain store system." Some of the testimony fell apart under cross-examination. But the weight of it—68 witnesses over three weeks—was telling. At the end of the trial, Luciano took the stand in his own defense. "I've never had anything to do with prostitution," he swore. "I've never gotten a single dollar from a prostitute or from a prostitution racket."

Jurors retired at 10:53 on the evening of June 6. They returned a verdict at 4:30 the next morning. "Guilty on all counts," read the foreman.

At the sentencing, Luciano looked the stony-faced judge squarely in the eye. "Your Honor, I have nothing to say outside of the fact that I need to say again, I am innocent," said the chairman of the board. The judge gave him 30 to 50 years in state prison. It was the longest sentence ever meted out for compulsory prostitution, and Tom Dewey was ecstatic. "This of course was not a vice prosecution," he told the press. "It is my understanding that criminals under Lucania have gradually absorbed control of the narcotics, policy, loan-shark, and Italian lottery syndicates." In

In 1935 the New York Mafia Commission led by Luciano ordered Dutch Schultz murdered to abort his plan to assassinate Thomas Dewey. On the night of October 23, Schultz was gunned down in the Palace Chop House in Newark, New Jersey, where police found him unconscious but alive *(right).* Hospitalized *(below),* Schultz lingered in a delirium as investigators waited to hear him name his assailants. But, when Schultz finally succumbed to his wounds 20 hours after the Palace Chop House hit, he took the killers' names with him.

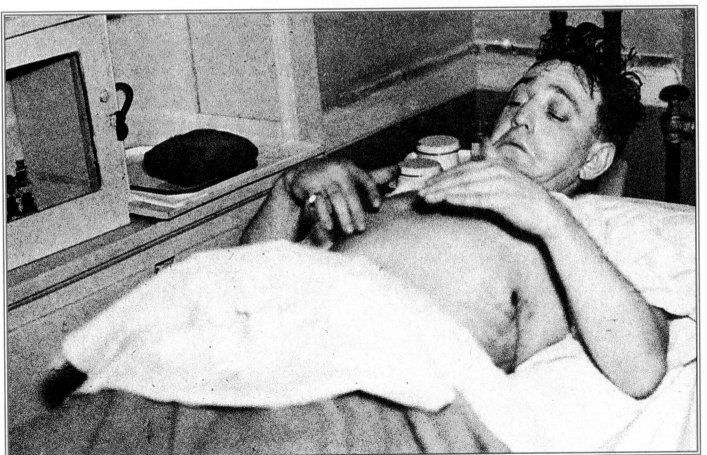

retrospect, Luciano raged that Dewey would openly admit "that he got me for everything else but what he charged me with. He's such a racketeer himself, in a legal way, that he crawled up my back with a frame and stabbed me."

Dannemora State Prison, looming bleakly over the flatlands of upstate New York, welcomed Luciano on June 18, 1936. He was 39 years old and would not be a free man again for nearly a decade. But whether he was behind bars or holding forth in his suite at the Waldorf Towers, Charlie Lucky remained the chief executive of the nation's greatest crime syndicate.

A procession of visitors journeyed north to do business with Luciano. The trusted Joe Adonis served as Charlie's general courier and vital link to the Commission. Frank Costello took over as caretaker of the Luciano family enterprises, with Vito Genovese as second-in-command. Meyer Lansky remained as treasurer. Charlie's orders were obeyed without question.

But it could not be the same as when he personally orchestrated matters, his nimble fingers roaming up and down the keyboard of crime. Costello increasingly focused on gambling, and Lansky spent more and more of his time in Havana. Inevitably, control over some of the subordinates began to erode.

From the reports, trouble was brewing with Louis Lepke, the violence-prone Jewish colleague who helped run the garment and foodstuffs rackets. Lepke spread the word that he planned to start using his muscle only for his own benefit; he was cutting out all his old friends. That was bad enough. But then he got himself into the dubious business of narcotics—and overall he came across as such a loud-mouthed, high-living hog that he attracted the attention of everyone from Tom Dewey, now Manhattan district attorney, to the FBI's J. Edgar Hoover, who proclaimed Lepke "the most dangerous criminal in the United States."

The situation had become hot enough toward the end of 1937 that a newly humble Lepke asked Joe Adonis to go to Dannemora and plead for help from Luciano in avoiding arrest. Charlie Lucky was of a mind to let Lepke sink, but he relented and passed word that Albert Anastasia could hide him.

The fugitive vanished, and for the next two years the law waged a fruitless manhunt. Hoping for a tip, the cops even went to see Lansky in Havana and Costello in New Orleans (both kingpins were often out of New York looking after far-flung business interests). And Luciano laughed aloud when Hoover sent an agent up to see him. "I told the agent I wanted to send a message back to J. Edgar—if he would arrange to commute my sentence, I could let him have Lepke in 24 hours."

Meanwhile Lepke was wearing out his welcome in Brooklyn, where Anastasia had him under close protection. Lepke still tried to out-muscle everybody in the rackets, and acting on his own, he dispatched killers to murder potential witnesses against him.

Killing Lepke would have been more trouble than he was worth, so Luciano tried another gambit. He first ordered Anastasia to stop shielding the fugitive. Then he devised a neat double cross.

With Lepke vulnerable again, Luciano led him to believe that he, Luciano, had made a deal on Lepke's behalf with J. Edgar Hoover. If Lepke would surrender on a federal narcotics rap, Hoover would guarantee that he wouldn't be turned over to Dewey for further New York State prosecution. Lepke was terrified of Dewey. Luciano went on to tell Lepke the state's case against him would probably collapse by the time he finished serving his federal sentence.

Lepke bought the idea. On August 24, 1939, Anastasia escorted him to a nighttime rendezvous with the FBI chief, who was waiting in a limousine at Fifth Avenue and 28th Street in Manhattan. Lepke was introduced to Hoover.

"How do you do?" the head G-man said coldly, motioning for Lepke to enter the car.

"Glad to meet you," Lepke mouthed inanely as he settled into the seat.

Exit Louis "Lepke" Buchalter. There was no bargain, of course. Lepke was quickly tried and sentenced to 14 years on a federal narcotics charge. Immediately thereafter, Dewey put him on trial and convicted him of extortion in the bakery business—with a term of 30 years to life.

Luciano thought it important for Dewey to know who had masterminded Lepke's downfall. Lansky and Costello made sure the word was passed. Charlie also wanted Costello to pass along another bit of information. Luciano was willing to have the Mafia back the ambitious Dewey to the hilt in his run for governor of New York. Charlie's lawyers had failed to get his conviction overturned on appeal, but he was developing other ideas about how he might get out of jail. Luciano reasoned that if Dewey won the State House,

Handcuffed to a police detective, Charlie Luciano steps out of a patrol wagon on his way into the New York State Supreme Court building in June 1936. He was found guilty of compulsory prostitution and sentenced to a record 30 to 50 years. After a brief stay in Sing Sing prison *(above),* he was transferred to the cold, damp confines of Dannemora prison in upstate New York, reviled as "Siberia" in gangland circles.

Duped into surrendering to federal authorities in the summer of 1939, a grinning Louis Lepke thought he had thwarted New York justice despite a $25,000 reward offered for his capture.

$25,000 REWARD
DEAD OR ALIVE

TWENTY-FIVE THOUSAND DOLLARS will be paid by the City of New York for information leading to the capture of "LEPKE" BUCHALTER, aliases LOUIS BUCHALTER, LOUIS BUCKHOUSE, LOUIS KAWAR, LOUIS KAUVAR, LOUIS COHEN, LOUIS SAFFER, LOUIS BRODSKY.

WANTED FOR CONSPIRACY AND EXTORTION

The Person or Persons who give information leading to the Arrest of "LEPKE" will be fully protected, his or her identity will never be revealed. The information will be received in absolute confidence.

RIGHT HAND

LEFT HAND

DESCRIPTION — Age, 42 years; white; Jewish; height, 5 feet, 5½ inches; weight, 170 pounds; build, medium; black hair; brown eyes; complexion dark; married, one son Harold, age about 18 years.

PECULARITIES—Eyes, piercing and shifting; nose, large, somewhat blunt at nostrils; ears, prominent and close to head; mouth, large, slight dimple left side; right-handed; suffering from kidney ailment.

Frequents baseball games.

Is wealthy; has connections with all important mobs in the United States. Involved in racketeering in Unions and Fur Industry, uses Strong-arm methods. Influential.

This Department holds indictment warrant charging Conspiracy

and if he was obligated deeply enough, he might be willing to invoke executive clemency.

Of course any such deal would obviously depend in part on what sort of public image Luciano and gangland in general continued to project. There could be no grisly revelations, no screaming headlines, no crushing prosecutions. Thus Luciano's heart sank when Costello reported in 1941 that one of Lepke's hoods, a savage killer named Abe Reles, was telling everything he knew to the Brooklyn D.A. to get off the hook on murder charges.

Reles's first disclosures filled 25 stenographic notebooks. His command of detail was staggering, and while he'd not yet gotten to Luciano, he clearly would take everyone down in time. He had already implicated Lepke in a 1936 murder that would eventually send his old boss to the electric chair.

The solution was obvious. Costello worked out the details and went to Dannemora for Luciano's okay. He reported that Reles was stashed away in the Half Moon Hotel at Coney Island. Police stood guard around the clock. A gunman wouldn't have a prayer of getting near him. And even if Reles could be hit, the job would be too messy.

"The cops will have to do it for us," said Costello, and Luciano approved that plan.

As Luciano would later describe it, the job cost $50,000 and was a masterpiece of simplicity. One night in late autumn a police bodyguard tapped Reles on the head with a blackjack while the informer was sleeping. Two other cops then picked up the unconscious form by the arms and legs, carried Reles to an open window, and hurled him out. Abe Reles dropped five stories. His body was found with two knotted bedsheets nearby, leading officials to surmise that he'd been trying to escape. The mob let out a collective sigh of relief.

December of 1941 came, and with it Pearl Harbor. Luciano always viewed things pragmatically, and in retrospect he thought the war "handed me a lot of favors." For one thing, it gave him a chance to document fairly thoroughly the frame that Tom Dewey had manufactured to put him in prison. For another, it offered a golden opportunity to play the patriotic, public-spirited citizen. Luciano thought both would be important in the campaign to regain his freedom.

Luciano had known since 1938 that immediately after his trial, the state's prize witnesses—the prostitutes—had been sent on an extended, all-expenses-paid trip to Paris. The idea may have been for them to remain there indefinitely. But the women had grown restive and resentful, and when their whereabouts became known, they were willing to talk to Luciano's lawyers. They signed affidavits recanting their testimony and stating that they'd been forced to lie on pain of heavy prison sentences for narcotics transgressions and prostitution.

The affidavits had formed the basis of Luciano's appeal, which had failed. But now, the fall of France to an invading German army had forced the prostitutes to return home, where Luciano's lawyers were waiting. "What I wanted most of all," said Charlie, "was a confession from all of them that it was Dewey himself that made them lie; that it was Dewey that coached them; that it was Dewey that paid them off."

With such testimony in hand, Luciano believed, he would have considerable leverage on Governor Thomas E. Dewey. But first Dewey had to get elected. The New York Mafia allegedly contributed generously to his campaign chest and otherwise worked hard to deliver the huge, normally Democratic city into Dewey's Republican column. How big a difference that made is unknown, but Dewey won. On January 1, 1943, the dapper little racket buster was sworn in as governor.

By then, Luciano's patriotic game was already in full swing. Once the United States entered the war, newspapers reported unsettling stories of spies and saboteurs operating along East Coast waterfronts. Navy intelligence officers swarmed over the docks, impressing the need for security on longshoremen. As Luciano would one day tell it, all this fear and frenzy gave him an idea: His boys would secure the docks for America.

Albert Anastasia had a creative thought in that regard. The French luxury liner *Normandie* was being fitted out as a troopship at a Hudson River pier. What if she were to suffer sabotage? Would that not galvanize the navy to seek allies? Albert worked out the idea with his brother, Tough Tony Anastasia, a boss in the International Longshoremen's Association. On February 11, 1942, the *Normandie* mysteriously caught fire at her pier. Within 24 hours, France's magnificent "Ship of Light" was a gutted hulk lying in the muck of New York harbor. The navy was frantic, and when word was passed that the underworld might cooperate in preventing future disasters, the admirals rose to the bait.

In no time at all, a naval officer was on his way to visit Luciano with a request for help with the waterfront unions. The help was freely given, and soon Charlie was transferred from the Siberia of Dannemora to much more comfortable quarters at Great Meadow Prison, just outside Albany. Relocating made it easier for him to confer with navy officers—and with his people: Adonis, Costello, Lansky, the two Anastasias. The warden even provided a private office for the meetings—which, when the navy was absent, concerned themselves with the theft and counterfeiting of ration stamps and black-market operations in gasoline, meat, and a dozen other items.

Once in a while the sympathetic warden at Great Meadow let Luciano out in the company of a guard to spend a few hours walking around the free streets of Albany. One evening two guards drove Charlie to a roadhouse near town to meet a longtime mistress, Gay Orlova. She had brought some thick steaks from a cache of Costello's, and the couple enjoyed a splendid dinner and a few hours of privacy.

With the invasion of Sicily in July of 1943, stories circulated that the Sicilian Mafia had assisted Allied troops. One tale had it that an American plane swept in low over a prominent church and dropped a packet containing a yellow flag with the letter *L* on it—*L* for Luciano. The flag was passed to the local Mafia capo, and when American ground troops landed, they were joined by a host of armed civilians eager to rid Sicily of the hated Fascists.

Luciano scoffed at such stories, but they had their effect. On May 7, 1945, the day the war in Europe ended, Charlie's lawyers sent a petition for executive clemency to Governor Dewey. Dewey declined to act on the petition, choosing instead to turn the matter over to the parole board that he had appointed. The naval officer who'd been dealing with Luciano wrote a laudatory letter, and the board unanimously recommended parole.

On January 3, 1946, Tom Dewey announced that Lucky Luciano would be freed. But Luciano could not remain in the United States. Dewey declared that as a condition of his parole, the mobster would be deported to Sicily. Amazingly, the Sicilian-born Luciano had never become a U.S. citizen.

The departure took place on a chill day in February. Immigration Service agents transported Charlie Lucky to the SS *Laura Keene*, a rusty Liberty ship berthed at Bush Terminal in Brooklyn. A horde of reporters and photographers jammed the terminal, but Luciano wanted no press confer-

Police investigators gather around the body of mob informer Abe Reles on the terraced roof of Coney Island's Half Moon Hotel. On the morning of November 12, 1941, Reles exited from a window six stories up—possibly tossed out by the very police officers assigned to protect him. Formerly a gunman for Louis Lepke and Albert Anastasia, Reles had turned informant to avoid prosecution on murder charges.

ence. At his behest, a wall of longshoremen armed with baling hooks stood between the ship and the press.

The *Laura Keene* had been set up for a party, with plentiful food and drink. Scores of Luciano's friends were escorted on board to say their farewells. Also on board were three beautiful women selected by Joe Adonis to keep Charlie company during the transatlantic voyage. Then the hour

arrived, and Luciano watched the skyscrapers of downtown Manhattan slide past. "I looked at the Statue of Liberty," Charlie would recall, "and I made myself think of only one thing—that I was taking a vacation trip and that pretty soon that Lady would be saying hello instead of goodbye."

Luciano meant it. In his last meeting with Meyer Lansky, he said that he already had connections in Italy for visas under his old name—Salvatore Lucania—that would be good for Mexico, Cuba, and certain places in South America. He told Lansky that if he couldn't find a way back into the United States, he would become a Cuban citizen and take back control of the mob from a new base in Havana. As always, the chairman of the board had big plans. But this time they wouldn't all work out the way he wanted.

The gutted hulk of the SS *Normandie* lies on her port side in a Manhattan berth in February 1942, several days after she was destroyed by fire started when a spark from an acetylene torch ignited a pile of life preservers. The U.S. Navy and a committee of the House of Representatives called the fire an accident; Charlie Luciano claimed the mob started it.

I don't have an
enemy in the world.

FRANK COSTELLO

4

Twilight of the Dons

The Manhattan courtroom was packed. At the witness table, Frank Costello squirmed and twitched in his well-cut suit. The man known to New York's tabloid press as the "Prime Minister of the Underworld" was starting to lose his cool, and that didn't happen every day.

The hearing causing Costello's discomfort was the high point of an extraordinary legislative investigation, and it riveted the attention of American TV viewers. Legislators who'd hopscotched through 14 cities to participate in Senator Estes Kefauver's hearings on interstate crime were hammering the mob leader with questions. They wanted to know about his gambling activities, his ties with politicians and judges, and his highly unusual business practices. Across the country, some 20 to 30 million citizens—perhaps twice the number that had watched the latest World Series—were mesmerized by what they saw and heard.

As the drama stretched on for more than three days in March of 1951, home viewers soaked up every word, but all they could see of the famed gangster were his carefully manicured hands. As a condition of appearing at the hearings, Costello had asked that he not be televised. His long-time lawyer, George Wolf, put it this way: "Mr. Costello doesn't care to submit himself as a spectacle."

In what turned out to be an inspired decision, television directors compromised on the request by keeping the camera away from the gangster's face and focusing instead on his hands—a tactic that only enhanced the drama for the TV audience. From moment to moment, Costello's expressive fingers would clasp one another nervously or drum staccato rhythms on the table. Sometimes a hand would shoot out to grab the water glass and raise it out of view to the witness's lips, or simply wobble it back and forth in a tremor of anxiety. On other occasions the hands would twiddle Costello's horn-rimmed glasses as he pondered a tough question, or tear up small bits of paper and crumple them into little balls to be rolled between thumb and fore-finger, or pick at themselves in tiny displays of irritation.

At one point the hands disappeared for a time: Costello had staged a walkout. But the hands were soon back as the mobster buckled before a threatened contempt-of-Congress citation. When Costello finished his long, evasive testimony, he was charged with contempt all the same. He'd refused to tell about his net worth, a topic of keen interest to the Bureau of Internal Revenue, soon to be renamed the Internal Revenue Service. In the end, as a sort of anticlimactic epilogue to the proceedings, viewers finally had a chance to look on the face of Frank Costello. He smiled weakly for the camera, his ordeal over, at least for the moment.

Those days of testimony marked a turning point for the man who was, in the absence of the exiled Charlie Luciano, America's most powerful criminal. Frank Costello was a man obsessed with proving his respectability, but he wound up disgraced and landed himself an 18-month stretch in the penitentiary. Moreover, the spectacle of the once untouchable don being grilled by the Senate panel helped accelerate Costello's downhill slide within the Mafia.

For organized crime as a whole, the Kefauver hearings were little more than an annoyance. Over 12 months, the senators heard more than 600 witnesses and amassed in excess of 11,500 pages of testimony, but the only immediate results were 45 citations for contempt, and only three of those led to convictions. Eventually, the five senators on the panel would recommend 19 new anticrime laws, but only one would pass, and it would prove to be unenforceable. The Immigration and Naturalization Service would review the citizenship status of 559 gangsters, but only 24 would be deported. The Bureau of Internal Revenue would do somewhat better, convicting 874 mobsters of tax violations over the next six years. One of the worst hit would be Costello himself. He would be found in arrears on his taxes to the tune of more than $586,000, and for this infraction he would get a five-year prison sentence and a $30,000 fine.

But if the hearings produced less-than-definitive results, they did provide a genuine revelation to the many Americans who'd been unaware that there was any such thing as big-time organized crime. Thousands of people stayed

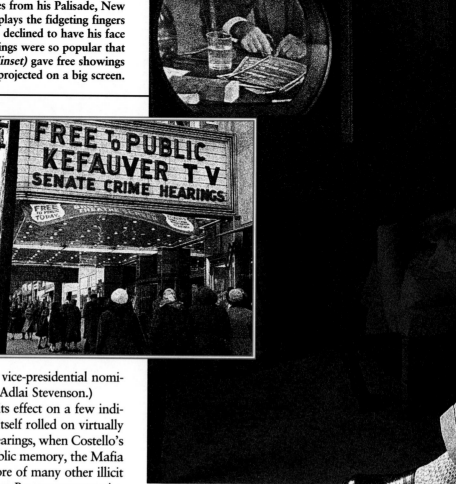

Aging mafioso Joe Adonis watches from his Palisade, New Jersey, home as national television displays the fidgeting fingers of crime boss Frank Costello, who declined to have his face appear in the broadcast. The hearings were so popular that theaters such as New York's Marine *(inset)* gave free showings of the filmed proceedings, projected on a big screen.

home from work to listen in; university and high-school classes were dismissed in some areas for the duration of the telecasts; and inmates at one New Haven jail petitioned the warden for a chance to watch. Newspapers gave the crime probe 10 times the space that they allotted for the Korean War. Estes Kefauver, an earnest Tennessee Democrat and a Senate freshman, hadn't previously cast much of a shadow. But he emerged from the hearings as a pop icon. Kefauver appeared on a popular quiz show and parlayed his fame into a vice-presidential nomination in 1956. (He lost alongside Adlai Stevenson.)

Despite the Kefauver probe and its effect on a few individuals, however, organized crime itself rolled on virtually unscathed. Two decades after the hearings, when Costello's televised grilling had faded from public memory, the Mafia controlled more gambling—and more of many other illicit trades—than at any time in the past. By one conservative estimate the Mafia's take in 1969 was $7 billion to $10 billion. The lion's share came from gambling, but cash also rolled in from loansharking, narcotics smuggling, prostitution, labor racketeering, and the infiltration of thousands of legitimate enterprises. "We're bigger than U.S. Steel," mobster Meyer Lansky crowed in 1966.

By midcentury, the Mafia could perhaps be best understood as a vast, enormously profitable segment of the American services industry: It was a vertically integrated, loosely knit conglomerate of spheres of influence, sometimes overlapping, that stretched from the meanest ghetto to the wealthiest neighborhoods in the land. Its personnel included only a few thousand made members—those who'd undergone the brotherhood's traditional initiation ritual, with its vow of silence. Although by this time the Mafia was no longer exclusively Sicilian, it was still open only to men of Italian descent. Nevertheless, the Mafia's extended family—the mob—took in many ethnic groups and included many thousands of associates, suppliers, and contract employees.

The mob's client base included nearly everyone, although most of the customers would never have suspected as much.

Anyone who put money into a cigarette vending machine may have been contributing to Mafia coffers; anyone visiting a brothel almost surely was. The Mafia was hauling America's garbage, doing America's dry cleaning, and, in many cases, singing America's songs: Mobsters had, after all, infiltrated Hollywood's entertainment unions decades earlier. Offshore branches of organized crime, under the direction of top criminals in exile, were pumping heroin and other drugs into the country at the same time as they pumped dollars out—billions to banks in Switzerland.

Even more insidiously, organized crime had acquired wide-ranging political influence. The Kefauver hearings had provided fascinating testimony on how mobsters had corrupted sheriffs in Florida, for example, and how they'd melded into the political machinery of Kansas City, New Orleans, and Los Angeles. Former Brooklyn district attorney and New York mayor William O'Dwyer, who'd since become the U.S. ambassador to Mexico, was forced to reveal his intimate ties with Frank Costello and other mobsters; he was then tarred with stories of payoffs from local firemen seeking pay raises and pension benefits. Within a

decade of the hearings, Mafia tentacles would reach farther still—all the way into the White House.

In the second half of the 20th century, the mob would become the shadow partner of the nation's intelligence apparatus, hatching plans with the Central Intelligence Agency to kill a common enemy, Cuban dictator Fidel Castro. No less astonishing would be the Mafia's infiltration of the highest law enforcement agencies: In 1963, for example, three days after a report on illicit mob profit skimming at Las Vegas casinos reached the office of Attorney General Robert F. Kennedy, the same document found its way into Mafia hands. As Kennedy described the situation in his book *The Enemy Within:* "The gangsters of today work in a highly organized fashion and are far more powerful now than at any time in the history of the country. They control political figures and threaten whole communities."

Despite all the power and influence, a kind of rot was setting into the Mafia, invisible at first, but quick to spread. The old code of omertà was weakening, and the public was getting brief but telling glimpses into the mob's dark methods. In time, these flashes of light, however brief, would arouse enough popular disgust and outrage to bring about new anticrime laws that would shake the brotherhood to its roots. But this ominous fate was unforeseen by most dons. On the whole, the 1950s and '60s were boom years, despite such annoyances as the Kefauver hearings and internal miniwars occasioned by the usual jockeying for power.

From the perspective of the Mafia leadership, the two decades were a time of turbulence and vicious competition —business as usual, in other words. Things might have been different had Charlie Luciano not been deported: Luciano had commanded absolute respect, and, while he never insisted on leadership, no one would have challenged him for it. Therefore, he kept the peace. But his departure created a gap no one else was big enough to fill, and in the breach, would-be bosses reverted to the old, violent tactics in their climb to power. In the wake of the Kefauver hearings, no rivalry better highlighted the renewed internal tensions than that between the mobster-diplomat, Frank Costello, and that other longtime Luciano associate, Vito Genovese.

In terms of personal style, the two Mafia leaders could hardly have been more different. For Costello, the title of Prime Minister was less a tribute to his power and influence than a reflection of his aspirations to gentility. At the height of his career, Costello was famed for the breakfast meetings that he held in his Manhattan apartment just west of Central Park. Powerful politicians and industrialists were regular guests at these gatherings, sharing a morning meal while currying favor with their host or seeking his O.K. for some pet project. Many of the guests owed their jobs to Costello. William O'Dwyer, for example, had sought Costello's blessing before running for mayor of New York.

Costello also flaunted his power in the trendy public places of his day, among them the Waldorf Astoria's Norse Grill and the King Cole Room at the St. Regis Hotel. He could certainly afford the upscale nightlife: Along with his oil leases, nightclubs, and gaming casinos, the mob kingpin owned substantial amounts of real estate in Manhattan and the Bronx. He likened himself to any other businessman and made much of the fact that he loathed violence. His frequent nights on the town proceeded without the services of bodyguards, and Costello himself always went unarmed. Perhaps to further bolster his image of respectability, he lobbied his fellow Mafia chieftains to stay out of the drug trade, which he considered a destructive business.

It's possible that Costello eventually began to believe his own public relations and to think of himself as a member of the establishment, more or less—a misconception that may have eventually contributed to his downfall. For the time being, however, many people believed in the gangster's public persona or at least made allowances for his notoriety. In 1949 the would-be pillar of the East Coast business community was invited to speak as the guest of honor at the Greater Los Angeles Press Club. He regretfully declined.

By way of contrast, Vito Genovese was the old-fashioned don personified. He wore cheap, rumpled suits and lived in suburban New Jersey. True to the stereotype, he loved to cook pots of spaghetti for his grandchildren. But behind the folksy facade was the same ferocious killer who'd served Charlie Luciano so long and so well. Genovese's reputation from that era still filled his colleagues with dread. Scores of gangsters who'd gotten in his way in the old days had paid with their lives—usually in ugly circumstances. Even romance seemed to bring out his murderous side. According to mob lore, he ordered the killing of the husband of his soon-to-be second wife and married her two weeks later.

As Luciano's underboss for several years, Genovese had actually outranked Costello. But investigative pressure involving a 1934 homicide left him little choice but to flee to Italy in 1937. (He was indicted for the murder, *in absentia*, in 1944.) In Italy he threw himself into the local rackets. Like Luciano, Genovese found a way to ingratiate himself with the Allies during World War II. He became a translator for the advancing American troops and served in that capacity until he was found to be up to his ears in a black market scheme involving stolen army supplies. By 1945 Genovese was back in the United States, having been extradited to stand trial on the homicide charge. That headache would soon go away, however. In 1945 a key prosecution witness died in prison, the victim of a poison-laced pain-killer. About a year later, the prosecutor announced that he had no case, and the murder charge was dropped. Once again Genovese was free to concentrate on regaining his lost status, and he did so with characteristic single-mindedness.

Genovese's differences with Costello were a matter of business as well as personal style. Genovese paid lip service to the Costello-inspired ban on traffic in narcotics, but when

Nine months before testifying to the Kefauver committee, Frank Costello (left) admires 1950's crop of spring blossoms with his wife, Loretta, at their Sands Point, New York, estate. Costello's genteel town-and-country style contrasted with the rumpled thuggishness of his successor, Vito Genovese, seen here in a 1945 New York police photograph.

it came to making money on drugs, he took to the business like a fish to water: The astronomical profits were irresistible. He likewise made no pretense of nonviolence. He surrounded himself with thugs and assassins.

This lifestyle apparently had only limited appeal for Genovese's second wife, Anna, who in 1952 broke with all Mafia decorum and sued for divorce. Her grounds were cruelty, but Anna was not content to leave it at that. She made it clear to the court that Genovese was the most ruthless of Mafia bosses. She identified safety deposit boxes in the United States and abroad where the government could, she claimed, recover some of her husband's stolen riches. She also gave considerable detail on Genovese's gambling, loansharking, and labor racketeering activities. Anna was apparently in a position to know: She'd helped run at least one of her husband's illicit businesses: the Italian lottery. Needless to say, none of this sat well with Genovese, who apparently loved his perfidious wife despite her unseemly revelations. For years to come, the mere reminder of Anna was enough to bring tears to his eyes. Of course, not many people were foolish enough to bring up the subject.

It would have been hard to imagine any such tacky domestic scandal touching the high-living Frank Costello, but for all his stylistic differences with Genovese, the two had much in common. Both had risen from poverty and obscurity. Genovese was born to poor parents near Naples, went to school there through the fifth grade before dropping out, and came to America with his family in 1912 at the age of 15. He immediately became a street thief, then graduated to being a collector for the Italian lottery. It was in that capacity that the young Genovese met Charlie Luciano.

Frank Costello, the youngest of six children of a poor Calabrian farmer, came to America as a child in 1896. By adolescence Costello was a hard-eyed thief; he robbed his mother's East Harlem landlord at age 14. In 1915, when he was 24, he served 10 months in jail for gun possession. According to his lawyer, Costello never carried a firearm again. Nor did he do jail time again—until the Kefauver debacle. After the first jail term, Costello began proving himself as a businessman, running a company that dealt in novelties such as Kewpie dolls while providing cover for Harlem crap games. His triumphs in the bootlegging trade cemented his ties with Charlie Luciano and were, for a time, tremendously profitable. But that was only a start.

Well before the end of Prohibition, Costello had expanded into big-time gambling, specializing in bookmaking operations and illicit slot machines. When reforming New York mayor Fiorello La Guardia went on a highly publicized slot-bashing spree *(page 81),* a miffed Costello moved his slot operations to Louisiana, where he found the business climate more to his liking.

During the same period, Costello's influence was growing alongside Luciano's. Thus after Genovese fled abroad and Luciano was imprisoned, Costello became the head of the Mafia, if only by default. Among his peers he was exalted as fair-minded, scrupulous, and — by mob standards — honest to a fault. "A complete gentleman and a guy that done business correctly," intoned fellow mobster Mickey Cohen. "He was a dignified man; class just leaked out of him."

A newspaper-man put it more pragmatically: "He kept the animals in line. He had so much power and prestige that he could settle a tense situation with a phone call."

Diplomacy notwithstanding, Costello was not always one to stand in the way of more violent solutions when his Mafia peers called for them. By all accounts he did little to prevent the 1947 murder of his old partner Ben Siegel. Costello and several other dons had advanced Siegel millions of dollars to build the Flamingo hotel in Las Vegas — an establishment that would be the cornerstone for the glittering gambling town that Siegel and Meyer Lansky had foreseen. But the partners discovered that Siegel was skimming a healthy portion of the proceeds from the loans and from construction funds. Costello had put his prestige on the line to get his mob partners to back the Flamingo venture. It fell to him, therefore, to pay off those investors when the Flamingo opened up to huge operating losses. Siegel's assassination followed shortly thereafter.

The Las Vegas fiasco cost Costello his ranking as the unofficial chairman of the Mafia board of directors. But his star may have already been on the wane. By the time of the Siegel murder, Genovese was back in America — arriving just as Luciano was being deported — and he was watching with wolfish interest the signs of Costello's weakened condition. More signs were not long in coming, as Costello faltered in his campaign to woo Manhattan society to his side. In a particularly vainglorious move, he threw a 1949 benefit dinner for the Salvation Army, inviting many of the city's brightest luminaries. The press was there, and New Yorkers were treated to the sight of various state judges and Tammany Hall bigwigs rubbing shoulders with the tough guys of Costello's underworld. Although a novelty, the charity event proved to be more of an embarrassment than a triumph.

Then came the Kefauver hearings, and no one was more attentive to Costello's tribulations before the Senate committee than Vito Genovese. As if Costello's testimony weren't humiliating enough, there was the appearance before the panel of a thug named Willie Moretti, one of his closest allies, dating back to their boyhood in East Harlem. Moretti directed mob operations in northern New Jersey, but advanced syphilis had impaired his mind and left him dangerously loose-lipped.

A picture of innocence, Ben "Bugsy" Siegel waits for Los Angeles police to question him in August 1940 about a gangland slaying nine months earlier.

There were no serious breaches of security in Moretti's Kefauver testimony, mainly because Costello saw to it that Moretti spent the bulk of his time sequestered under strict medical supervision. But then a New Jersey grand jury called on Moretti to testify, and — worse — Moretti began talking to reporters. A number of Mafia leaders, led by Genovese, argued that Moretti posed a threat to them all. Genovese argued that Moretti's execution was a sad but necessary act to keep the ailing man from talking. Several other members of the Commission went along, and Moretti was gunned down. Mafia members referred to the murder as a "mercy killing" and gave Willie Moretti an elaborate funeral. The whole problem could only be seen, however, as another black mark against Costello.

Genovese's final bid for supremacy didn't come until 1957, but it arrived amid a welter of bloodshed. The first victim was Costello himself. On May 2 the aging don arrived home late after an evening on the town. Unarmed and — as usual — unaccompanied by bodyguards, he strolled into the lobby of his apartment building to be confronted by hulking gunman. "This is for you, Frank," muttered the hit man as he raised his weapon and fired once at Costello's head. Costello collapsed into a chair, and the killer moved quickly out of the lobby, brushing past the terrified doorman.

But the shooter hadn't finished the job. The bullet merely burrowed under Costello's skin in front of his right ear and came out just in back of the ear. The Prime Minister was wounded, but not all that seriously, and he was utterly determined to keep secret the identity of his attacker. "I don't know who could have done it," Costello told the detectives.

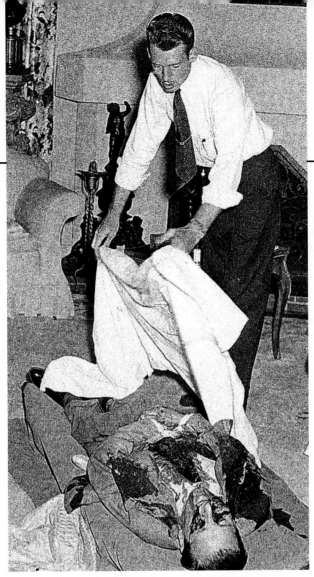

A coroner's assistant covers the riddled remains of Bugsy Siegel, gunned down in 1947 in the Beverly Hills mansion of his mistress, Virginia Hill. Siegel was executed for skimming mob money.

"I don't have an enemy in the world." He refused to help police, even insisting that his back had been turned to the killer when all the forensic evidence — including bullet holes in his fedora — proved otherwise. Costello's studied noncooperation did not prevent the arrest and subsequent trial of a hulking former boxer named Vincent "the Chin" Gigante — a soldier in the Genovese ranks *(pages 149-150)*. With Costello's refusal to finger Gigante, the triggerman's lawyer made hash of the eyewitness account of the doorman, who turned out to be nearly blind in one eye. The trial ended with Gigante's acquittal, and the hit man thanked Costello publicly.

In that he was still alive, Costello was lucky: certain other top Mafia bosses were not. On June 17, 1957, Francesco Scalise, the irascible number two man in Albert Anastasia's crime family, was shot to death in front of a Bronx fruit store. According to informer Joe Valachi, Scalise's sin was selling Mafia memberships for prices that ran as high as $50,000. In the eyes of most dons, this amounted to crass commercialization, devaluing a right that other thugs had killed for. Scalise's brother was soon murdered as well, but that slaying was kept secret. According to Valachi, the body was dismembered for disposal by a mob heavy who controlled garbage collection for New York nightclubs and restaurants.

Valachi fingered Albert Anastasia as the man behind the Scalise murders. As one of the mob's most ruthless enforcers, Anastasia was widely feared within Mafia circles. He was also close to Frank Costello, having provided much of the muscle that backed up the Prime Minister's diplomacy. According to one mob legend, it was this alliance that led

His fedora clamped over a bandage following a shooting in May 1957 that merely creased his scalp, a fortunate Frank Costello finds that he can't identify his assailant when questioned at a New York police station.

to Anastasia's death. As this story goes, Vito Genovese needed to eliminate Anastasia in order to feel completely secure in his victory over Costello. So the wily Genovese made quiet contact with an ambitious member of Anastasia's private army, a long-nosed, soft-spoken killer named Carlo Gambino. On October 25, 1957, Anastasia was getting a shave in the barbershop at Manhattan's Park Sheraton Hotel when his bodyguard strolled away. With the boss defenseless under a pile of hot towels, two gunmen walked into the shop and riddled him with bullets.

With Anastasia dead and Costello on his way to jail for tax evasion, Genovese's reign was assured. All that remained was the coronation. Within three weeks of Anastasia's death, a great event was planned to take place in the town of Apalachin, a tiny rural hamlet in upstate New York. But before Genovese could lay claim to his title, there ensued one of the most humiliating debacles in the history of organized crime. It would have the flavor of comic opera, and for a moment the Mafia grandees would be exposed like so many cockroaches, frozen in the glare of light.

The New York State police officer who discovered the conclave of Mafia chieftains on November 14, 1957, was as startled as the rest of the country. That is not to say, however, that Sergeant Edgar Croswell wasn't already suspicious of the prosperous local beer and soft drink distributor who was hosting the gathering. His name was Joseph "Joe the Barber" Barbara, and Croswell had heard rumors that the man was up to his hips in bootlegging. High excise taxes on alcohol meant that there was still good money to be made in the illicit manufacture and distribution of booze even though Prohibition was long gone. A year before the Apalachin meeting, Croswell had discovered links between Barbara and Carmine Galante, a New York gunman and

drug trafficker. Since then, the sergeant had kept Barbara under observation.

On November 13, 1957, Croswell was struck by a snatch of conversation that he overheard in a motel. He and his partner were following up on a complaint about a bad check when Barbara's son strode into the lobby and booked three double rooms for the next two nights. Croswell decided to cruise by the old man's estate. When he did, he was surprised to find four large cars parked in the driveway, two of them bearing out-of-state plates. The officer called for federal help.

By the next day there were more than 30 swanky cars parked on Joe the Barber's property, and a large party was in progress out by the barbecue pit. Before long, the guests noted the presence of the police, and some of them began to rush about, seemingly in a panic. Croswell hurriedly set up a roadblock on the only lane leading away from the house. He called for additional backup and waited.

The first car to leave contained Vito Genovese, who produced identification and was allowed to proceed on his way. Then a whole line of cars approached the roadblock, and Croswell spotted other guests hightailing it over a fence and into the nearby woods. The fleeing gangsters made a bizarre sight, taking to the forest in their silk suits and elegant shoes. Croswell had seen enough and decided to haul everyone who left the Barbara mansion to police headquarters for questioning. By the time the roundup ended, some 60 mob heavies were in custody. A number of others may have eluded the police in the woods.

All the detained mobsters were released after questioning: At the time authorities began rounding them up they were not, after all, committing any crimes. And that in itself was fairly unusual. Of those detained, 50 had police records, 35 of those had been convicted of crimes, and 23 had served time. All were Italian or of Italian descent, and around half

Albert Anastasia's bloody body lies under barber's smocks in the New York Park Sheraton Hotel barbershop, where he was ambushed by two mob gunmen.

were interrelated either by blood or by marriage. Their misdeeds ran the gamut from homicide and armed robbery to extortion and drug trafficking. The majority of the detainees were from New York or New Jersey. They included four current and two future heads of New York City crime families. But there were also representatives from across the nation and three men from foreign countries. Along with the New York bosses, three other members of the ruling commission were found to have attended the aborted meeting, although they escaped the police roundup at the time. They were Stefano Magaddino of Buffalo, Joe Zerilli of Detroit, and Sam Giancana of Chicago.

The stated occupations of those detained at Apalachin were concentrated in areas such as labor management, the restaurant and hotel trades, the garment industry, real es-

tate, and the import-export business. Nine said they had interests in vending machines, and nine others cited heavy construction. One of those questioned by the police was a former Buffalo city councilman: John C. Montana, who alleged that he owned a taxi company, was actually a lieutenant in the Magaddino organization. Montana was caught when his camel's-hair coat got tangled on a barbed-wire fence. He claimed he didn't know any of the guests at Joe the Barber's estate. He'd merely been driving through town, he said, when his car developed brake trouble.

Montana's story was at least original. Virtually all the others stuck to the yarn that they'd stopped by on the spur of the moment to inquire about the health of poor Joe Barbara, who purportedly had a heart condition.

In reality, the Apalachin meeting probably had a number

of issues to resolve in addition to the feting of Vito Genovese. High on the list was the need to mediate the long-simmering dispute over trade in drugs. As Frank Costello's power was waning, the drug trade was growing in importance to the Mafia, a fact due in no small measure to the organizational genius of the exiled Charlie Luciano. Charlie Lucky, shipped to Italy in February of 1946, traveled from there to Cuba eight months later to meet with American mafiosi. He was deported from Cuba in February of 1947 and wound up in Naples, where he opened a popular café catering to Americans. He also assumed a key role in channeling drugs to the United States. The subtle Luciano had inveigled officials from the major Italian pharmaceutical companies to serve as his main suppliers of heroin, which could, at the time, be dispensed legally in Italy for medicinal purposes. In addition, Luciano forged alliances with French criminals who produced illicit heroin in factories near the port of Marseilles.

The Mafia's role in drug smuggling, as Luciano defined it, amounted to a monopoly on distribution: No major drug shipment could leave Italy without the approval of him or one of his underlings.

During this time, the U.S. government was devoting increased attention to policing drugs. Special agents had been stationed in a number of foreign countries in hopes of finding a way to cut off supplies at their source. This new heat from the government hadn't gone unnoticed by the American Mafia, and it was almost certainly high on the agenda as the Apalachin meeting convened.

The bust outside Joe the Barber's estate did little immediate harm to the people involved. Almost all of those detained were on their way home within a day or two. And in a series of ensuing meetings throughout the country, the business slated for Apalachin got transacted: Genovese was confirmed as boss, Gambino was given Anastasia's organization, and an official ban was issued against drug trafficking—a prohibition that would be widely ignored.

Nearly two years after the Apalachin incident, 27 of the mobsters who'd attended the meeting were indicted for conspiracy to obstruct justice. The charges stemmed from their unresponsiveness to questioning by the police; 36 others were named as co-conspirators. The indictments resulted in numerous convictions, but in 1960 the verdicts would be overturned by a federal appeals court.

The reprieve on appeal was temporary at best, however, because enormous publicity was lavished on the Apalachin story—enough to light a fire under a whole new congressional hearing that was already under way. The chairman of this latest probe was Senator John L. McClellan, a cautious, conservative Democrat from Arkansas. High on McClellan's agenda was exploring the link between the Mafia and organized labor. The ambitious chief counsel to the investigation was fiery young Robert F. Kennedy. Kennedy's desire to take on organized crime in the union movement had been forcefully opposed by his father, former U.S. ambassador to Great Britain Joseph P. Kennedy, but to no avail.

The Senate Select Committee on Improper Activities in the Labor or Management Field had been in session since January 30, 1957. Over 30 months, it would hear more than 1,500 witnesses and amass more than 20,000 pages of testimony attesting to the intimate linkage between criminals and organized labor. Particularly tarred by the committee for its ties to the mob was the largest, richest union in the country, the International Brotherhood of Teamsters. The Teamsters had a membership of approximately 1.3 million and a virtual stranglehold on anything that moved by truck in the United States.

Organized labor was McClellan's chief target, but the committee's work also furthered the uncloaking of the Mafia. Seven years before the McClellan group began its business, Estes Kefauver had started his Senate hearings on organized crime with the pronouncement that he didn't believe in the existence of a secret criminal conspiracy rooted primarily in the Italian-American community. He would change his mind, and his hearings would raise among the public the specter of a nefarious underworld brotherhood. After the Apalachin incident and the McClellan hearings, very little doubt remained as to the Mafia's existence. Just one day before the Apalachin meeting, the McClellan panel heard testimony from Joseph Amato, a Mafia specialist in the U.S. Bureau of Narcotics. Amato affirmed the existence of a "loosely organized" criminal society responsible for a lot of the crime in America. Nothing could have underscored his point more dramatically than the raid on nearly five dozen known gangsters in upstate New York.

Not even J. Edgar Hoover could hold out against the mounting evidence. Prior to the Apalachin incident, the powerful director of the FBI had confidently asserted that there was no such thing as a nationwide organization of criminals. The only conspiracy that interested Hoover was the supposed threat of communism within U.S. borders. While the FBI churned out statistics on car thefts and armed bank robberies, it did virtually no research on the Mafia. "They're just a bunch of hoodlums," Hoover once remarked. Members of the mob rarely turned up on the bureau's highly publicized lists of public enemies and most-wanted criminals.

This neglect ended, however, after stories of the Apalachin raid saturated the press. An embarrassed Hoover ordered his subordinates to collect everything they could on the Mafia, but the nation's chief law enforcement agency was getting off to a late, slow start. Robert Kennedy demanded for the McClellan committee all the FBI files on the Apalachin conferees, only to discover that the cupboard was bare. By contrast, Kennedy got mountains of files from the FBI's rival, the Federal Bureau of Narcotics. FBN chief Harry J. Anslinger had been collecting material on the nation's top 800 gangsters for decades.

Hoover's demand for crash action resulted in a two-volume FBI report on the Mafia the following year, 1958, but the report merely turned out to be another embarrassment. It thoroughly proved that the Mafia had been in business all during the time that Hoover had been denying its existence. The document was pulled out of circulation almost the minute it was printed.

Despite this initial awkwardness, Hoover began crafting a high-profile image as a mob foe. In November of 1957, just days after the Apalachin raid, he initiated the Top Hoodlum Program, under which regional FBI chiefs were asked to identify the top 10 gangsters within each of their jurisdictions. Some of the agents came up with nothing. The Dallas office even insisted that Joseph Civello, the Dallas underboss for New Orleans don Carlos Marcello, was nothing more than "a counselor to the Italian community at large." But other regional heads began naming names and keeping records. In a move that went

Summit Meeting

The sleepy, tree-lined main street of the upstate New York village of Apalachin seems a postcard image of small-town innocence *(right)*. But some two miles away, at the estate of Joseph "Joe the Barber" Barbara, the Mafia held its most famous—and most disastrous—national summit meeting. In November 1957 Apalachin's tiny population swelled with an influx of beefy, hard-faced men riding in big cars, many of them with out-of-state license plates. It turned out that the visitors were the top dons in the American Mafia, gathering to anoint Vito Genovese as their new boss of bosses and to cover an agenda of mob business—notably, whether to get into the narcotics trade in a major way. Before the conclave properly began, however, police showed up and turned it into a rout. Subsequent national publicity gave the peaceful hamlet an association that's been hard to shake: The very name of Apalachin still evokes a meeting of the masters of organized crime.

In a Syracuse, New York, hotel room, Joseph Barbara *(be-low)* clutches his chest prior to a 1958 court appearance for income-tax evasion. Barbara had a heart ailment, said mobsters who claimed they visited Apalachin to inquire after his health—and, indeed, he died in 1959 of a heart attack.

New York State police sergeant Edgar G. Croswell *(above)* shows a June 1958 session of the McClellan committee an aerial view of Barbara's estate, 58 acres dominated by a rambling stone mansion *(below)*.

A bold sign steers Apalachin's visitors to the late Joseph Barbara's estate, once seen by some entrepreneurs as a possible tourist attraction. Barbara himself moved away from the property soon after the abortive Apalachin summit, and residents concerned for their town's image quickly squashed the idea of a Mafia Disneyland in upstate New York.

OPEN
JOSEPH BARBARA SR'S Former ESTATE
Site of the APALACHIN SUMMIT CONFERENCE
RUSSELL C. TERRY Realtor
147 FRONT ST.   VESTAL, N.Y.

Chairman John L. McClellan of Arkansas *(far left)* speaks at a 1957 session of his Senate committee, attended by chief counsel Robert F. Kennedy *(center)* and his brother Senator John F. Kennedy *(far right)*, a member of the committee.

well beyond cosmetic attention to the problem, Hoover started using wiretaps against suspected mobsters. The tactic, which struck certain civil libertarians as illegal, was a bid to fill the FBI's intelligence void quickly, and it would prove very effective. Electronic surveillance would soon become a vital weapon—perhaps the most important one—in the war against organized crime.

Eavesdropping would also turn the spotlight on another major crime figure, whose career would eventually bring him into contact with both the Central Intelligence Agency and the White House. The high-flying escapades of Momo Salvatore "Sam" Giancana would be cut short by assassination in 1975, but by then he'd risen to the top of the heap in the Chicago mob—known as the Outfit—and had acquired considerable national influence as well.

Chicago Mafia leaders came in for attention early in Hoover's overdue antimob crusade because of some loose talk by a mobster who should have known better. John Michael Caifano was a veteran mafioso, and he soon figured out that he was being tailed by an FBI agent. Accustomed to the bureau's longstanding disinterest in Mafia doings, Caifano was puzzled. So he confronted his pursuer, a

young agent named Ralph Hill, to point out that none of his rackets—gambling, protection, and loansharking—had ever been of interest to federal agents.

Hill made it clear to Caifano that things had changed, but the gangster apparently failed to grasp the full import of the FBI's new interest in the mob. He casually discussed the names, territories, and business interests of other Chicago racketeers in such detail that Hill returned to his boss, Special Agent in Charge Marlin Johnson, with a pretty good overall picture of organized crime in Chicago. Johnson then asked headquarters in Washington for permission to start electronic surveillance on the Mafia big shots, and the go-ahead was quickly granted.

Chicago FBI men initially planted one bug. It was installed in the summer of 1959 in a second-story tailor's shop on North Michigan Avenue where a number of the local Mafia chieftains held regular morning meetings. The tailor's shop bug would run for the next five years, giving the FBI extraordinary access to Mafia planning sessions. The mobsters never knew there was a listening device in the room, but one of them, a valued legal tactician named Murray Humphreys, liked to entertain his pals by pretending that everything they said was being overheard. "Good morning,

Frolicking at a London nightspot in 1962, Chicago mobster Sam Giancana and his longtime mistress, singer Phyllis McGuire, share a happy toast.

gentlemen, and anyone listening," he would intone as the group convened. "This is the nine o'clock meeting of the Chicago underworld."

The information taken in through this secret surveillance was so rich that other bugs were soon installed. Before long, J. Edgar Hoover was able to read about the latest in the Outfit's murder techniques or monitor the ebb and flow of mob influence in Chicago politics. Within two years, agents had overheard a discussion by Sam Giancana of what was later described as "a small group of persons representing groups in various sections of the United States and referred to as 'The Commission.' "

By that time, Giancana himself had been a part of the Mafia governing body for several years. It had been a long climb for him. Giancana was born in 1908—not in Sicily, but in Chicago's Little Italy to Sicilian-born parents. His father, a native of the village of Castelvetrano, was a street peddler, and, by some accounts, an exceptionally brutal man. According to Chuck Giancana, Sam's brother, young Salvatore was badly abused as a child and took to the streets to escape his father's rages and beatings.

By the time Sam was 10 his teachers had declared him a hopeless delinquent. He spent six months in a reformatory, and when he emerged, he signed on with a local street gang called the '42s. This pack was regarded as the most vicious gang in the neighborhood, and by the time Sam Giancana was 13 years old, he'd distinguished himself as its most violent member. His buddies called him Mooney, a reference to what they considered to be his lunatic outlook on life. His mental quirkiness was one of two of young Giancana's distinguishing characteristics in those days. The other was his skill as a wheelman, or driver.

Giancana's ascent owed a great deal to Al Capone, who figured the young thug would make an excellent triggerman. In 1926, Giancana was jailed on a robbery-murder charge, but the case never went to trial because the sole witness turned up dead. Giancana went on to become one of the premier hit men in Chicago. He also showed signs of growing business sense, and for an amoral young man on the make, he was in the right place at the right time. Even after Capone was jailed for income tax evasion in 1932, the Chicago mob flourished, establishing itself as one of the most innovative criminal organizations in the country. In the 1930s it sent an emissary to Hollywood, and mob influence took root in the entertainment unions. After gam-

bling was legalized in Nevada, Chicago Mafia men were quick to establish a presence in Las Vegas and at the resort community of Lake Tahoe. Giancana had a taste for the glitzy show-biz life, especially if it involved show girls. He had married in 1933 a young Italian woman, Angeline De Tolve, and the couple had three daughters before the sickly Angeline died in 1954. In his widowhood Giancana became an enthusiastic womanizer. In 1960 he met Phyllis McGuire of the singing McGuire Sisters trio at the casino of the Desert Inn in Las Vegas, and she became his mistress.

In Chicago and out west, Giancana retained his reputation as a fearsome and ruthless enemy. Unlike Frank Cos-

While starlets hold cue cards, Hollywood's notorious
Rat Pack—from left, Peter Lawford, Frank Sinatra,
Dean Martin, Sammy Davis, Jr., and Joey Bishop—re-
hearse a skit at Las Vegas's Sands Hotel in January
1960. Sinatra was believed to be a major link between
the Kennedy clan and the Mafia.

tello, he had little desire to be thought of as anything other than what he was. During World War II, for instance, he avoided the draft by answering a question about his occupation with a terse, "I steal." Military authorities passed him over, declaring him to be a psychopath.

The diagnosis certainly wasn't unreasonable; Giancana seemed to enjoy killing, both personally and by proxy. And he liked inventiveness in his murders. Once, when a 300-pound mobster had incurred his wrath, Giancana sent thugs to take the man to a meat rendering plant. There the wayward soldier was impaled on a hook and tortured for

two days with methods that included some particularly brutal uses of electric shock. Only death spared him additional suffering.

Political corruption had always been a specialty of the Outfit, and by the time Giancana took over as boss in 1957 at least three wards in Chicago were firmly in the Mafia grip. The First Ward in particular was a strategic treasure, since it contained the business district known as the Loop, City Hall, and a number of posh hotels. A variety of city officials were more or less openly on the Mafia's payroll.

Giancana seemed able to dismiss local legislators at will:

He once denied permission for an alderman to run for re-election after observing the politico shaking hands with an FBI agent. It was a measure of Giancana's self-confidence that when he appeared before the McClellan committee in 1959, he was taken to task by counsel Robert Kennedy for giggling during the questioning. The snickers were, however, the most honest response the committee got: The Chicago capo took the Fifth Amendment 34 times in his testimony, refusing to discuss much of anything lest he incriminate himself.

With his power and visibility, Giancana was courted by a great many people who needed political help in Chicago. One of those who may have sought his help was Robert Kennedy's father.

Joseph P. Kennedy had founded the family fortunes partly on bootlegging money from the Prohibition days, and long after he'd become a pillar of the business community, he continued to hobnob with mobsters. He liked to hang out in gangster-owned clubs and satisfied his appetite for gambling by paying frequent visits to a casino called the Cal-Neva Lodge at Lake Tahoe. The FBI at one point had 343 separate case files on the Kennedy patriarch, detailing, among other things, his fondness for meeting with gangsters at the Cal-Neva.

An alleged part-owner of the casino was Sam Giancana, who once disparaged Joe Kennedy as "one of the biggest crooks that ever lived." For a time, an owner of record of the Cal-Neva was Frank Sinatra, whose close acquaintance with mobsters has long been a source of speculation. Sinatra was a good friend both to Joe Kennedy and to actor Peter Lawford, who was Joe Kennedy's son-in-law and thus the brother-in-law of then-U.S. senator John F. Kennedy. Lawford was one of the founding members of the so-called Rat Pack, a group of high-living entertainers with strenuous partygoing habits. These men—among them Sinatra, Dean Martin, Joey Bishop, and Sammy Davis, Jr., found a kindred soul in the young senator from Massachusetts.

In early 1960 FBI agents were reporting wild parties involving John Kennedy. The future president's now-notorious sexual appetites and his connection with Sinatra apparently bound him up in a fateful relationship with the Mafia. Sinatra, who once declared that "I'd rather be a don of the Mafia than president of the United States," seemed determined to be a friend to both.

On February 7, 1960, just as his lengthy primary campaign for the presidency was getting under way, Jack Kennedy was sitting at Sinatra's private table at the Sands Hotel in Las Vegas when he was introduced to Judith Campbell, a stunning, dark-haired party girl who liked to hang out with celebrities. A month later, Campbell would allege, she and Kennedy were having an affair. A week after their first tryst, she acquired another admirer: Sinatra introduced her to Sam Giancana, and the mobster also courted her. According to Campbell's subsequent account of this period, she eventually had sex with Giancana, but only after her liaison with Kennedy ended. Meanwhile, she claims, she became a courier between the mobster and the senator and set up several meetings between them. Fund-raising may have been the subject of these meetings, as Kennedy's campaign was headed toward a crucial May primary in West Virginia, a showdown between him and his chief rival, liberal Minnesota senator Hubert H. Humphrey.

FBI wiretaps from that period have shown that the Mafia put large amounts of money into that primary campaign—funds that had allegedly been doled out by the obliging Sinatra. Some historians believe that the money was used to pay off ward organizers to get out the vote for Kennedy. He won the West Virginia primary handily, in the process eliminating Humphrey from the presidential race. Humphrey decried the methods used to beat him. "I don't think elections should be bought," he said. "I can't afford to run

Judith Campbell Exner, seen in a series of 1962 photographs, claimed to have had an intimate relationship with John F. Kennedy both before and after he became president. She was also mobster Sam Giancana's mistress.

through this state with a little black bag and a checkbook."

The mob also helped Kennedy in the 1960 general election. One of the most crucial states for the Democratic candidate was Illinois, where the urban Chicago vote had to outweigh the results from the traditionally Republican rural areas and small towns. Chicagoans turned out for Kennedy in huge numbers—results attributed to a combination of solid support in the African American community and big margins in wards controlled by Giancana.

Kennedy won Illinois by fewer than 9,000 votes—a tissue-thin margin, but enough to ensure the electoral votes that would edge him past then-vice president Richard M. Nixon at the finish line. The narrowness of the victory led Giancana to boast to Judith Campbell, "Listen, honey, if it wasn't for me your boyfriend wouldn't even be in the White House."

Giancana's assessment of his influence on the election was open to question, but he had another reason to feel confident of being in with the Kennedys: Cuba. Like other mobsters, the Chicago don had suffered a major financial set-

back when Fidel Castro's Communist revolution ousted the regime of mob-friendly Cuban strongman Fulgencio Batista. Losses stemming from Castro's closing of mob-owned gambling casinos may have run as high as $100 million per year. According to a number of witnesses, the mob planned vengeance in its own fashion, offering as much as $1 million for Castro's murder. And in the final years of President Dwight D. Eisenhower's administration, the Central Intelligence Agency came to see merit in the Mafia approach.

In one of the more bizarre chapters of American history, the spy agency commissioned a former FBI agent named Robert Maheu to put out a contract on Castro. Maheu contacted Johnny Rosselli, Sam Giancana's man in Las Vegas, and Rosselli brought Giancana into the loop. Giancana in turn contacted Florida mob boss Santo Trafficante, Jr., once a power to be reckoned with in Cuba. According to the CIA plan, Trafficante would be in charge of organizing the Castro hit.

A couple of inept assassination attempts involving poison ensued. They failed, and in the aftermath of the disastrous

President John F. Kennedy sits with Frank Sinatra at the January 1961 Inaugural Ball that the singer helped organize. Their friendship waned because of Sinatra's alleged ties to the mob.

CIA-backed Bay of Pigs invasion of Cuba by anti-Castro fighters, the assassination scheme was put on hold. It would be briefly revived in 1962, but nothing ever came of it. It's possible that the mob never intended for anything to come of it. Many observers of mob doings believe that the Mafia was only stringing the CIA along, using the agency as a pawn to keep the FBI at bay.

If Giancana hoped to gain anything personally from his cloak-and-dagger flirtation with the Feds, it was immunity from government prosecution. Apparently, the CIA tried to give him exactly that, telling the Justice Department of his part in "clandestine efforts against the Castro government." But Robert Kennedy, now serving as U.S. attorney general at the pleasure of his brother the president, was not entirely impressed. Whatever tangled relations existed between Giancana, Joe Kennedy, and John Kennedy apparently did not extend to Bobby, who made it known that he'd still like to see Giancana behind bars.

One link between the mobster and John Kennedy—a shared acquaintance with Judith Campbell—apparently persisted after Kennedy's inauguration. White House telephone logs show that about 70 phone calls were made between Campbell and the president during 1961 and 1962.

After her days of backstairs liaisons with power, Judith Campbell married and took her husband's surname, Exner. Needing money, she collaborated on a book about her life and began freely discussing her relationships with Kennedy and Giancana. In 1988, gravely ill with cancer, she added more details in a magazine interview. Her assertions included these claims: that she acted as a go-between on several occasions, carrying envelopes between Kennedy and Giancana; that in April of 1960 and again a year later she set up meetings between the two men; and that Kennedy once told her, "Don't worry about Sam. You know he works for us." There is no confirmation from other sources of any of her story.

This much is known with certainty, however: In February 1962, J. Edgar Hoover—no friend of the Kennedys—informed Robert Kennedy about his brother's involvement in the highly unorthodox triangle. A month later Hoover took a memorandum on the same subject to a White House lunch with the president. After that, Campbell's welcome at the White House was withdrawn.

Frank Sinatra was about to get the same treatment. In the days immediately following Kennedy's election, the singer was made to feel entirely welcome by the Kennedys. He even sang at JFK's inaugural gala. But Sinatra seemed no less interested in maintaining his friendship with Sam Giancana, who was a frequent guest at the crooner's Palm Springs home. In the spring of 1962, Sinatra was expecting to play host to the president himself, during a Kennedy trip to California. Sinatra had even gone to the expense of installing a helicopter landing pad. But JFK canceled the visit quite unexpectedly and stayed instead at the estate of rival crooner Bing Crosby, even though Crosby was a Republican. Sinatra never forgave the snub.

It was probably Robert Kennedy's influence that turned the president away from his Mafia associations. As soon as the younger brother was appointed attorney general, he made it clear that he had no intention of backing away from his longstanding opposition to organized crime. In Robert Kennedy's first speech as head of the Justice Department, he declared that organized crime had become big business and vowed to root it out. In his aggressive, no-nonsense fashion, he pressured J. Edgar Hoover to gather more intelligence. Miffed at being ordered about by his young upstart boss, the autocratic FBI director nevertheless eventually threw himself energetically into the effort. His bugging program had already garnered a great deal of useful information, but it was expanded even further until anywhere from 75 to 100 listening devices were active at any one time.

Robert Kennedy meantime beefed up the Justice Department's organized crime section. He added 43 lawyers to its staff, bringing the total to 60, and opened new field offices in Chicago, New York, Los Angeles, and Miami. He also ordered a report documenting Frank Sinatra's mob connections; the resulting 19-page memo outlined Sinatra's connections with 10 top mafiosi.

Robert Kennedy encouraged his new crime busters to prosecute aggressively, and they did. In the last year of the Eisenhower administration the number of indictments handed up against suspected mobsters was 49. That figure more than doubled, to 121, during Kennedy's first year as attorney general, and it rose to 350 the following year. By 1963 the total was 615. Kennedy also won support for a number of important new anti-Mafia laws that criminalized interstate travel in support of illegal gambling or racketeering.

In addition, the young attorney general solicited information from other federal agencies—in particular, the Fed-

Kept company by his miniature pinschers, a dapper and relaxed Lucky Luciano enjoys his exile, reading the local paper over coffee in his richly appointed apartment in Naples.

Luciano's body *(below)* is lifted into a coffin after
the Mafia chief died of a heart attack at the Naples
airport in January 1962. He'd gone there to meet an
American film producer.

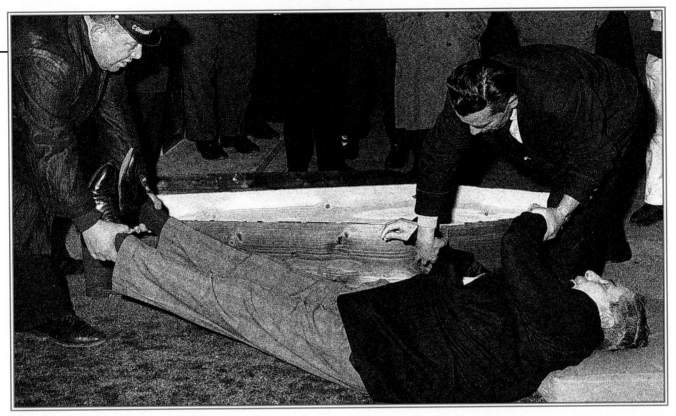

eral Bureau of Narcotics, which was only too happy to oblige. As bureau chief Harry Anslinger put it: "The attorney general wasn't afraid to admit that there was an association of highly organized gangsters in the country, and he wasn't afraid to term this organization the Mafia. It was a revelation to me to see what a strong, courageous, and intelligent attorney general could do." The Mafia, of course, saw it another way. "They're hypocrites," a Boston mobster complained of the Kennedys.

In the midst of the government's anticrime drive, the Mafia suffered a loss far removed from the frenetic activity in Washington: Charlie Luciano, the greatest godfather of them all, met with sudden death in Naples. In January 1962, Luciano had traveled to Capodichino Airport to meet with American movie producer Martin Gosch to discuss a film about the gangster's life. As Luciano walked to his car, he suddenly called out, clutched his chest, and fell dead. The father of the modern mob and mastermind of the transatlantic drug trade had fallen victim to a heart attack. He was driven to his burial through busy Neapolitan streets in a 30-foot-long funeral coach pulled by eight black horses.

It was a fitting send-off for the ultimate mafioso, capping an exile that had been both comfortable and productive.

While keeping an interested eye on the distant doings of the American mob and ramrodding the organization of the international drug trade, he lived in a quietly elegant apartment in Naples and took to giving interviews. He got married at last, to an Italian ballerina who was a comfort in his autumn years, and he passed some of his time dispensing handouts to fellow exiled mafiosi who hadn't fared as well as he after leaving America. "Some of them would break your heart," he told an interviewer. The role of the revered and generous elder statesman seemed to suit him, and he could look back on a career unparalleled in Mafia annals. But one dream had gone unrealized. He died in exile, never able in life to return home. After his death, he was permitted back into the United States for burial at St. John's Cemetery in New York City.

About six months after Luciano's death marked the end of a Mafia era, another death on another continent would prove equally momentous in the mob's fortunes, although it didn't seem so at the time. On June 22, 1962, at the U.S. penitentiary in Atlanta, a stocky Mafia foot soldier named Joseph Valachi bludgeoned a fellow prisoner to death with an iron pipe. It was a tragedy for the victim, of course, but it was also the biggest break that Robert Kennedy's anti-Mafia crusade would ever get in terms of focusing public attention on the underworld.

Valachi had made a terrible mistake: He'd killed the wrong man, someone he didn't even know. He'd acted in panic, thinking that the man was a prisoner who'd been assigned to kill him. Valachi, it seems, was under an unofficial sentence of death from one of his fellow inmates— none other than New York crime boss Vito Genovese.

Don Vito had been linked to a large-scale drug smuggling ring, and in 1958, he entered the Atlanta penitentiary to begin serving a 15-year sentence. In 1959 Valachi went to the same prison, having been sentenced to two concurrent stretches—one for 15 years and one for 20—on drug-related charges. Genovese was Valachi's friendly cellmate for a time, but he came to believe that Valachi had turned informant for narcotics agents. In fact, Valachi, bidding for a reduced sentence, supplied some fragmentary information about drug dealing, but none of it involved fellow mafiosi. More or less innocent, he nevertheless received the traditional kiss of death from his don.

Valachi was filled with terror at the thought of Genovese putting out the call for his death. But he was also seething with anger at the injustice of his plight: He felt himself to have been Genovese's loyal soldier. The two men had known each other for decades: Genovese had been the best man at Valachi's wedding, and the stolid, gravel-voiced Valachi had been a gunman and midlevel racketeer in the service of Genovese's crime family. But there the common ground ended, for in terms of the Mafia pecking order, Valachi was several rungs down the ladder. Born in 1904 in East Harlem, he'd been singularly afflicted with bad luck throughout most of his life. He committed his first theft at the age of nine, and by the time he was 18 he'd become a petty thief and the driver for a smash-and-grab street gang known as the Minute Men. He'd once been shot in the head during a robbery; a few years later he survived a prison knifing that required 38 stitches. Valachi was formally inducted into the Mafia in 1931, during the crime wars that brought Charlie Luciano to power.

During more than 30 years in the mob, Valachi had been involved in at least 33 murders. He'd supervised small pieces of several rackets, including slot machines and drugs. In performing these services he'd answered to a succession of crime kingpins, including Luciano himself. But none of Valachi's bosses ever saw fit to advance his career, nor did anyone ever seem to go out of his way to protect him.

If Valachi had a talent, however, it lay in his knack for survival: During his latest prison stay, he'd already lived through three murder attempts, and the fatal bludgeoning that he gave to the wrong man was a desperate effort to avoid yet another attack on his life. Valachi had already made a bid to get himself tucked away in solitary confinement. But prison authorities withdrew their protection when he refused to say why he needed to be isolated. Valachi had written to his wife, asking her to get another Mafia boss to intercede to stop the attempts on his life. The letter was returned by prison officials.

Killing his fellow inmate finally attracted the kind of serious attention that Valachi urgently needed. It also brought talk of the death penalty, however, and when Valachi got wind of this he was quick to send word to U.S. Attorney Robert Morgenthau in New York City that he was finally ready to cooperate. In exchange, he was promised a life sentence on the murder charge, and he was flown to a jail a few miles north of New York City. There he was given a false name and installed in isolation in the prison's hospital wing.

It was still more than a month before Valachi actually started to talk; the closemouthed habits of a lifetime weren't easy to shed. But when he did begin to tell his story, Attorney General Kennedy got into the act. Valachi's public testimony, Kennedy felt, might mobilize public support for additional anticrime legislation. On September 9, 1963, Kennedy had Valachi flown to Washington to appear before a new round of Senate hearings being chaired by Senator John McClellan.

Valachi's nationally televised appearance before the Senate Permanent Subcommittee on Investigations was not, in itself, impressive. The rough-hewn, taciturn mobster was hardly eloquent—or even, at times, very coherent. But he had a vivid memory for the events of his life, and his testimony held the country riveted. For the first time that anyone could recall, a mafioso was publicly breaking the oath of omertà.

Valachi introduced a new term to the American vocabulary: *La Cosa Nostra,* or, roughly, "this thing of ours." It was, he claimed, the American Mafia's name for itself. He also made public the existence of the Commission, the mob's supreme council. In addition, Valachi outlined

Facing a prison murder charge, Mafia soldier
Joseph Valachi breaks his code of silence at
a 1963 session of Senator McClellan's subcommittee on investigations.

the hierarchical structure of the Mafia families and discussed the geographic distribution of criminal organizations
across the nation.

In all, Valachi named 289 specific individuals as members
of the secret society. He provided a vivid picture of the
mob's casual recourse to murder and violence, and he spun
out detailed accounts of a Mafia initiation ritual. The rite,
very similar to the initiation ceremony of the old Camorra,
involved the initiate's swearing to live and die by the gun
and knife—and his blood oath never to reveal the secrets of
La Cosa Nostra.

For breaking that vow, Valachi earned federal protection—and a $250,000 price on his head.

Six weeks and one day after Valachi finished his public
testimony, John F. Kennedy was assassinated in Dallas.
Any number of fanciful theories are still being put forward
regarding the assassination, and several of them involve the
Mafia. One holds that the Mafia-CIA coalition that had
formed to kill Castro killed the president instead, angered

because he turned on the CIA after the Bay of Pigs disaster
and threatened to disband the agency. Another theory has
it that Sam Giancana and other mafiosi, who felt particularly betrayed by Robert Kennedy's anticrime crusade, saw
the murder as a way to stop the attorney general in his
tracks. Whatever the truth about the assassination, the de-
railing of Robert Kennedy's crusade was indeed part of the
tragedy's aftermath. After his brother was killed, the attorney general never again met with his elite corps of organized
crime busters at the Justice Department.

Nevertheless, the pressure on Giancana continued. Before
President Kennedy died, the FBI had placed the Chicago
mobster under what it called lockstep surveillance. Agents
dogged him every minute, night and day—even following
him onto the golf course. In an odd move for a mafioso,
Giancana went to court and demanded an injunction
against the snooping. He won a temporary ruling that on
the links the agents would have to play at least one four-
some behind him. The FBI appealed, and the ruling was
quickly overturned.

Mafioso Joe Bonanno reaches out to shake a well-wisher's hand during a 1959 appearance before a Los Angeles federal grand jury investigating criminal conspiracies in America.

By 1965 the Justice Department felt it had enough of a case against Giancana to bring him before a grand jury for potential indictment on a charge of violating the Federal Communications Act; that is, making interstate phone calls in furtherance of crimes. For this occasion, federal attorneys tried a tactic that would become increasingly popular in going after mobsters: They granted the witness immunity from prosecution for crimes related to anything he might say, while at the same time threatening him with contempt charges should he refuse to talk. This method virtually guaranteed a conviction for contempt, if nothing else. And that's what happened with Giancana. He refused to talk and was jailed for a year.

Once Giancana got out of jail, he left the United States and set up a baronial hideout in the Mexican city of Cuernavaca. In the process, he gave up day-to-day control of the Chicago mob but remained a power behind the scenes.

The year 1963 proved to be a watershed for the Mafia. As Giancana went into exile, an abortive attempted coup brought to the fore a new don in New York City in the person of Joseph Colombo, a mafioso who, like Frank Costello before him, would try and fail to laminate the Mafia with a respectable veneer.

Colombo rose to power as a consequence of the overreaching of another Mafia chieftain—Joseph "Joe Bananas" Bonanno. Bonanno was the head of one of the original crime families formed by Lucky Luciano and was thus a member of the Commission. A dangerous, flat-nosed hood from Brooklyn, Joe Bananas was credited by his peers with inventing the "split-level coffin." As owner of a Brooklyn funeral home, he found that he could secretly dispose of murder victims by burying them in secret compartments under the bodies of people who'd died more conventionally. Bonanno's inventive streak was appreciated by his fellow mobsters; his Napoleonic ambitions were not.

In addition to his stronghold in Brooklyn, Bonanno had carved out scattered territories in the American Southwest and in Canada. He hoped to use these fiefdoms as a base for seizing control of the entire Mafia. Bonanno quietly put out contracts on four of the most important crime figures in the country: Stefano Magaddino of Buffalo, Tommy Lucchese and Carlo Gambino in New York City, and Frank DeSimone in Los Angeles. He assigned the killings in the East to Joe Magliocco, the beefy head of the Profaci crime family, who in turn passed the job down the line to a young gun-

man named Joe Colombo. Colombo was shrewd enough to spot a losing proposition, and he figured that his best course was to expose the plot to the Mafia Commission. His instincts served him well.

At an emergency meeting called by the Commission to consider the charges, Magliocco told all. Fined $50,000 and banished from the Mafia, he would die shortly afterward of a heart attack. Bonanno refused to present himself to the Commission and instead went into hiding. In 1964 he surfaced in Canada, but in September of that year he refused again a summons from the Commission. The ruling council then decided to put an end to the troublemaker.

On October 21, 1964, Joe Bonanno, who seemed to suffer from the illusion that he was bulletproof, turned up in New York City. He met for dinner with a gaggle of mob lawyers, one of whom alerted Bonanno's enemies. The renegade don was hauled off to a hideout in the Catskill Mountains but—astonishingly—was not killed. Over the span of six weeks, Bonanno apparently persuaded his captors by a combination of threat and bribe to let him live. He warned of a nationwide gang war that would come to pass if he were killed, and he promised to turn over control of all his business interests in return for his life. The Commission agreed and released him in December 1964—an injudicious move, as it turned out, since Bonanno broke his word. Fighting to regain and extend his power, he launched what became known as the Banana War. It lasted until heart trouble forced the contentious don into retirement to Arizona in 1969.

In 1963 Joe Colombo had become a don. In return for exposing Bonanno's plot, he was given the Profaci family, which had once been the fiefdom of the incautious Magliocco. At 40, Colombo was the youngest crime boss in America, and that wasn't his only distinction: The Mafia didn't know it yet, but it had something new on its hands— a quick-tempered, outspoken leader who believed that he could manipulate public opinion in ways that would do great things for the mob.

Colombo's accession represented a generational shift of power. The new boss was a son of the mob. His father, Anthony, had been a mafioso, albeit one who came to a bad end: Anthony Colombo was strangled to death for going to bed with a fellow mobster's wife, thus violating one of the brotherhood's oldest and most sacred rules. After Anthony's death, son Joe dropped out of high school to support his mother and sister. During World War II he enlisted in the Coast Guard, but he exhibited such a wild streak that his superiors thought he had psychiatric problems and saw to it that he got a medical discharge. A civilian again, Colombo fell into a life of small-time thuggery on the Brooklyn waterfront, where—among other things—he spent his time organizing low-stakes dice games. He was arrested at least 12 times and wound up with two convictions for gambling and one for contempt for refusing to talk to a grand jury.

Eventually young Colombo showed the requisite viciousness to move up in his chosen field. He was appointed to a five-man hit team in the service of the Profacis. According to police, the squad performed at least 15 murders prior to 1959, when its members were ordered to kill one of their own. They complied but were left to wonder which of them might be next. Such misgivings undermined loyalty, and in time two members of the group, brothers Larry and Joseph "Crazy Joe" Gallo, rebelled against Profaci in a play for a bigger piece of the action. The mob family was plunged into a three-year civil war that left it profoundly weakened. Colombo stepped in to engineer a truce between the warring factions, in the process making enemies of the Gallos. Later, after Colombo had become a don, the brothers staged an ambush aimed at killing him on his way home from the country club where he played golf. Once again, Colombo was lucky and survived.

The fact that killers would look for Colombo near a golf course said something about the style that the young don affected. Fond of posing as an investor in property, he even acquired a real estate salesman's license by having a stand-in pass the exam for him. This allowed him to account for about $18,000 a year in legitimate earnings, and he claimed additional income from a flower shop and a funeral home. Of course, the serious money came from none of these enterprises, but from his interests in gambling, loansharking, and cargo hijacking at Kennedy Airport.

The illicit take financed a more-than-comfortable lifestyle. Colombo's home was a modest split-level house in Brooklyn, where he lived with his wife, two of his four sons, and a daughter, but he also maintained a lavish estate in Blooming Grove, New York, complete with swimming pool, tennis courts, and stables.

Along with his pretensions to middle-class legitimacy, what set Colombo apart from his fellow Mafia big shots was his refusal to keep a low profile. His insistence on being treated like any other upstanding citizen first made itself felt in 1966 when he applied for a real estate broker's license—a big step up from his salesman's permit and a possible avenue toward an expanded front operation. Colombo was apparently unaware that this move would entail a rigorous security check. The state of New York refused his application and, four years later, in March 1970, indicted Colombo for having lied on the application. That same month, a federal grand jury indicted him for tax evasion. And only one month later came an even bigger blow: His son Joseph junior was arrested for allegedly taking part in a scheme to melt down coins and extract the silver—a federal offense.

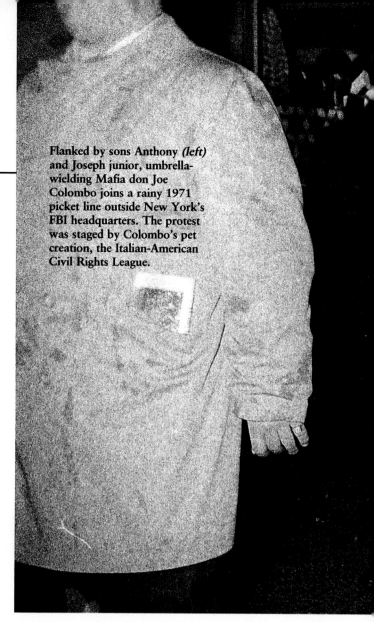

Colombo senior was indignant, convinced that he and his family were targets of a full-scale FBI harassment campaign. An eyewitness to the father's volcanic rage remembers Colombo shouting that his son's arrest was discriminatory. "It's because the kid's named Colombo," he announced, "because his name ends in a vowel." The mobster therewith packed his friends and family off to Manhattan, armed with picket signs. They marched in front of the regional FBI headquarters in a demonstration that marked the beginning of the Italian-American Civil Rights League.

The sight of a Mafia boss engaged in public protest must have left Colombo's mob colleagues greatly bemused, so far removed was such behavior from Mafia practice and tradition. But the fact that such a thing was even thinkable to a second-generation Mafia chief reflected some evolving attitudes of the American public. To some degree, it seemed that the Mafia was moving out of the shadows of secrecy and into the national mainstream. Exposed to public scrutiny, the Mafia, while still exotic, was no longer particularly alien; the mob was moving toward a new status as just another fact of life.

Much of this change in perceptions was due to the testimony of Joseph Valachi. But the Mafia mystique was further dispelled by two 1969 best-selling books, one fiction, the other fact. The nonfiction work was *The Valachi Papers,* written by journalist Peter Maas with Joe Valachi's cooperation. It sold two million copies and was translated into 14 languages. The fictional effort was an even bigger success: *The Godfather,* by Mario Puzo, was the saga of the powerful Corleone family (named for the Mafia-dominated village in Sicily). The work's grand theme was the integration of a huge criminal enterprise into the American mainstream. Puzo's novel became a nine-million-copy bestseller and won critical praise both for its literary merit and for its accuracy in depicting the Mafia's history and heart. It also became the basis for a trilogy of successful films.

Growing familiarity with the Mafia didn't seem to dampen the public's fascination with the brotherhood—nor did it blunt the federal government's assault on it. By now hardly anybody, least of all in Washington, still denied the reality of the Mafia, and this acceptance made it possible to push legislation facilitating the prosecution of mafiosi.

Even before the blockbuster Mafia books and films, Congress—largely in response to Joe Valachi's testimony in 1963—passed the 1968 Omnibus Crime Control and Safe Streets Act, which included provision for court-ordered wiretaps and bugs and the use of electronic surveillance evidence in criminal trials.

In 1970, while Americans were avidly reading *The Valachi Papers* or *The Godfather,* lawmakers passed the Organized Crime Control Act, which included a radical statute covering "Racketeer Influenced and Corrupt Organizations." RICO, as the law was called, provided that persons convicted of two or more of a dozen designated crimes over a 10-year period could be prosecuted for being part of a racketeering enterprise. Even the planning of such crimes could constitute guilt. Adding teeth to the new law was a stipulation that the property of convicted racketeers could be seized. It would be a decade before the Supreme Court upheld the constitutionality of the RICO provisions, but the new weapon clearly had ominous implications for mobsters.

It was in this atmosphere of increased mob visibility and

I.A.C.R.L.
IS DEMANDING
CONGRESSIONAL
HEARING INTO THE
F.B.I.
STRIKE FORCE

J.EDGAR HOOVER
WAKE-UP !
THIS
STRIKE FORCE
IS RUNNING
YOUR F.B.I.

vulnerability that Joe Colombo launched his public relations assault on the nation's law enforcement agencies. He took as his model the civil rights movement, and he was able to tap into simmering resentment among millions of law-abiding Italian-Americans who were appalled by the spotlight focused on the criminal minority in their ethnic group. Politicians, sensing an issue with voter potential, began flocking to the gangster's standard. In a moment of high enthusiasm, Colombo reportedly exclaimed, "We're gonna make Brooklyn the Selma, Alabama, of the Italians!"

Colombo had struck a nerve, and chapters of the Italian-American Civil Rights League began springing up across Manhattan. On June 29, 1970, tens of thousands of Italian-Americans and their supporters rallied at Manhattan's Columbus Circle. Much of the activity was spontaneous, but some of it had been orchestrated by the mob. Stores in Mafia-dominated neighborhoods were closed. Longshoremen walked off the job, bringing the city's docks to a virtual

standstill. New York deputy mayor, Richard Aurelio, turned out for the Italian-American Unity Day rally, and Colombo led the crowd across town to picket the local FBI headquarters.

No doubt the movement had some merit, but its leader was hardly its greatest asset. A month after Unity Day, Colombo and 23 other defendants were indicted on state charges of criminal contempt, loansharking, and gambling. In a concession to the ethnic fervor that the gangster had raised, the indictments didn't use the terms *Mafia* or *La Cosa Nostra*. Both of these names had been banned from Department of Justice reports by U.S. Attorney General John Mitchell, and officials in New York followed the same course.

Despite Colombo's personal transgressions, the issue he espoused resonated in certain intellectual and social circles. A number of academic writers, largely with backgrounds in sociology, began to question the whole notion of the Mafia as defined by law enforcement agencies. And in March 1971, Colombo—free on bail—was honored at a $125-per-plate testimonial dinner in front of 1,300 people. The celebrants came to toast the don's "undying devotion to the Italian-American people and all humanitarian causes." The guest of honor declared to his admirers that his aim was to make the league "the greatest organization in the world, so that people will be proud of us, no matter what we do, where we are, even if we are in prison." About three months later, he staged a repeat of his triumphant Unity Day rally in Columbus Circle. This time, however, enemies from within his own organization would see to it that the event turned out differently.

Thousands of people showed up once again, waving banners that featured the red, white, and green of the Italian flag. But the crowd was down to about a fifth the size of the previous year's. Once again mobsters made the rounds of the neighborhoods, but this time they carried orders to keep the shops open. Longshoreman stayed on their jobs. All these factors were signs that some powerful dons who'd once given the event at least tacit approval had withdrawn their support—both from Unity Day and its chief organizer. Colombo's high-profile style, so alien to the privacy and secrecy that had always characterized the Mafia, was wearing thin.

Detractors didn't seem to deflate the mood of the Italian-American champion of ethnic rights, however, as he moved through the crowd on his special day, shaking hands and posing for photographs. But the rumors proved right: Shots rang out, and Colombo collapsed, bleeding from the head and neck. More shots followed, as the don's bodyguard gunned down Jerome Johnson, a black man who was posing as a photographer.

A rapist and thief, Johnson was not known to be linked with any of Colombo's rivals. An hour after he died, an organization called the Black Revolutionary Attack Team claimed credit for shooting the don and warned that it would carry out further assaults on anyone who exploited the black community. Two days later the group warned that an apartment owned by a white drug dealer in Harlem would be bombed, and such an attack was indeed carried out. No one, however, had ever heard of this revolutionary group before, nor would it be heard from again.

Colombo actually survived the shooting—but barely. He would linger in a coma for seven years before finally slipping away. Despite the claims of the mysterious Black Revolutionary Attack Team, many knowledgeable people suspected that the Gallo brothers were the true authors of the Colombo hit. Their hatred for the victim was well known. Moreover, they could easily have recruited a black gunman: The brothers had long since broken with Mafia tradition and inducted African Americans into their organization.

Guilt in this matter was far from certain, however, since Colombo had plenty of enemies who may have countenanced the execution. The success of his Italian rights campaign had been mixed: The crusade raised the valid point that most Italian-Americans were good, honest citizens. Still, it had little substantial effect in blunting the crackdown on organized crime, and it embarrassed traditional dons who were profoundly suspicious of high visibility. Soft-spoken Carlo Gambino, for one, who inherited Albert Anastasia's family after he had him killed, was scornful of Colombo. He felt that members of an organization founded on secrecy and muscle had grown too talkative and too soft. Another Gambino family conservative, Aniello Dellacroce, also feared declining discipline in the ranks and saw big problems in the mob's future. "People don't train their people no more," Dellacroce observed. "There's no more respect. There's no more nothing."

Dellacroce's glum comment stood as an epitaph for a Mafia generation that had brought the organization to the peak of its power. By the time Joe Colombo fell, Frank Costello had long since been put out to pasture, enjoying a genteel New York town-and-country retirement troubled only by the nagging attentions of the Internal Revenue Service. Costello died in 1973 at the age of 82. His longtime rival, Vito Genovese, died in prison in 1969. He was 72. (Joe Valachi outlived his don by two years and also died in prison.) Back from his Mexican exile, 67-year-old Sam Giancana was cooking sausages in the basement kitchen of his home in the Chicago suburb of Oak Park on the night of June 19, 1974, when someone shot him in the back of the head, killing him. The murder went unsolved; the sadistic don had a lot of enemies.

With the ranks of powerful dons so thinned, only Carlo Gambino remained of the ranking mobsters who'd been present at the Apalachin meeting, and he was suffering from a serious heart condition. Increasingly beset, from without and within, the Mafia faced the coming decades richer—but less confident—than at any time in its past. ◆

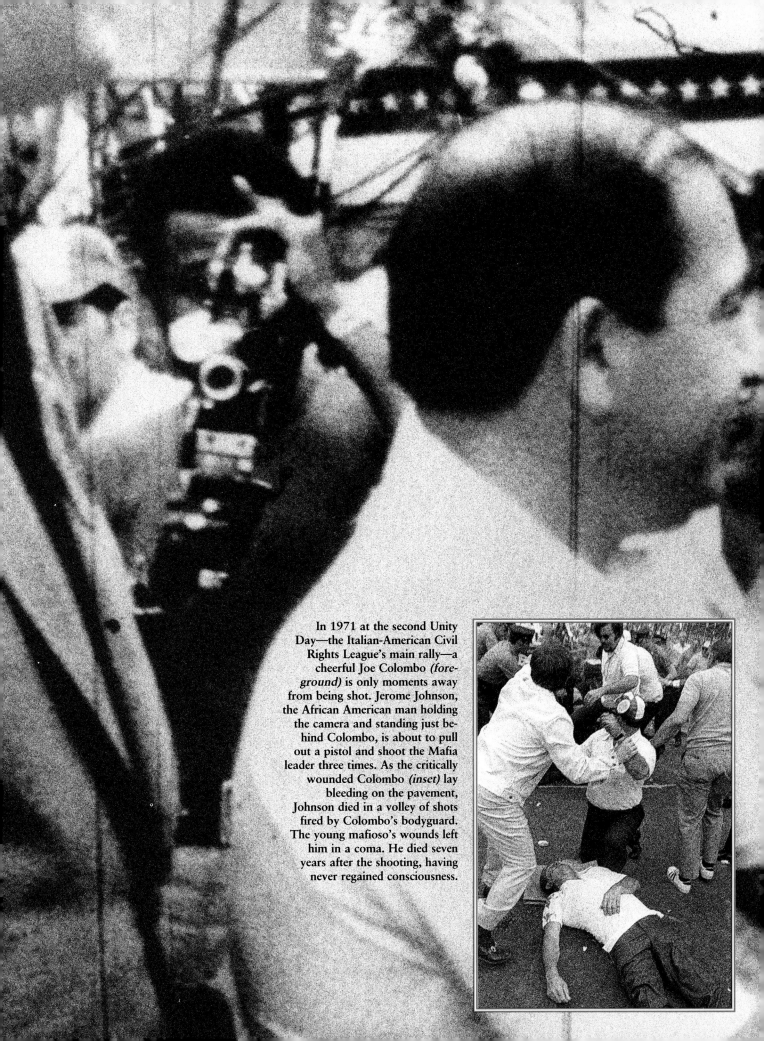

In 1971 at the second Unity Day—the Italian-American Civil Rights League's main rally—a cheerful Joe Colombo *(foreground)* is only moments away from being shot. Jerome Johnson, the African American man holding the camera and standing just behind Colombo, is about to pull out a pistol and shoot the Mafia leader three times. As the critically wounded Colombo *(inset)* lay bleeding on the pavement, Johnson died in a volley of shots fired by Colombo's bodyguard. The young mafioso's wounds left him in a coma. He died seven years after the shooting, having never regained consciousness.

Y ou don't get released from my crew. You have lived with John Gotti and you will die with John Gotti.

JOHN GOTTI

5

The Death of the Code

People tend to take their meals at an earlier hour as they get along in years, and Paul Castellano, at 70, was no different from most. It was around 5:30 p.m. on Monday, December 16, 1985, when Big Paul, as he was respectfully known, arrived at a favorite restaurant, Sparks Steak House, on Manhattan's East 46th Street. He was already thinking about what he would have to eat: a prime rib, the third cut from the end, the cut that his early butcher's training had taught him to favor. His youthful days as a butcher were long past, but the old Mafia don might even now make a show of examining the meat to be served before actually ordering.

Castellano's driver, bodyguard, and chief lieutenant, 45-year-old Thomas Bilotti, parked the black Lincoln limousine in a towaway zone directly by the restaurant's entrance. The two men opened the doors and started to get out. They were not aware of it, but at that moment they assumed the perfect posture for prey—heads down, bodies bent over. They never saw the three men in khaki trench coats and Russian-style fur hats striding swiftly up to the Lincoln.

With practiced ease, the trio whipped out semiautomatic handguns from their coats and started firing. Castellano was hit five times, Bilotti six. Not a shot went wild. Bilotti pitched forward, rolled, and lay flat, his head tipped back, his riddled body pumping blood into the street. Castellano, boss of New York's dominant Carlo Gambino family and capo di tutti capi in all America, slumped from the Lincoln onto the sidewalk, his head propped grotesquely against the floorboard of the car's front seat. His rose-tinted tortoiseshell glasses spun into the gutter. His half-smoked cigar tumbled from his lips and later was found, along with a sizable piece of his skull, resting on the curb.

One of the shooters moved closer and calmly fired a final bullet straight into Castellano's head. Then the three killers turned and jogged, like businessmen hurrying for a cab, to the corner of Second Avenue, where they piled into a dark-colored Lincoln with New Jersey license plates. The Lincoln slid smoothly into traffic and disappeared.

A few seconds elapsed, and the engine of yet another Lincoln, this one parked near the steakhouse, came to life. The big car moved slowly past the bodies already cooling in the chill December dusk. A pale face peered briefly from a window, and then this car, too, blended into the midtown traffic and was gone.

The execution of Paul Castellano and his underboss in 1985 would not have come as a great surprise to the leaders who had carried the Mafia to the zenith of organized crime. Charlie Luciano, Frank Costello, Joe Bonanno, and their businesslike colleagues understood perfectly that men rise, outlive their usefulness, and become nuisances that require elimination; they themselves were experts in the matter. What would have utterly appalled Luciano and his fellow giants from the mob's glittering heyday were the circumstances that led to the hit on Castellano: The old don was both a victim and a symbol of the deep decay and massive disarray that had come to afflict the modern Mafia.

Since the late 1970s the once-mighty brotherhood had been under siege on all sides, its chieftains toppling before the onslaught of the law, its soldiers scurrying for cover, its organization and discipline crumbling, its cherished code of silence, honor, and respect disintegrating. It seemed likely that the decline would be irreversible. No new leaders worthy of the name were rising from the ranks; increasingly, the men at the top were simple thugs—killers and drug dealers who focused their energies solely on raking in a pile of money before the other ethnic gangs got to it.

But the rot seeping into the brotherhood was not wholly evident in 1976, when Carlo Gambino died of a heart attack at the age of 74, and his cousin and brother-in-law Paul Castellano stepped into his shoes. Once a lieutenant of Albert Anastasia, Gambino had learned the business well. He'd put together an enormously successful and diversified family of perhaps 800 men: 250 "made"—or formally inducted—Mafia members, plus another 550 associates. Not only were the Gambinos the largest of the five New York

The sheet-covered body of Gambino family boss Paul Castellano *(opposite)* lies outside Manhattan's Sparks Steak House on December 16, 1985, as plain-clothes police discuss the killing. Shot six times by three gunmen as he got out of his black Lincoln limousine, Castellano collapsed on the sidewalk *(inset, right)* with his head cradled by the car's doorsill. Also killed was Castellano's driver and underboss, Thomas Bilotti *(inset, above)*, whose bullet-riddled body sprawled in the street.

Announcing indictments of New
York's five Mafia family leaders in
1985, U.S. Attorney Rudolph Giuliani
shows a five-tiered organization chart
of the Mafia's Commission.

families, they were the biggest and most powerful clan in the nation, with a vast array of enterprises from gambling, loan-sharking, and prostitution to labor racketeering, real-estate scams, and a host of legitimate businesses. Naturally, the Gambino godfather sat at the head of the nine-man commission that served as board of directors for the activities of all 24 Mafia families in the United States.

To many mafiosi, Castellano seemed properly suited to his inherited position. An imposing presence at 6 feet 2 inches, he was shrewd and ruthless, and had a knack for shedding trouble. He'd been jailed only twice in his long life. In 1934, when he was still in his teens, he served three months for a bungled burglary. The law didn't catch up with him again until 23 years later. Then he served a mere seven months of a five-year contempt-of-court sentence meted out for his steadfast refusal to explain his role in the aborted 1957 Apalachin convocation of mob bosses.

Castellano's silence, his loyalty to the code of omertà, had earned him much respect among his peers. And at the Apalachin meeting, brief as it was, the rapidly rising 42-year-old captain had shown himself to be on the right side of a number of important issues that had been on the agenda. One involved vengeance against lawmen; most of the wise heads in the mob, Castellano among them, favored outlawing cop killing as counterproductive overall, however individually satisfying.

The dons also favored — at least as an official stance — a ban on drug trafficking. Like killing police officers, dealing drugs aroused the law. Besides, the drug business was a filthy enterprise that tarnished the Mafia's image of itself as a provider of more or less harmless goods and services such as untaxed liquor and tobacco, gambling, labor peace, loan money, and women. Official posturing aside, some mafiosi took the antidrug edict more seriously than others: Some bosses adhered religiously; some paid lip service but tacitly allowed their underlings to ply the drug trade and profited from those dealings. Castellano was among those who took the ban with deadly seriousness.

Such old-fashioned rectitude didn't sit well with some of the younger members of the Gambino family. Their candidate for boss had been Aniello "Mr. Neil" Dellacroce, a year older than Castellano, and Gambino's second-in-command since the late 1950s. Not a subtle man, Dellacroce favored crime's blunt instruments: holdups, hijacking, and extortion. He viewed narcotics with some sympathy

and counted a sizable constituency among the money-lusting young hotheads in the family. Dellacroce was in jail at the time for tax evasion. Nevertheless, he was Castellano's superior and in line for the top job, so he and his followers suffered bitter disappointment when Gambino chose a relative as his successor and not his old comrade in crime. Yet Dellacroce was a sensible man, not given to fratricide and intratribal warfare. He stayed on as Castellano's cooperative underboss, helping run the family and keeping a rein on the mavericks. But events were about to overwhelm both the aging heirs of the Gambino family.

By the 1980s federal attorneys were using as a principal weapon against the mob the RICO statute, which made it possible to prosecute a person simply for being a member of a "criminal enterprise" that was engaged in a "pattern of racketeering." Even if specific crimes were committed by other individuals, all members of the enterprise were guilty, just as accessories to a crime are considered guilty. Penalties were severe: up to 20 years per charge. In addition, RICO enabled the government to confiscate illegal profits — a proviso that spelled tremendous damage for the underlying organization.

One young lawyer sensitive to the possibilities in the RICO statute was Rudolph Giuliani, an associate U.S. attorney general who in 1983 would become U.S. attorney for the Southern District in New York. Giuliani was a major strategist in an anti-Mafia offensive that used RICO as the legal base for going after the brotherhood's leaders. The FBI and the New York City police created special task forces to investigate the five New York families. With court orders permitting them to wiretap the mobsters' phones and bug their hangouts, the authorities soon had stacks of evidence. There were photos of men talking in doorways and audiotapes of what they said in their vulgar, boastful, disjointed, code-laden, and often vivid idiom. There were descriptions of killings, extortion demands, drug deals, and the corrupting of public officials and union leaders. The mafiosi bragged about their toughness, their money and power, the "respect" they were shown. The FBI and local police had opened a window on the mob's soul.

What police called the "Enterprise Theory" of gangbusting under RICO worked better than most dared dream. The first flood of indictments, trials, and convictions washed away some of the Mafia's vaunted discipline. Afraid for their hides, informers crawled out from the deepest recesses

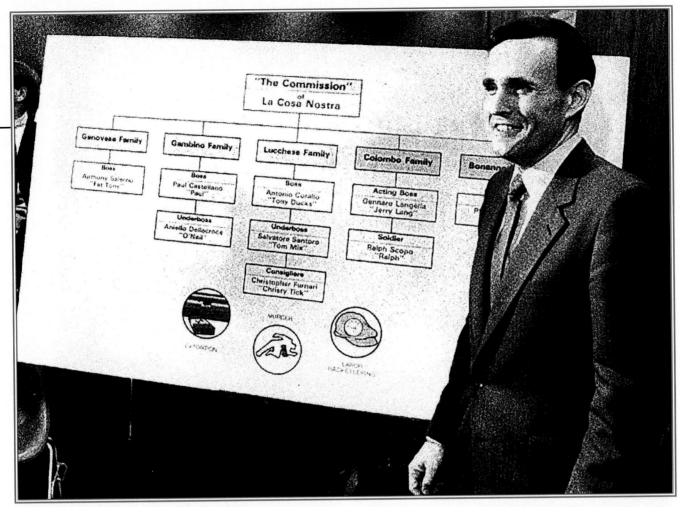

of the families, first by the handful, then by the dozens. Their testimony led to further convictions and still more informers. By 1983 FBI Director William Webster could tell a congressional committee that the government had convicted almost 500 mafiosi and their associates in organized-crime investigations dating back to 1979.

Under the new onslaught the Gambino family was faring better than most, and Big Paul Castellano's leadership seemed secure. However, that leadership was about to suffer a calamitous lapse. The error, plus associated complications in Castellano's personal life, would raise dire questions among his peers about what sort of mafioso Paul Castellano really was. For one thing, the august don whom some family members called "the Pope" would soon be seen as a hypocrite, mouthing Mafia platitudes about honor and respect while dishonoring his wife and acting like nothing so much as a lecherous old goat. And if Castellano had lost his honor, what next?

The decline of Paul Castellano began in his home. On assuming command of the Gambino family in 1976, the don had built himself an enormous 7,000-square-foot mansion on Staten Island's swank Todt Hill. The place had 17 rooms and eight baths, an Olympic-size swimming pool, a boccie court, and an inspiring view of the Verrazano-Narrows Bridge, which connects Staten Island to Brooklyn. The house's imposing white-columned portico reminded some visitors of the White House in Washington, and Castellano didn't discourage the comparison.

There he lived from 1980 on with his wife, Nina; his daughter, Connie; and a live-in housemaid named Gloria Olarte. Olarte was 30 and moderately pretty, an immigrant from Medellín, Colombia. She was uneducated and not notably bright, but she was certain of one thing: She wanted to leave her poverty-blighted Hispanic past behind her and associate with what she viewed as real Americans—rich ones. The big house on Todt Hill and Paul Castellano were just the ticket, she thought, and she didn't object in the least when Big Paul began making passes at her.

So open was Castellano about his craving for Olarte that his wife quickly caught on. Emotions flashed and thundered through the white house on Staten Island. When the storm finally subsided, Nina Castellano had moved out, and Gloria Olarte was coming and going through the mansion's front door. Castellano bought her a flashy red sports car,

Head of the most powerful organized-crime family in America, Paul Castellano *(right)* forfeited the respect of Mafia colleagues when he began an affair with Gloria Olarte *(far right)*, a housemaid at the mansion *(inset)* that Castellano shared with his wife on Staten Island's fashionable Todt Hill.

cooed to her in sentimental baby talk, and even had a surgical penile implant to remedy the damage that diabetes had done to his sexual function.

As maid, Olarte had been obsequious; now, as mistress, she was ill-mannered and imperious, interrupting conversations and annoying guests. There was something else about Gloria. Not being a good Sicilian woman, she didn't know any better than to believe whatever her sugar daddy told her—that he was a successful meat wholesaler, for instance. Olarte apparently had no instinct for legal trouble, for when the FBI came snooping around she happily made friends with an amiable agent named Joe O'Brien. Partly as the result of conversations between O'Brien and Gloria—most of them at a coffee shop that she favored—the FBI soon knew a great deal about Castellano's habits and his home—the places he liked most to talk, for example.

With Olarte's disclosures and a few other breaks, agents were able by March of 1983 to finish planting bugs in the house on Todt Hill and begin listening in on the private world of the Mafia's capo di tutti capi. Castellano had no idea what Gloria had done to him. Nor did she.

There followed 600 hours of recorded conversation over the next five months. The listening agents learned far more than anyone ever wanted to know about Castellano's relationship with Gloria Olarte. And there were fascinating insights into the mind of Paul Castellano. "This life of ours, this is a wonderful life," the don told an old colleague. "If you can get through life like this and get away with it, hey, that's great. But it's very, very unpredictable. There's so many ways you can screw up."

The FBI must have chuckled at that, since the Castellano tapes would eventually lead to more than 100 indictments against scores of mafiosi. The tapes constituted the worst breach of security the organization had ever experienced. And since by law an accused person has the right to review the evidence against him, everyone knew where the damaging information had come from.

As the end of 1985 approached, about 10 percent of the Mafia's membership nationwide was under indictment, including perhaps 50 of the top bosses, underbosses, captains, and lieutenants. Castellano was one of the big losers, of course. With a number of others, he was on trial in federal district court in Manhattan, charged with operating a hugely profitable auto-theft ring. He was also accused of conspiring to murder witnesses and competitors, among them his former son-in-law, who had unwisely beaten and deserted Castellano's daughter, Connie. Most important, he was one of nine men, including the heads of the four other New York families, accused of sitting on the commission that directed the Mafia—dividing profits, adjudicating disputes, and authorizing the necessary killings. The trial of the Commission case, as it was known, was due to start in March of 1986, only three months away.

Meanwhile, further pressure was building against Castellano inside the family. The issue was drugs. The don remained vehemently opposed to narcotics; it was his view that no one with drugs in his history should ever become a made Mafia member, and members caught dealing drugs should pay for the infraction with their lives.

Castellano's stand enraged many of the younger men. Every dimwitted street punk was getting rich from heroin and cocaine, so why not the mafiosi? The old fool Castellano was cutting them off from the age's biggest opportunity, the restless faction reasoned, and it was not to be borne: The followers of underboss Neil Dellacroce decided that Castellano had to go.

Two members of the anti-Castellano faction had ignored the antidrug dictum in any case. They were Angelo Ruggiero, 45, and Gene Gotti, 39. The pair had been part of the heroin-smuggling operation of Salvatore Ruggiero, Angelo's brother, and when Salvatore was killed in a plane crash in 1982, Angelo and Gene took over the business. They were arrested in 1983, partly on the strength of evidence from bugs planted in Angelo Ruggiero's Long Island home.

It was inevitable that Castellano would hear about the incriminating tapes and, as boss, demand to hear them. By 1985 he was impatiently waiting for his underlings to bring them to him. Gotti and Ruggiero stalled—with very good reason. The drug issue aside, the tapes would expose beyond all doubt their disloyalty to their don; Castellano would hear them disrespectfully referring to him as a "pansy" and worse. He might be sick and aging, but he was not so far gone that it was safe to question his manhood. Gene Gotti and Angelo Salvatore knew this, and so did their immediate superior: John Gotti, 45, Gene's older brother and a man who was the very flower of the changing Mafia.

Stocky and muscular at 5 feet 10 inches and 200 pounds, John Gotti was headstrong and violent by nature; his idol from the mob's old days was the crude and bloodthirsty Albert Anastasia. Gotti had acquired a certain street craftiness and considerable criminal knowledge but was otherwise of unexceptional intelligence. His greed knew no bounds. One lawman scorned him as "a barely articulate low-life, a thug even by Mafia standards." That assessment was a bit unfair; Gotti could be highly articulate in his own gutter way, and he was extremely efficient at certain enterprises. Because of those qualities, he was a leader in the Dellacroce faction and personally close to Dellacroce.

Whether John Gotti was actively involved in brother Gene's drug dealing or not, Castellano undoubtedly would hold him responsible for his men. As Gotti knew, Castellano might have him killed for letting his subordinates disobey the antidrug rule. Or, the boss might order Gotti to kill his own brother, along with Angelo Ruggiero.

While this matter remained unsettled, the issue of the Gambino family's future leadership was coming to a head in another way. Neil Dellacroce had been fighting cancer for the past several years, and on December 2, 1985, after two weeks in a hospital, the 71-year-old underboss lost his struggle for life.

It might be said that Paul Castellano died along with him. With Dellacroce's death went the restraining hand that had for nine years kept the John Gottis of the family in check. Suddenly, the younger, pro-drug faction was free to challenge Castellano. And Big Paul himself made it easy by committing two more major errors. One was so egregious as to be incomprehensible: He failed to attend Dellacroce's wake and say his good-byes to the man who'd done so much to keep him in power. For the Mafia, which still set great store on ritual and tokens of respect, this was inexcusable. John Gotti, grieving like a son for Dellacroce, took it as an insult beyond calculation.

Then Castellano compounded the affront by naming Thomas Bilotti, his longtime driver and bodyguard, to be the family's new underboss. A savage pit bull of a man, Bilotti had his talents. Leadership was not one of them, however. Again, Gotti was furious. He felt that as Dellacroce's protégé, he should have gotten the job.

The law was on his heels and mutiny threatened within his own family, but those were not all of Paul Castellano's troubles. Increasingly, he was viewed as a liability by the highest of powers, the leaders of the other New York families. With the Commission trial coming up, rumors went around that Big Paul wanted to deal: his testimony in exchange for a sick old man's last few years of freedom. Such

When the FBI bugged this Long Island home of heroin smuggler Angelo "Quack Quack" Ruggiero *(inset),* a lifelong friend and associate of John Gotti, agents recorded insults that might have moved Castellano to vengeance had the Gotti faction not murdered him first.

a betrayal could not be allowed, of course, so when someone went to the Commission for authorization to put out a contract on Castellano, consent was apparently granted.

At first, there was no word on the street about who had requested that Castellano be killed. But from the moment the echo of gunfire died on 46th Street, nearly everyone agreed that John Gotti was behind the hit. It was a logical assumption. Eight days after Castellano was killed, FBI agents on Christmas Eve stakeout in front of the Ravenite Social Club on Little Italy's Mulberry Street watched as dozens of shiny cars pulled up and scores of ranking mafiosi strode through the crowd to embrace and kiss both cheeks of the new Gambino godfather-elect. A month after the killing, Gotti and Angelo Ruggiero entered a Queens bar much favored by Gotti's crowd. "Meet your new boss," a smiling Ruggiero told those present. And Gotti said, "It's gonna be nice, you watch."

John Gotti was only 45 when he became boss of the Mafia's most powerful family. Considering what kind of man he was and what sorts of activities he found most congenial, his elevation was a measure of how far the Mafia had descended.

Born John Joseph Gotti, Jr., on October 27, 1940, the future chieftain grew up poor in the South Bronx, one of 13 children born to a Neapolitan immigrant couple. John's father was a God-fearing day laborer with no ties whatever to the Mafia. That is not to say, of course, that he was unaware that the mob existed. He knew. Everybody in the South Bronx knew. It's probable that John Gotti was already an admirer of the mafiosi when, at the age of nine, he started running with the street gangs that staked out turf in his neighborhood. When he was 12 the family moved to Brownsville-East New York, a working-class section of Brooklyn where Gotti followed his older brother Peter into the Fulton-Rockaway Boys, a gang whose colors were a sinister purple and black.

Some of the gangs were relatively innocent; others were juvenile criminal cartels, incubators for the mob. The young punks loved to hang around the Italian-American social clubs that served as headquarters for the Mafia decinas, or crews of soldiers. The kids acted tough, eagerly ran errands for the adults, and tried to peddle what they'd stolen to the minor mobsters. The Fulton-Rockaway Boys were such a gang—a hopeful bunch of bush leaguers dealing in stolen property. Before long other Gottis, including John's younger brother Gene, joined the gang, and there were new friends as well. One of them, Angelo "Quack Quack" Ruggiero, would become John Gotti's lifelong sidekick.

The social club where the boys hung out the most was run by Carmine Fatico, a capo for Albert Anastasia and later for his successor, Carlo Gambino. John Gotti and his pals admired the men who, while seldom seeming to work, always had lots of money. The mafiosi appeared to the boys to live the good life, idling away their days gambling, joking, and sipping endless cups of espresso. Gotti, who would become a gambler of fierce dedication, watched the games with particular fascination.

In 1956 John dropped out of Franklin K. Lane High School and his real life began. At 16, the handsome, self-assured youth already had the erect, square-shouldered stance that he'd bring to court 36 years later for his toughest battle of all. And he faced the world with the same hard stare and aggressive manner. He wore his Fulton-Rockaway bruise-colored jacket like the mantle of a potentate.

Gotti got a straight job right out of school—as a coat presser in Brooklyn. But most of his energy was not devoted to his work: When he was 17 he began his long contest with the law. The first entry on his criminal résumé noted that he and some friends were caught stealing copper from a construction firm. He pleaded guilty and got probation. At 19, already flirting with the passion that would cost him millions, he was caught in a raid on a gambling den. At 20 he was arrested for disorderly conduct and drew a 60-day suspended sentence.

Gotti clearly had his wild side, but it didn't discourage a sanitation worker's daughter named Victoria DiGiorgio—a petite, darkly pretty girl two years younger than John—from appraising him as suitable husband material. By 1962 the two were married, and Gotti was a father. He shed his Rockaway Boys colors for the sturdy jacket of a working man and took a job as a truck driver's helper for the Barnes Express Company. For the future mobster, this was a smart move. In his new post Gotti learned much about shipping manifests and bills of lading that would be useful in his later labors as a hijacker.

With his new domestic situation, the future don had serious obligations to meet. He also liked to be out most nights gambling and raising hell. To carry the resulting two-pronged financial burden cost a lot of money. Gotti started

Charged in 1968 with theft from an interstate shipment, aspiring mobster John Gotti, 27, offers the police camera a poker face.

heisting cars, and when he was 23, he and Salvatore Ruggiero were caught driving a stolen rental car. Now, for the first time, Gotti went to jail. But it was only for 20 days and scarcely counted.

Two years after that he was jailed again, for two attempted thefts. This time he got a year behind bars. With no money coming in, Victoria and their three children went on welfare. When Gotti emerged from jail at the age of 26, he badly needed money, both to support his family and to move out of the South Bronx. Blacks were coming into the neighborhood, and he didn't like that. The answer was obvious: Crime had to pay better than a job, so Gotti started hijacking trucks loaded with salable goods.

The trough that virtually all of the mob hoods fed from was the immense John F. Kennedy Airport in Queens, a veritable banquet of air cargo from all over the world. At 5,000 acres, with literally hundreds of warehouses, the place was simply too huge to protect and still remain a civilian facility. Crooks who managed to bribe or extort inside help at the airport stole everything from high-tech Japanese cameras and electronic equipment to the latest European fashions and furs.

One day in November 1967, Johnny Boy, as he now was called, made off with a $30,000 mixed cargo of women's dresses and aircraft and machine parts. (Still a rather clumsy crook, he missed a crate of furs.) He dumped the parts, fenced the 10 cartons of clothes, and was back at the airport for another go four days later. But this time he bumped into FBI agents struggling to put a crimp in the rampant interstate larceny. Gotti had no room for maneuver on the federal theft charge. He pleaded guilty and went to the maximum-security Lewisburg Federal Penitentiary in Pennsylvania for 30 months.

Thus far, Gotti was no more than a small-time hood, scoring now and again but unlucky with the law and frequently in jail. Yet he'd made some important friends in the Italian-American social clubs. Carmine Fatico, the Gambino capo, thought Gotti promising because of his work ethic and earning potential and made him an associate in his crew. Better still, Gotti was introduced to "Mr. Neil" Dellacroce, number-two man in the entire Gambino family. Dellacroce also took a liking to him. Johnny Boy's luck was about to change.

While Gotti was in prison, Fatico moved his headquarters, which for some reason he decided to call the Bergin Hunt & Fish Social Club—informally known as the Bergin—to Ozone Park, Queens. A considerable virtue was its location next to Kennedy Airport. When John Gotti was released from prison in January 1972, he gravitated to the Bergin, and its clientele became his constant companions. There were about a hundred regulars, most of them Mafia-connected. Gotti knew them as Frankie Pickles, Mike the Milkman, Tommie Tea Balls, Tommy Sneakers, Johnny Cabbage, Joe Pineapples, Joe the Cat and Buddy the Cat, Tony Pep, Joe Dogs, Eddie Dolls, Philly Broadway, Nicky Nose, Jackie the Actor, and Old Man Zoo. Gotti and his set shared the time-honored mob fondness for nicknames.

Ambitious and aggressive, Johnny Boy soon became something of a star among his peers. The pecking order at the Bergin was largely determined by how much money a man brought in from hijacking, loansharking, auto theft, robbery and fencing, graft, killing, and bookmaking and other gambling—a broad spectrum of crime. Whatever his talents as a hijacker, Gotti's fascination with gambling made him an absolute whiz at that end of the family business. Not that he was a good gambler himself; he almost always lost. But he knew everything there was to know about the games and how to manage them.

Fatico put Gotti in charge of his gambling operations, and Johnny Boy took it from there. The gang controlled a number of small but profitable casinos around Queens, presided over major dice games, installed push-button poker machines in many of the borough's bars, operated bookie parlors, and ran a thriving numbers racket. Overseeing this array of gambling enterprises demanded unceasing vigilance. The manager had to make sure that no one skimmed off profits, that money was available for the high rollers and

Gotti would have to wait a few years for that honor. Meanwhile, he went briskly to work at his expanded job. One nice score came when he put together a hijacking team that made off with 57,000 watches from a JFK airport warehouse; everybody at the Bergin sported new timepieces to go with the suits stolen in earlier jobs. As acting capo, Gotti reported directly to Dellacroce. When Mr. Neil went to prison for contempt of court and tax evasion, Johnny Boy started dealing directly with Carlo Gambino himself.

Gotti greatly enjoyed passing on the big boss's orders. Early in 1973 he told his men not to hijack trucks controlled by other families. That only made sense. Also, Gambino wanted to avoid counterfeiting, securities theft and fraud, drug dealing, and kidnapping. These were federal crimes, and, the don reasoned, it would be stupid to draw any more heat from federal agents than there already was.

Gambino had another reason for banning kidnapping. Certain lowlifes made careers of snatching other criminals for ransom, and there was one wild Irish gang in particular that Gambino was interested in. The previous May, some suicidal crazies had grabbed Gambino's own 29-year-old nephew, Emanuel, off a Manhattan street and contacted his wife with a $350,000 ransom demand. The family got up $100,000, but Emanuel never returned home. On January 23, 1973, excavators at a federal ammunition depot in New Jersey dug up his body. There was a bullet in the skull.

It is not totally clear who killed Manny Gambino. But his uncle Carlo blamed a gang led by a hulking 32-year-old Irishman named James McBratney. Gambino ordered McBratney's death. Preferably, the killing would be protracted and inventive. And who better to carry it out than the family's rising star, Johnny Boy Gotti?

that they paid up when they lost, and that there was enough protection from the police—or from anyone else interested in interfering with the games.

Gotti was a tireless watchdog. He worked 18 hours a day. Nor was he the sort of boss who minded getting his hands dirty; Johnny Boy quickly became noted for personal problem solving, usually by threatening a transgressor, sometimes by beating the man to a pulp. A delinquent might be encouraged to mend his ways at the mere mention of an impending visit from Johnny Boy. "What you got there is a hoodlum's hoodlum," said one admiring colleague.

So spectacular was Gotti's rise that it came as no surprise when he offered himself for a higher position in mid-1972. His opportunity was Fatico's misfortune. Already on probation for a murder conspiracy, the capo now was indicted for loansharking, and he retired temporarily to prepare for his trial. Gotti proposed that he fill the vacuum. Dellacroce agreed, and Gotti, at 31, became acting capo of an important Gambino contingent. Amazingly, he got the job while still a candidate mafioso, not yet a fully fledged made man.

James McBratney, the alleged kidnapper of Mafia boss Carlo Gambino's nephew, lies dead after the contract killing in which John Gotti "made his bones" to become a full-fledged Mafia member.

On May 22, 1973, three men walked into a Staten Island bar called Snoope's and peered closely at the few customers. The barmaid recognized them. A month before, they'd entered in just this way, looked around as if searching for a friend, and then left without having drinks. This time they found the man they were looking for. McBratney was sitting at the bar sipping a 65-cent crème de menthe on the rocks. He was probably expecting some sort of trouble because he'd recently taken to carrying a submachine gun. Unfortunately for him, on this occasion he'd chosen to leave it in his car so as not to upset the folks in Snoope's.

The avengers were astonishingly brazen. Instead of waiting to grab their quarry outside, they simply walked up to him at the bar. One had a gun; another had handcuffs. They announced that they were cops, seized McBratney, and said he was under arrest. McBratney, who knew perfectly well that the men weren't police, resisted, and a drunken customer tried to intervene on his behalf. The fake policeman with the gun then fired a shot into the ceiling, and customers began scurrying for the exits. McBratney tried to leave too, but two of the men held him by the arms and the one with the gun pumped three slugs into his body. The killers were probably not as imaginative as Carlo Gambino might have wished, nor did they draw out their victim's suffering. Still, they got the job done.

From mug shots, it was easy for the barmaid to identify Ralph Galione and Quack Quack Ruggiero, and not much harder for police to learn that the third man, who'd held one of McBratney's arms while Galione fired, was John Gotti. All three men were charged with the Irishman's murder.

There was nothing quite like personally killing someone to earn respect in the latter-day Mafia. Carlo Gambino was grateful to the assassins, and he hired as their defense lawyer the wily, amoral, and widely loathed Roy Cohn, who'd played a pivotal role in Senator Joseph McCarthy's Communist witch hunts of the 1950s. Somehow, the very expensive Cohn managed to finagle a remarkable plea bargain under which Gotti and Ruggiero got four-year terms for attempted manslaughter. Galione wasn't in on the deal because he was dead by the time it was negotiated—shot to death by an unknown assailant.

Gotti went to New York State's Green Haven Correctional Facility, 90 miles north of New York, where he swept floors, spent his leisure time lifting weights, and survived the prison's pervasive ethnic-racial tensions. At least three times he bribed guards to drive him home to Howard Beach, Queens, for family visits. He was still behind bars in 1976 when Carlo Gambino suffered a massive coronary at the age of 74, setting in motion events that would carry Gotti to the top within a decade.

When Johnny Boy emerged from Green Haven in July of 1977—having served less time for killing a man than he had for hijacking a load of dresses—a new blue-and-tan Lincoln Mark V was waiting for him as a gift from the Gambino family. He drove it to the Bergin, where he proudly hung a plaque that fellow inmates had given him at a farewell party the night before his release. It read: "To John Gotti—A Great Guy." Later that summer Johnny Boy was one of nine candidates formally inducted into the Mafia. Neither Gotti nor the others ever described the ceremony, but one of them later reminisced: "They held it up for him. They were waiting for him to come home."

The Gambino family, now technically the Castellano family, was already embroiled in the family feud between the Castellano and Dellacroce factions, and Gotti was an important player in the latter group. The leader of his Bergin-based crew—which included his brothers Gene, Peter, and Richard, and old friend Angelo Ruggiero—Gotti left his neat frame house in Howard Beach each morn-

During the 1970s Gotti moved his family to this unassuming frame house in the New York City borough of Queens, supposedly purchased for the couple by Gotti's parents-in-law.

ing and went off to work. He was on the payroll as a plumbing supplies salesman for Arc Plumbing and Heating Company, which had done a thriving business on such public jobs as the 106th Precinct station house, Shea Stadium, and the National Tennis Center in Flushing Meadows. "What John does," said the firm's president when asked, "is point out locations."

Gotti's true offices were the street and the Bergin, and from those headquarters he labored tirelessly. He worked seven days a week, managing his crew, setting up meetings, adjudicating disputes, organizing crimes. His colleagues considered him diligent, dedicated, and reasonably reliable, if somewhat hotheaded. He drank very little—a virtue in the view of his superiors. But the gambling was a serious flaw, one that began to take on a kind of radioactive glow as his income rose. The mob doesn't keep records of its members'

earnings, and Gotti didn't keep track of his losses. But it came to light over the years that Johnny Boy often dropped $30,000 to $40,000 in a single weekend of shooting craps, playing the horses, or investing in the football pools.

His usual practice was to bet in "dimes"—a dime, two dimes, four dimes. A dime was $1,000. Once, at a gambling joint around the corner from Dellacroce's Ravenite Social Club in Manhattan's Little Italy, Gotti lost $60,000 in a dice game that he and his partners had financed with a bank of $120,000. And the don-to-be was no gentleman gambler. When he was behind he would borrow heavily from the house—and not always make good his debts: Like the bully he was, he capitalized on his knowledge that nobody was going to argue with him. Angelo Ruggiero once wondered out loud if Johnny Boy was "abusing his position, or what?" Gotti had so much riding on some games, and got so dangerously enraged at each loss, that his friends began switching off the Bergin's TV set when sport scores were about to be announced. But that only postponed the fury.

As Gotti's power grew, his personality seemed to change for the worse. Many other things besides gambling brought on the explosive temper tantrums. He required a lot of deference from his followers, and he could fly into a rage at the tiniest perceived slight. Law enforcement tapes, dripping venom and laced with obscenities, would show numerous examples of his touchiness. In one, he threatened to kill a man whose only sin was his failure to promptly return his phone calls. "Let me tell you something," Gotti raged. "I need an example. Don't you be the —— example. Do you understand me? Listen. I called your —— house five times yesterday. If you're going to disregard my —— —— phone calls, I'll blow you and that —— house up. I'll —— kill you." (A restoration of the deleted expletives would expand the passage considerably.)

Gotti insisted on total control and domination. He owned his men. When a member of his crew asked about a possible release and transfer to another crew, Gotti snapped: "You don't get released from my crew. You have lived with John Gotti and you will die with John Gotti."

By the time Gotti ascended to the capo's job, he and his wife, Victoria, had five children—two girls and three boys. John was no homebody, but he was a prideful, protective husband and father—to a fault, actually. One day in March

1980, the Gottis' middle son, 12-year-old Frank, borrowed a friend's motorized minibike and rode it out from behind a Dumpster and into the path of a car driven by John Favara, one of the Gottis' neighbors. Favara, 51, was service manager for Castro Convertibles, the sofa maker. His son was a friend of one of the Gottis' other boys; the kids had spent nights at each others' houses. The setting sun was shining into Favara's eyes when his car hit Frank Gotti. The boy was killed.

The death was ruled accidental, and no charges were filed. But the Gotti household, frantic with grief and fury, didn't see it that way. The days after the boy's death were followed by a series of threats against Favara. At one point the epithet "MURDERER" was spray-painted on his car. Favara was a stolid, mild-mannered man, not easily excited or frightened, but the succession of threats rattled him. He asked a friend, who happened to be a soldier in the Castellano family, what he should do. The friend advised him to get rid of the death car: The sight of it enraged Victoria Gotti—so much that in May, two months after the accident, she attacked Favara with a baseball bat. He went to a hospital for treatment of his injuries but refused to press charges. Nevertheless, Favara followed a second piece of advice from his friend: He put his house up for sale.

Toward the end of July, John Gotti decided to take Victoria off for a week's vacation in Florida. "My wife is still mourning my son and I took her down there to get her mind off things," he would later say. "She's still on medication."

On July 28 John Favara came out of the sofa factory and headed for his car. He'd nearly reached it when a stocky man rushed him, clubbed him with a two-by-four, seized him by his belt, and heaved him into the back of a van.

"Our friend is sick," the stocky man explained to a witness who wondered what was happening. "We're taking him home." The van disappeared down the road. Another man got into Favara's station wagon and drove it away after the van. John Favara would never be seen again.

Several days later the Gottis returned from their holiday in Florida. When Queens police asked John Gotti about his neighbor's disappearance, the bereaved father replied: "I don't know what happened. I'm not sorry if something did happen. He killed my kid."

Soon after, an informant told the FBI that "the individual responsible for Frank Gotti's death was killed recently at Gotti's direction, and Gotti wanted a solid alibi of not even being in New York at the time." Another told a New York cop that Favara was kept alive until Gotti's return from Florida so that Gotti could kill him himself. The informant claimed that Gotti cut Favara in half with a chain saw and had his body crushed in a compactor along with his car.

Gotti grieved for his son the rest of that year, and his misery seemed to aggravate his gambling habit. He lost hugely, as much as $30,000 every single weekend. He began to taper off a bit in the new year, possibly because he was short of funds; he lost only $21,000 one January football weekend and $16,000 the next. Meanwhile, his men were complaining about their own financial straits and grumbling that their capo was not providing properly for them. About this time, a police informant predicted that Johnny Boy was getting ready to solve everybody's problems by jumping into the drug trade in a big way.

There is no direct evidence that Gotti got deeply involved with drugs then, but logic certainly argues that he did. Some of his closest associates, as well as his brother Gene, were in the drug trade up to the hilt. Besides, the business was so big and so easy, the sums so huge, and Johnny Boy's need for gambling money so great that it's reasonable to assume that he was part of it. Informants, in fact, insisted that he pulled the strings. Yet there was nothing that would stand up in court, and Gotti managed to escape the August 1983 round of arrests that netted Angelo Ruggiero, Gene Gotti, and seven other men on a variety of RICO charges.

Among other things, said the government, the nine were "organizers, supervisors, and managers" of a heroin ring. As befitting a man of his stature, Ruggiero's bail was set at $1,000,000. Eventually, after a long, drawn-out case plagued by jury tampering, Gene Gotti was found guilty and sentenced to 50 years. Only death from lung cancer saved Ruggiero from a similar fate.

It was ironic that the breakup of a drug ring that John Gotti may well have had an interest in should help propel him to the head of the Gambino-Castellano family. But it did. It led Paul Castellano to demand the incriminating tapes and vent his displeasure on Johnny Boy as a disloyal capo. That in turn led Gotti, or those who favored him, to start plotting against Castellano. And in December of 1985, when Castellano finally was removed, there stood Johnny Boy Gotti ready and willing, if not notably able, to take his place.

A John Gotti look-alike, younger Gotti brother Gene *(foreground)* **and his codefendant John Carneglia make their way to a Brooklyn courtroom in 1989 to defend themselves against racketeering and drug charges.**

As though mindful that a don should look like a don, Gotti cut an imperial figure. Gone were the clothes of the workingman. Now Johnny Boy favored $1,800 hand-tailored double-breasted worsted suits and matching top-coats, white scarfs, silk shirts, monogrammed socks, and Italian loafers. He had his graying dark hair styled daily and drove a Mercedes-Benz. The one-time hijacker started showing up in the trendiest Manhattan nightclubs and cafés. Brawny men held doors open for him, shielded him from the rain with umbrellas, accorded him elaborate courtesies befitting a Renaissance Florentine prince. News stories breathlessly depicted him as a man who'd risen above his violent past to become a sort of Mafia statesman. *Time* magazine put him on its cover. Suddenly, he was the Dapper Don, as gaudily, assertively visible as self-promoting businessman Donald Trump. Coarse and utterly foulmouthed in private, Gotti projected a public air of rugged class—the dimples deepening, eyebrows curling sardonically as he grinned for the cameras. He swaggered and boasted, especially in his sanctum, the back room of the Bergin club, where a photo of his dead son, Frank, held an honored spot.

But the bombast might have been considerably deflated had Gotti known how thoroughly the FBI had bugged the Bergin and his other haunts. Agents heard Gotti bragging to a colleague about how easy it would be, given his own power, to replace the family's longtime and highly respected consigliere, 74-year-old Joe Gallo. "Yeah," agreed the friend. "Who's going to go against you?" And the agents heard about Gotti's big ambitions. Standing in the doorway of the Nice N EZ Auto School in January 1986, under another FBI bug he didn't know was there, Johnny Boy told a new capo: "If they don't put us away, for one year or two, that's all we need. But if I can get a year run without being interrupted—get a year—gonna put this thing together where they could never break it, never destroy it."

For a while, he did seem invulnerable. In a little less than 12 months, Gotti beat two cases that could have put him in prison for a total of more than 40 years. The first was a New York State charge that stemmed from a typical tough-guy altercation. On September 11, 1984, one Romual Piecyk, a 35-year-old refrigerator mechanic, found his car blocked by a vehicle double-parked outside the Cozy Corner Bar in Maspeth, Queens. So Piecyk leaned on the horn. And then again, and again.

The next thing he knew, Piecyk later told police, a man came boiling out of the Cozy Corner. He punched Piecyk around and took $325 from his shirt pocket. When Piecyk began to fight back, a second man came out. He slapped Piecyk hard across the face, made a motion as if to draw something from his waistband, and told him to get out of there. Piecyk did, but being something of a tough guy himself, he decided not to swallow such indignity and returned with a police officer. He pointed out Gotti, sitting at a next-door restaurant, as the man who slapped him.

Then Piecyk read the newspapers and realized who his assailant was. The refrigerator mechanic had a pregnant wife, and he began to have doubts about things. According to a lawyer involved with the case, he kept thinking about how he might wind up as a slab of meat in one of those walk-in refrigerators he serviced. That made him shiver—chills that got worse when he got scary phone calls in the night and then found the brake lines of his van cut. "I ain't testifying," he finally told police just before the March 1986 trial. Piecyk added that if he did appear in court, it would be on Gotti's side. "I'm not going to go against Mr. Gotti," he said earnestly. "I'm going in his behalf. I don't want to hurt Mr. Gotti."

And he didn't. Forced to testify, Piecyk remembered absolutely nothing. Case dismissed. "I FORGOTTI," the press howled gleefully.

The second trial was considerably less farcical. Along with underboss Neil Dellacroce and eight other mobsters, Gotti had been indicted in March 1985 for racketeering and conspiracy under the RICO statute; each man faced 40 years and a $50,000 fine on the two counts, and each was charged with a number of "predicate acts"—specific crimes committed to further the illegal enterprise. Of Gotti's seven predicates, three were crimes he'd already served time for: two hijackings and the killing of James McBratney, now elevated in the RICO indictment to murder. The government contended—and the courts upheld the notion—that already punished crimes simply served as evidence of the new crime: racketeering to benefit the illegal enterprise.

By the time the case came to trial in August 1986, Dellacroce had died of cancer and Gotti was the prime defendant. The prosecutor, a smart and very thorough assistant U.S. attorney named Diana Giacalone, took seven months to present her evidence, which included nearly 100 witnesses and 30 hours of taped conversations. Gotti's volatile lawyer, Bruce Cutler, a one-time assistant district attorney, tore

Highlife

After his rise to power late in 1985, John Gotti abandoned the apparent austerity of Windbreakers and work clothes for $1,800 suits, fancy restaurants, German cars, and the elegant nightlife of New York's trendy rich. Here, the tuxedoed don dances with Victoria DiGiorgio Gotti, his wife of many years.

Seen sharing Bastille Day festivities at fashionable
Manhattan nightspot Regine's in 1987, John Gotti
(opposite) had by then seized the helm of the Gambino family. He still lived in the unpretentious
Howard Beach home in Queens, protected by a
no-nonsense guard dog *(inset, right).* But Gotti
and his family were spending their upscale vaca-
tions in Fort Lauderdale, Florida, and at their
hideaway in the Pocono Mountains of Pennsylvania, seen in an aerial surveillance photograph *(inset, above)* that shows the swimming pool and
handball court. Neither name nor number graced
the front of the palatial Pennsylvania spread—just
a sign with one word: Love.

into the case. Giacalone had distorted the tapes' meaning, he argued. These were innocent conversations. Seven of Giacalone's witnesses against Gotti were confessed criminals—some of them kidnappers and murderers—who'd received favors for their testimony. Could decent people believe them? And was it fair to revive those old charges of hijacking and manslaughter, no matter what the RICO law said?

In the end, the jury agreed with Cutler. Gotti was acquitted on both RICO counts and went home to a rousing welcome in Ozone Park. Neighbors had tied yellow ribbons to the trees, and people shouted "Way to go, Mr. G" as he drove past. The press painted Gotti as something of a folk hero: the Teflon Don. Nothing could be made to stick.

The legend was enhanced in 1990 when Gotti beat another rap. He'd been indicted for assault for allegedly ordering the 1986 shooting of a carpenters' union boss named John O'Connor, who was feuding with the Gambino family. After long deliberation, the jury acquitted him.

The law, however, was having better success in the 1980s with other mafiosi, both in New York and elsewhere around the country. New York's Colombo family boss Carmine "the Snake" Persico, his underboss, and three capos and two soldiers and an associate were sentenced to 469 years among them for Cosa Nostra control of legitimate businesses. A handful of Lucchese and Genovese family members were convicted in a case involving corruption in the construction industry in New York City. In Chicago, in what was called the LIUNA case, FBI agents uncovered incontrovertible evidence of fraud, kickbacks, and embezzlement in the Laborers' International Union of North America. A Chicago capo named Alfred Pilotto and 11

union members and mob associates were sentenced to lengthy prison terms. Elsewhere, bribery cases ended with the conviction of New Orleans boss Carlos Marcello.

Focusing on gangland control of the Teamsters Central States Pension Fund, the government successfully prosecuted Teamster President Roy Lee Williams, Chicago Mafia capo Joseph Lombardo, and three other mob-connected men. A related investigation uncovered a Mafia conspiracy to milk the same pension fund for capital to buy Las Vegas casinos and then skim profits from the tables; Chicago boss Joseph Aiuppa and a Kansas City underboss were among those put away for that aborted scam.

By the mid-1980s, 17 leading members of 24 Mafia families—in Chicago, Cleveland, Boston, New Orleans, Kansas City, and Los Angeles—had been or were about to be indicted for crimes. Meanwhile, in New York, prosecutors were proceeding with the Commission case, in which the late Paul Castellano was to have been a principal defendant. Although the Commission had been one of the Mafia's most closely guarded secrets since Charlie Luciano created it in the 1930s, security had fallen apart in recent years. Joe Bonanno, the retired New York family boss who was perhaps the last die-hard defender of omertà and the other old Sicilian ways, had even written about it in his confessional 1983 autobiography, *A Man of Honor*. "If he could write about it," said one top lawman, "we could prosecute it."

A tape from a bug inside the dashboard of a Jaguar driven by Anthony "Tony Ducks" Corallo, boss of the Lucchese family, got the case rolling. Corallo was heard talking about meetings among the heads of the New York families, and he used the word "Commission" to describe them. The

Attorney Bruce Cutler *(far left)* defends Gotti and co-defendant Anthony Guerrieri *(near left)* at a 1989 arraignment on assault charges stemming from the 1986 shooting of union leader John O'Connor. Acquitted in February 1990, the Teflon Don *(right)* defiantly salutes his third victory in the courts in four years.

tapes referred to kickbacks, loansharking, labor racketeering, and murder. Enough evidence quickly accumulated to indict the bosses of all five New York families under the RICO statute.

When the Commission trial ended on November 19, 1986, the jury in the U.S. District Court for the Southern District of New York returned guilty verdicts against all the defendants: Genovese family boss Anthony "Fat Tony" Salerno, Colombo boss Carmine Persico, Lucchese boss Anthony Corallo, and five lesser mobsters. The sentences totaled 740 years, plus fines of more than $2,000,000.

Mob leaders were coming and going as if through a revolving door. The Colombos split into factions and started fighting among themselves; so did the Luccheses, who saw three different bosses in the space of a single year. The Bonannos were hamstrung by ever-shifting leadership and steadily diminishing stature.

Only two families were maintaining any semblance of stability by the late 1980s. One was the Gambino-Castellano clan under Gotti, and the other was the Genovese organization, with 200 made men the second-biggest in the country after the Gambinos. Its boss was Vincent "the Chin" Gigante, a lantern-jawed one-time prizefighter and a remarkable man by any measure.

The things that set Gigante immediately apart were his supposed stupidity and mental instability. From time to time doctors testified variously that he was brain-damaged, mentally ill, and possessed of the IQ of a moron. He certainly acted moronic, slopping around the streets of Little Italy, stooped and muttering, in his bathrobe and slippers, usually with an aide acting as attendant. Once, when FBI agents tracked him down at his mother's apartment and tried to serve a subpoena, they found the six-foot-tall, 200-pound Gigante standing naked in the shower, the water drumming down on an open umbrella in his hand.

Most cops, however, thought the Chin crazy like a fox. One investigator called him "probably the most clever organized-crime figure I have seen."

In the early years, Gigante reportedly served as a Commission hit man who executed certain mafiosi caught trafficking in heroin and thus unfortunately susceptible to pressure from the law. He first came to serious notice in 1957, when Frank Costello, head of the family created by Charlie Luciano, was shot in the lobby of his Manhattan apartment. The bullet merely grazed Costello's scalp, but it persuaded him to step aside for his old colleague Vito Genovese. Gigante, a Genovese strong-arm, was charged with firing the shot. In court, however, Costello could not—or would not—identify him as the shooter. The case collapsed.

Two years later, with Don Vito, Gigante was convicted of dealing in heroin—quite a switch in roles for the Chin. He served five years of a seven-year sentence, and had only been arrested once thereafter: In 1970 authorities charged him with conspiring to bribe the entire police department of Old Tappan, New Jersey, to get information about an ongoing investigation of him. That interesting case occasioned more than 30 front-page articles in the local press, but it never went to trial. According to the Old Tappan police, the "bribery" consisted of Gigante's wife, Olympia, sending the department a five-dollar bill enclosed in a Christmas card.

Gigante's rise to boss dated from the early 1980s, when Anthony Salerno took over after Genovese died in prison. Some investigators believed that Gigante and Salerno had an arrangement to share power; others suspected that the Bathrobe Don was the real boss and that he merely allowed Salerno to front for him. In any event, Gigante took over the family outright when Salerno was convicted and went to prison in the 1986 Commission case.

The law took another swing at the Chin in May 1990, when Gigante was indicted along with Vittorio Amuso, then head of the Lucchese family, in a bid-rigging scheme for $142 million in window contracts at the New York Housing Authority. But the police might have guessed what would happen. As the trial date approached, Gigante was declared mentally unfit to participate in the proceedings— and went back to running his outfit as before.

Aside from the pretend dimwit in the slippers, the only longtime don in New York City in 1991 was Johnny Boy Gotti. He was 51 and riding high, seemingly invulnerable, not only to the law but to enemies within the Mafia. Once, in 1987, the authorities had overheard a bugged conversation in which members of the Genovese family put out a contract on Gotti and his brother Gene. Gigante wanted to prevent Gotti from expanding into his territory; moreover, the Chin felt endangered by the glare that Gotti's celebrity cast on the mob in general. FBI agents warned Gotti about the contract. In response, he ordered a preemptive hit on Gigante but succeeded only in killing his rival's underboss.

Yet for all his seeming success, Gotti remained his essential self—a street thug, not a Mafia general; a hijacker and compulsive gambler looking for the quick score, not a sophisticated planner and visionary businessman of crime. Gotti met openly with drug traffickers, which law enforcement officers took as a certain sign that the family was dealing heroin and cocaine in a big way. But the carefully constructed traditional parts of the Castellano family business seemed to be decaying—the kickbacks for bid rigging in the construction and garment industries, for example. Gotti was apparently losing many of Castellano's complex, lucrative contracts.

Nevertheless, the younger mafiosi continued to admire Johnny Boy's flash and glitter. His capos proudly attended noisy Wednesday-night dinners at the Ravenite Social Club, and the soldiers were awed by his fancy suits, his gaudy jewelry, his press coverage. All the outward signs of his preeminence seemed only to increase as time went on. The patriotic don started a tradition: Every Fourth of July, beginning in 1977, he hosted a mammoth fireworks bash for the citizens of Ozone Park—to approving notices in the New York tabloids. "Gotti's people" became characters in cartoonist Gary Trudeau's nationally syndicated Doonesbury comic strip. And when the organizers of a Columbus Day celebration in Brooklyn were considering how to get more television coverage for their 1988 Italian-American parade, they thought of asking John Gotti to be grand marshal. (He was probably asked, but apparently he declined the honor.)

With old consigliere Joe Gallo in prison on RICO charges, Johnny Boy installed in his place Salvatore "Sammy Bull" Gravano, a thick-necked, gravel-voiced contractor who watched over the old family interests in construction and, investigators thought, passed along $100,000 a month in kickbacks to Gotti.

It seemed that the new don was consolidating his control, but trouble waited in the wings: Attracted by Gotti's high profile, the FBI began pursuing him in a single-minded way. Agents painstakingly assembled a RICO case based on the Teflon Don's command of a criminal enterprise and the murder of his predecessor, Big Paul Castellano. The federal agents planted a bug in the apartment above the Ravenite Social Club and settled back to listen while Gotti discussed crime after crime, murder after murder. He'd ordered one of his soldiers "whacked," he said, for refusing to come

Although a young Vincent "the Chin" Gigante *(inset)* beat the 1957 rap for the attempted assassination of Mafia boss Frank Costello, he later affected bathrobe attire and an addled air to bolster his claim of being mentally unfit to stand trial for several alleged offenses. Photographed on a New York street in 1990 wearing his trademark 'robe, Gigante was one of the very few Gotti rivals who managed to stay out of jail.

Under Surveillance

Unknowingly performing for hidden FBI cameras, John Gotti conducts mob business on the sidewalk outside the Ravenite Social Club on Mulberry Street in Manhattan. The steady surveillance by camera and wiretaps was part of a massive investigation aimed at making charges stick to the slippery don. In 1992 the five-year-long effort finally paid off: Convicted of racketeering and murder, Gotti was sentenced to five life terms, four without parole, plus 65 years.

Gotti managed to elude punishment until police and FBI agents were able to penetrate an apartment upstairs from the Ravenite and hide bugs in the living room *(above)* and kitchen *(left)* where Gotti entertained high-level Mafia colleagues. But even wiretaps might not have put Gotti away without the corroborating testimony of Salvatore "Sammy Bull" Gravano *(opposite)*, Gotti's turncoat friend and underboss.

promptly when he was summoned. Another soldier was slain because Gravano told Johnny Boy that the man had talked about him behind his back. Gotti trusted Sammy Bull. "Soon as anything happens to me, I'm off the streets, Sammy is acting boss," Johnny Boy was heard saying on an FBI surveillance tape.

Gotti and Gravano were indicted in December 1990. The charges were operating a criminal enterprise, income-tax evasion, obstruction of justice, illegal gambling, loansharking, and ordering four mob executions. Denied bail, Gotti went to jail; he was off the streets, but he still ran the family through his son, John Gotti, Jr.

Gravano was in another cell. Sammy Bull had carried a reputation as a killer since his twenties. He was first indicted for murder in 1974. After his acquittal, he'd become a made man in the Gambino family and had participated in numerous slayings, he told authorities. Both he and Gotti had come up through the Dellacroce faction of the Gambinos, and all along Gravano had been fiercely loyal to Johnny Boy. Sammy Bull, in fact, told government investigators that he'd personally passed $60,000 in bribe money to one of the jurors who'd acquitted Gotti in the 1986-87 RICO trial.

But Gravano, languishing in jail, was a very unhappy fellow. Despite a life of violent crime, he'd never served time and was now discovering that he didn't like it at all. He was 46, and he had a wife and teenage son and daughter. He missed them, and it looked as if he might be missing them for a long time to come: The FBI told him that the bureau had a witness who would link him to a murder. If he couldn't think of some way out, Sammy Bull might easily spend the rest of his life in prison. And prison was not what it once was. There'd been a time when the Mafia ran the prisons for all practical purposes, and life behind bars was soft for important people. Now, however, as one lawman put it, "the blacks run the jails, and mobsters are second-class citizens."

In March 1992 Gravano stepped to the witness stand in federal district court in New York, started talking, and didn't stop for nine days. He described his initiation ceremony, at which Big Paul Castellano presided. Castellano had pricked Gravano's trigger finger, dripped symbolic blood onto a saint's picture, and set the picture afire. This was how Sammy Bull's soul would burn, Castellano told him, if he ever divulged Mafia secrets.

With John Gotti staring at him from 20 feet away, Gravano went on to describe in minute detail how the Mafia operated. He also narrated woefully the difficulties of mob life: trying to find a safe place to talk business, wondering whom to trust and how to handle people who—yes, like himself—became rats. He admitted taking part in 19 murders in one way or another. "Sometimes I was the shooter," he said. "Sometimes I was a backup guy. Sometimes I set the guy up. Sometimes I just talked about it."

Ten of those killings, Gravano said, were ordered by John Gotti, and among them were the murders of Castellano and Bilotti. Yes, he and Gotti were there that night, parked nearby. They watched the shooting, then Gravano started the car and drove along 46th Street past the bodies. "I looked down at Tommy Bilotti," he recalled. "I said he was gone."

The jury of seven men and five women deliberated for 13 hours. When the jurors reentered the courtroom, John Gotti straightened the starched French cuffs peeking from the sleeves of his double-breasted gray pinstriped suit and winked at courtroom spectators. "I think we walk," he said to his lawyers.

The forewoman read off 13 guilty verdicts.

Gotti turned to his codefendant and put a finger to his lips, as if to say, "Hush."

"The Teflon is gone," said an FBI man. "The don is covered with Velcro, and all the charges stuck."

Johnny Boy Gotti received five life terms—four without parole—plus 65 years, plus a fine of $250,000. He is serving his time in the maximum-security federal penitentiary at Marion, Illinois, among the toughest prisons of them all. His case is on appeal.

With Gotti put away, the government could take considerable satisfaction in the results of its campaign against the Mafia in America. An FBI report stated that "many of their lucrative criminal conspiracies have been dismantled, their status and secrecy have been weakened, and their influence and intimidating powers have waned." But no one has claimed that the Mafia is at death's door—not now or in the near future.

The large Genovese organization continues to thrive in New York under the leadership of Vincent "the Chin" Gigante. The unlikely heir to the old Luciano-Lansky-Costello outfit has maintained the numerous, carefully forged links to construction, trucking, and textile and food distribution. According to the police, Genovese soldiers are better schooled in their criminal crafts, more wisely selected, and less trigger-happy than their contemporaries in other families. True, the Genovese tribe has lost some important people recently. But authorities do not feel that they've inflicted crippling damage.

The other families are in grave trouble, but they haven't been immobilized. Without the old bosses, without the peacekeeping efforts of the Commission, with the street work being done by greedy and impatient young soldiers, there is great confusion everywhere. But there is no less Mafia crime. The Apalachin edicts of 1957 have been overturned by the realities of the 1990s. The FBI believes that at least 19 of the country's 24 Mafia families are presently dealing drugs, and the bureau has identified 373 Mafia members actively engaged in the trade. As much as anything else—perhaps more than anything else—narcotics fuel the modern Mafia.

It's possible, however, that the new Mafia is no more crass, brutal, or greed driven than the old. Perhaps time has burnished fact in a way that enshrines in flattering legend Vito Cascio Ferro as a courtly diplomat, or Charlie Luciano as a criminal genius. The truth may have been otherwise, but the romantic myths persist. Most likely the myths are real enough to a few mafiosi who still mourn the passing of the Mafia that supposedly used to be, the old Sicilian bandit brotherhood with its vaunted code of silence, honor, and respect.

Those were the values that men like Joe Bonanno claimed to hold close to their hearts, but there appears to be little place for them today. "My tradition has died in America," lamented Bonanno bitterly in his autobiography. "The way of life that I and my Sicilian ancestors pursued is dead. What Americans refer to as 'the Mafia' is a degenerate outgrowth of that life-style." ◆

A Dons' Gallery

Whatever else they may be, the Mafia dons are hugely individual. Each leaves a trail littered with the expected acts of greed and murder, but often there is something more—a special signature. This distinctive mark may derive from some extreme: remarkable skill at corruption, cruelty, and murder, for example. Some are notable for painstakingly avoiding the spotlight, others for seeking it out.

Dons may be remembered more for their cravings than their crimes—especially an itch, which evidently plagues the species, to mingle with high society, to have the ear of people with wealth or power. And, because the don's most resilient vow is one of secrecy, they have sometimes been credited with engineering impossibly complex conspiracies.

Whoever they are, princes of the brotherhood share a precarious existence, with rewards and hazards that more commonplace men can only imagine—extremes that constitute what the dons on these pages would proudly call the Life.

The Corruption of Robin Hood

On July 5, 1950, the world press proclaimed the news: Salvatore Giuliano, the most elusive, dangerous bandit in Sicily's outlaw-ridden history, had gone down, guns blazing, in a hail of bullets from hundreds of federal policemen. It seemed a fitting end for the 27-year-old folk hero. To many Sicilians he'd been a kind of modern-day Robin Hood, one of the last great idealist-bandits on an island with a centuries-old tradition of bold brigandage.

Stories were told—and, indeed, songs were sung—of how he waylaid the wealthy on the roads around Palermo. "I am Giuliano," the dashing highwayman would announce magnificently before taking his victim into custody for a huge ransom or plundering a woman's jewels. It was said that Giuliano often slipped money under the doors of starving villagers and that he would kill his own men for stealing from the poor.

The stern but good-hearted rogue painted by mythology matched well the legends of the Mafia's origins in noble banditry. But the image hardly squared with the real Salvatore Giuliano. Although undoubtedly idealistic, Giuliano was also naive, vain, violent, and power-hungry, finally obsessed exclusively with escaping the consequences of his crimes. Inflated heroically by legend, Giuliano styled himself the enemy of both the landowners and their Mafia protectors. However, there are scholars who believe that the handsome highwayman was a mafioso himself. And dissenters who doubt that Giuliano was an actual member of the brotherhood concede that he lived, thieved,

kidnapped, and murdered at the pleasure of the powerful dons on whose stage he strutted as a puppet for seven brief years.

Conceived in a two-room Brooklyn flat, Giuliano was born in the sun-blasted mountain village of Montelepre—Rabbit Mountain—on November 20, 1922. His father had emigrated to the United States nearly two decades earlier; then, like many of his compatriots, he'd returned to his roots—only to find the life harder, the poverty deeper, and the government more corrupt than he remembered. In this poor village only 15 miles—and several centuries—away from Palermo, Salvatore grew up on tales of a promised land across the ocean, where such Sicilian heroes as Lucky Luciano drove grand cars and had money to throw around.

When Giuliano dropped out of elementary school as a child, he stepped into a world that was very different from his American fantasies—a world of ancient privilege, vested in landowners and guarded by powerful Mafia bands, overlain by the authority of Benito Mussolini's Fascist regime. In 1942 the 20-year-old Giuliano went into hiding to avoid service in the Italian army and, like so many of his contemporaries, made a living in the black market.

With the successful Allied invasion of July 1943, Sicily became littered with abandoned matériel, its black market engorged with stolen weapons and supplies. Giuliano was carrying an illegal pistol on the fateful September day when police stopped him and his load of contraband wheat. Giuliano fled. When the police

opened fire, he fired back and killed his first officer. Now a hunted man, the young fugitive headed into the mountains around Montelepre, where, within a few months, he had assembled a small guerrilla army of convicts and bandits.

An avowed enemy of landowners and the Mafia, Giuliano in December 1943 made common cause with the young movement to separate Sicily from Italian rule. The Mafia also backed the separatists, who'd advanced no schemes for disturbing the economic status quo. Clad in the mantle of a patriotic cause, Giuliano quickly became a legend, ranging his northwest corner of the island with impunity.

Giuliano's forces were superbly effective. Over and over again, his bandit army, outgunning police with German and American military weapons, ambushed and routed government forces. He held up trains in broad daylight, then slipped away to high mountain caves. Every effort to encircle him failed; shepherds along the ridges would signal the approach of soldiers by shrill whistles, allowing the outlaws to slip away. But the enemy seldom got that close. Salvatore Giuliano's intelligence network was so good that he often knew of intended raids even before the carabinieri left their barracks.

In fact, his success was truly too good to be true. Perhaps unwittingly, the young bandit chieftain had conducted his little war under the quiet protection of the powerful gangs of the nearby towns of Monreale and Partinico. Nor was his Mafia shield a secret: Even the carabinieri knew

Mounted on a marble plaque, this photograph of dashing Sicilian bandit king Salvatore Giuliano was added to his gravestone 30 years after his death in 1950. Buried in his native village of Montelepre, the legendary brigand lives on as a tourist attraction, immortalized in postcards, romantic histories, photographs, and film.

that Giuliano survived only because the Mafia let him.

The young bandit held the rank of colonel in EVIS, the Voluntary Army for the Independence of Sicily. In 1945 EVIS lost a key battle with the Italian army and saw its commander jailed. The separatists' force was further diluted a year later, when the referendum that made Italy a republic handed Sicily virtual autonomy at the local level. His cause evaporating around him, Giuliano suddenly found himself less a patriot than a thief on the run.

Buoyed by the corrupt possibilities of Sicilian autonomy, the Mafia began exterminating the other bandits they had once helped. But they preserved Giuliano's band because they had one further use for the gullible young man. In September, peasants squatting on five unoccupied estates were given the property, to the outrage of landowners who already felt threatened by political promises involving a redistribution of wealth. The squatters' victory sparked a series of skirmishes in which 40 peasants died, most of them Communists, and the left was further thwarted by being suppressed in Mafia territory by dons who believed in nothing if not capitalism. Nevertheless, a socialist movement was rising that Giuliano, properly coached, could do much to derail.

The dashing bandit was offered a new patriotic cause: keeping the leftists from destroying his native land. This put the easily steered Giuliano on the side of the landowners and pitted him against the peasants he had originally set out to liberate. If he felt any qualms, however, he concealed them with rabid anticommunism. In fact, his motives were more personal than ideological. He wanted amnesty for his crimes and believed he could get it by portraying himself as the enemy of socialism. He even wrote U.S. President Harry Truman to ask

that Sicily be made the 49th state, noting that he, Giuliano, hoped for American support in his war against communism. To others he wrote asking for artillery to continue the good fight.

In 1947 Giuliano and his men began a campaign of antileftist terror. On May Day, they took up a position on the flank of Monte Pizzuta, overlooking a peaceful left-wing rally outside the small town of Portella delle Ginestre. As the town's Socialist leader began his speech, Giuliano's five Breda 38 machine guns opened up on the crowd. Eight people were killed and 33 wounded, many horribly, in the hail of bullets. Police later found 800 spent shell casings where the guns had been set up. Late in June Giuliano struck again, ruthlessly attacking and torching a number of trade-union halls and Communist party offices in towns around Palermo.

By the time of Sicily's April 1948 election, 498 murders had occurred on the island that year, most of them at Mafia instigation. The terror evidently curbed the people's appetite for socialism: They returned a solid majority of Christian Democrats, the party of landowners and the Mafia, to power. The Socialist collapse also removed any pretense that Giuliano's motives were political; he was just a thief and murderer trying to stay alive.

The Portella delle Ginestre massacre had been a turning point for the bandit—the Robin Hood who machine-gunned women and children—and Giuliano sealed his fate two years later. In August 1949 he ambushed a motorized column of carabinieri, killing seven. A storm of public outrage caused a special police unit to be established under the command of carabinieri colonel Ugo Luca, a tough, tenacious veteran of the Italian secret service. Soon some 2,000 police scoured the rough country around Montelepre for Giuliano. At the

same time, Giuliano also turned against the Mafia, which, having no further use for him, not only suspended his protection but ordered him killed.

The following July brought reports that the brigand died in a barrage of carabinieri fire in the town of Castelvetrano, some 40 miles from his Montelepre haunts. He was there, according to some accounts, waiting to be flown to safety in Tunis. In fact, the story of Giuliano's gallant death was an official lie. He'd come to Castelvetrano as a rat to a trap. Dozing off around 3 a.m., he was shot in his sleep by his lieutenant and best friend, Gaspare Pisciotta, and his body was dragged into the open where the waiting police officers could riddle it with their bullets.

This revelation came less than a year after Giuliano's death and seemed to solve the mystery of the bandit's end, but it shed no light on the larger puzzle of Giuliano's long survival as a hunted man. The testimony of Pisciotta, among others, indicated that Giuliano had held off his betrayal by letting it be known that he'd written a lengthy document revealing the identity of his secret supporters in the Mafia and, some say, in the highest echelons of the Italian government. Supposedly placed in the hands of Giuliano's brother and taken to the United States, the document disappeared. Some say it never existed, others that the practical-minded General Ugo Luca—the colonel was promoted soon after the bandit's death—had found, read, copied, and then somehow lost the incriminating record.

Giuliano's assassin survived for less than four years after betraying his friend. On February 9, 1954, Gaspare Pisciotta, held in Palermo's Ucciardone Prison on banditry charges, drank a cup of coffee prepared by a trusted relative—and died of strychnine poisoning. ◆

The Organizer

The nicknames awarded John Torrio by his friends and enemies summed up his complex character. Terrible Johnny, his fellow mobsters called him. Internal Revenue Service agents dubbed him the Fox. His unusual blend of brutality and organizational skills helped put the Mafia on a kind of industrial footing, leading the way to a cartel approach to crime. But Torrio was no prisoner of ambition. Unlike many of his peers, he knew when and how to get out.

A native of Naples, Johnny Torrio grew up on New York's Lower East Side, where he developed exceptional ability with knife, club, and fists. Although he was small — barely five and a half feet tall — he found employment as a bouncer and eventually became a top lieutenant in the vicious Five Points street gang.

In 1909 the 27-year-old Torrio was called west to Chicago by Big Jim Colosimo, who was, by some accounts, a distant cousin by marriage. A restaurateur and racketeer with a firm grip on South Side vice, Colosimo was being threatened by Black Hand extortionists, and he sensed that his young relative could help. Torrio obliged by killing the blackmailers. Torrio moved to Chicago permanently around 1915 and rose rapidly in Colosimo's organization, enriching its ranks with such imported talent as a young tough from New York named Alphonse Capone.

From his vantage point high in the Chicago rackets, Torrio saw an irresistible opportunity. Prohibition was coming, and Terrible Johnny wanted to take over the local breweries and stitch them into a unified bootlegging network to slake Chica-

Johnny Torrio, out on bail and masked with a handkerchief, is trailed by curious Brooklyn kids in 1941.

go's thirst. But Colosimo didn't share his vision. Big Jim was already rich, had recently married a young show girl, and was wary of tangling with federal liquor agents. Torrio dealt with the difficulty in 1920 by arranging for Colosimo's liquidation by another New York colleague, Frankie Yale. Then, with the savage Capone at his side, Torrio began assembling Chicago's ethnic factions into a criminal coalition, guaranteeing them exclusive beer distribution rights in their precincts as long as they respected the general peace.

In addition to providing the overall strategy, Torrio masterminded the buying of protection. He dispensed payoffs at every level of government and even hired cops to ride shotgun on hijack-prone beer convoys.

The good times ended in 1923, when a reform ticket swept in, and the new mayor and police chief cold-shouldered Torrio, greatly weakening his imperial grip. Soon rival gang leaders were again warring for turf. One of them, a North Side Irishman named Dion O'Banion, set up Torrio for a federal alcohol bust at a brewery Torrio owned. Terrible Johnny used his pretrial freedom to have the double-dealing Irish-

man killed. The hit was one of Torrio's serious mistakes, for it ignited the West Side Beer Wars, which raged among competing gangs until 1926.

To O'Banion's Polish-American successor, Hymie Weiss, Torrio became the number-one target. On January 24, 1925, as Terrible Johnny returned to his Chicago home after shopping with his wife, gunmen opened up on him, wounding him several times. The mobster was rushed to a hospital, where Al Capone stationed 30 men to keep guard. Torrio slowly recovered.

The brush with death seemed to inspire Torrio to reflect on his life. He was 43 years old and worth perhaps $30 million. After pondering his close call and the probable hazard of trying to restore order among Chicago's warring gangs, he decided to take the mortal hint. "It's all yours, Al," he reportedly told his protégé. "I've retired." Torrio left Chicago and went back to New York.

Retirement did not mean oblivion, however. Torrio became an adviser to such rising stars as Frank Costello, Lucky Luciano, and Meyer Lansky, sharing with Luciano especially the vision of the mob as a cor-

porate business. In the late 1920s Torrio also took on the role of banker and financial brain for mob operations in New York. Always cartel-minded, he set up a rumrunning collective that at one point served 22 gangs, from Maine to Florida.

When mob leaders from across the country gathered in Atlantic City in 1929 to discuss the mob's future, Torrio led the New York delegation. He argued persuasively for a national crime federation along the lines of what he had attempted in Chicago. He also accepted an important diplomatic assignment: Al Capone's bloody reign in Chicago had fueled a dangerous degree of citizen anger, and Torrio—who had handed Scarface Al the crown of Chicago crime—was given the job of persuading him to step down.

Torrio lived another three decades, savoring his role as adviser to a crime empire he had helped shape. In 1957 he sat in a Brooklyn barber's chair, warily facing the door, when death suddenly stepped in to claim him. But it was not with a hail of bullets. Torrio's heart failed, and hours later he died, fulfilling his often-expressed wish to meet his end in bed. ◆

GIUSEPPE RUSSO
The Little Bull

Squat, pudgy Giuseppe Genco Russo had the nickname Zi Peppi Jencu, meaning "Uncle Joe the Little Bull." Mafia boss Lucky Luciano had another characterization: "Peppi isn't even a rooster, let alone a bull," Luciano said. "He's just a big fat hen." Barely able to read and woefully unpolished—he spat everywhere he went—Russo stood at the top of the Sicilian Mafia, holding the reins of great power in his chubby hands. His influence was felt on both sides of the Atlantic: When American and Sicilian dons met in Palermo in 1957 to discuss the future of the international drug business, the Little Bull helped plan their leap into narcotics.

Born on a hardscrabble farm in central Sicily in 1893, Russo had clawed his way up through Mafia ranks by excelling at robbery, extortion, and murder; he was said to have personally killed 11 men. He reportedly was also one of the mafiosi who, at the behest of American dons Charlie Luciano and Vito Genovese, smoothed the way for the 1943 Allied invasion of Sicily. In 1946 he received the Order of the Crown of Italy from the Italian parliament, and he was elected mayor of his native Mussomelli some years later.

Family connections played a part in Russo's rise to power. One of his uncles, Don Calogero Vizzini, was capo di tutti capi for many years (pages 17-19). When Vizzini died in 1954, the Little Bull succeeded him.

As Russo rose in power, he tried to smooth some of his rougher edges, although his piggish nature was hard to camouflage. Having relatives in the church, he spent a lot of time with priests, and the association seemed to marginally improve his manners and his tailoring. His picture was often taken with civic and business leaders, even bishops. He controlled the bank in Mussomelli and acted as an arbiter of political disputes all across the island.

But Russo's position was less secure than he thought. In 1963 authorities on both sides of the ocean cracked down on narcotics traffickers. In the first significant strike against the Mafia since Mussolini's time, Italian police arrested almost 200 men, including Russo and other leading dons. Russo fought his conviction. He presented the court with a testimonial to his good character signed by 7,000 supporters. He also threatened to release telegrams from top Italian officials thanking him for his help in getting them elected.

The trial unfolded in typical Mafia style: Evidence mysteriously disappeared, and witnesses recanted. Russo beat the drug charges, but not the lesser ones of associating with criminals, for which he drew three years in jail. An earlier judicial proceeding had banished him from Mussomelli and ordered him to a far northern corner of Italy for five years. Nearly blind with cataracts, his health shattered, Russo returned to Sicily in 1972 and lived there until his death in 1976 at 80. In these last years, he was a broken man, abandoned by his friends and dismissed by his enemies. But, to the end, he remained true to the code of silence. "Mafia? Mafia in Sicily?" he would respond to questioners. "I don't know anything about it." ◆

His eye bandaged after a cataract operation, Sicilian Mafia chief Giuseppe Genco Russo boards a train in March of 1964 to begin a five-year exile to a village in northern Italy.

The Reclusive Don

Although little of a criminal nature could take place in Detroit without the concurrence of Mafia boss Joseph Zerilli, the man himself managed for much of his long career to stay in the shadows, never very clearly defined. He was an old-style don, one of the last of the breed that cherished privacy and secrecy above almost all else.

A native of Terrasini, Sicily, Zerilli had come to America in 1914, when he was 17, and worked his way up through mob ranks as a rum-runner and occasional hit man. Although arrested many times and convicted twice—once for robbery and once for murder—he never received a penalty heavier than a fine. Even within the Mafia he kept a low profile: He sat on the national Commission but often skipped meetings, and he avoided interfamily scraps except to serve as conciliator.

So reclusive was Zerilli that for many years Mafia watchers were not certain that he was really the boss in Detroit. Eventually, though, his authority became clear—as did his success. Detroit mobsters took in an estimated $150 million a year in the 1960s. Their operations included the usual drugs, gambling, loan-sharking, extortion, prostitution, and labor racketeering. But they also had a hand in such legiti-mate businesses as beer distribution, a bus line, trash hauling, and horse racing. By one estimate the family had infiltrated 100 businesses valued at $50 million. The don claimed, of course, that he knew nothing of organized crime. He identified himself as the owner of the Detroit Italian Baking Company, nothing more.

Zerilli's cherished anonymity was shat-

This 1931 news photograph is one of the few extant images of elusive Detroit Mafia boss Joseph Zerilli, who managed to maintain a low profile while amassing enormous power in the underworld in a criminal career that lasted half a century.

tered in 1975, however, with the sensational disappearance of former teamsters' union leader Jimmy Hoffa. While the mystery of Hoffa's fate persists, investigators have always assumed that he couldn't have been killed in Detroit without the approval of don Joe Zerilli. After all, Hoffa did have close links with the Mafia, and on the day that he disappeared he was reportedly on his way to meet top Zerilli lieutenant Anthony "Tony Jack" Giacalone.

Nevertheless, no one has ever proved Zerilli's complicity in Hoffa's vanishing, and two years after the labor leader disappeared, the don died. Reporters were politely turned away from the funeral home where the Detroit boss lay, but a small contingent of undercover cops set up a surveillance post in a van parked across the street and noted who came and went. Zerilli's relatives later bought newspaper space to bemoan what they called prejudicial and often sadistic media coverage. Doubtless the don would have agreed with that sentiment and would have appreciated the rest of the family's newspaper tribute, which ended with this verse: "Your gentle face and patient smile / with sadness we recall / you had a kindly word for each / and died beloved by all." ◆

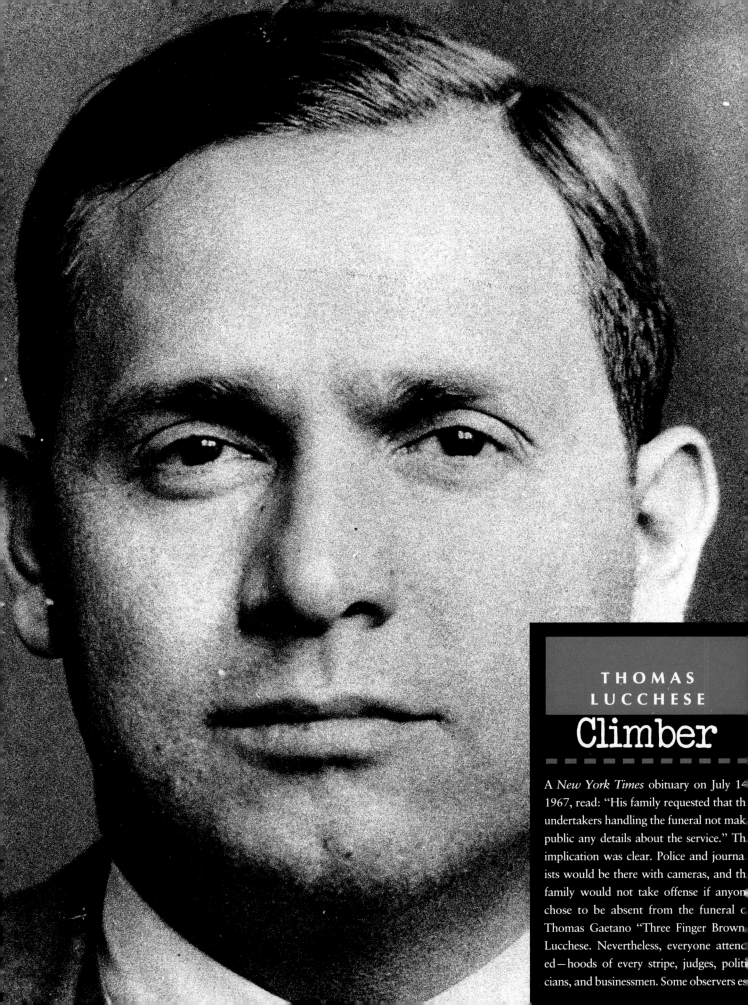

THOMAS LUCCHESE
Climber

A *New York Times* obituary on July 14
1967, read: "His family requested that th
undertakers handling the funeral not mak
public any details about the service." Th
implication was clear. Police and journa
ists would be there with cameras, and th
family would not take offense if anyon
chose to be absent from the funeral c
Thomas Gaetano "Three Finger Brown
Lucchese. Nevertheless, everyone attenc
ed—hoods of every stripe, judges, politi
cians, and businessmen. Some observers es

timated that a thousand people came to say farewell. It was one of the largest turnouts ever for a Mafia funeral, and perhaps the most diverse assembly of power brokers in New York's long and checkered history.

In life, the tiny man receiving the tributes—Lucchese stood only five feet two inches tall—had been regarded by his Mafia peers as perhaps the most capable crime chieftain America had yet produced. While never attaining the power of a Frank Costello or the imperial reach of a Vito Genovese or Carlo Gambino, Lucchese oversaw the steady expansion of his own crime family and did it without the in-house squabbling and intrigue and bloody coups that so often roiled Mafia ranks. Within the mob he was regarded as the classiest of dons, esteemed for his generosity and fairness, and also admired for his ability to avoid jail. Although he engaged in virtually every criminal racket for decades and may have been involved in as many as 30 killings, he served only a single stretch in prison—a few months in 1921 for car theft.

Lucchese came to New York in 1911 from Palermo, where he was born in 1899. Somewhere along the line he lost a finger and was given the nickname Three Finger Brown after a famous baseball player. Despite his small stature, he began his career as a street tough, running with the Italian gangs of Harlem. In the 1920s he became a bodyguard for Lucky Luciano—and, ac-

cording to some accounts, he was Luciano's favorite hit man during the Castellammarese War *(pages 73-75)*. In the biggest hit of all—Luciano's elimination of Salvatore Maranzano—Lucchese served as finger man: Luciano chose him to be in Maranzano's Park Avenue office to point out the victim as the killers arrived.

Lucchese showed a smart business sense early in his career. In 1922 he set up a window-cleaning business with some built-in incentives. Shopkeepers who didn't sign on to have their windows cleaned had them broken by brick-tossing toughs. Five years later, Lucchese started a dried-fruit importing firm that fronted for a bootleg alcohol plant. About the same time, he moved in on the Garment District, using his brick tossers as labor goons and eventually going partners with Louis "Lepke" Buchalter *(page 68)*. Rackets in the rag trade would remain a Lucchese mainstay, along with his acquired string of clothing manufacturers, which served as an invaluable legitimate front.

With the creation of the five New York families in 1931, Lucchese became underboss to Gaetano Gagliano and inherited the top spot after the boss's death in 1953. By then Lucchese was so highly regarded as a power broker within the mob that there was talk of his replacing Frank Costello, then the New York underworld's Mr. Big. Meanwhile, Lucchese's stakes in legitimate

businesses—not just in clothing but also in real estate, sand and gravel, construction, and other fields—helped him cultivate important political friendships. One chum was U.S. Attorney Thomas Murphy, who had successfully prosecuted Alger Hiss, a State Department official accused of spying for the Soviet Union. Lucchese was also close to Congressman Vito Marcantonio, who espoused a Communist line but was really a front for the right-leaning mob in his Harlem district, where he shielded all illicit activities. Working through Marcantonio, Lucchese engineered the rise of Vincent R. Impellitteri as New York's mayor in 1950, over the wishes of Tammany Hall and Costello.

The little don's passage into virtual respectability was now nearly complete. He lived in the suburbs of Long Island and was a rich man. His son got a congressional appointment to the U.S. Military Academy at West Point. His daughter married the son of Carlo Gambino.

Lucchese's only scrape in later life—a minor one—was with the Internal Revenue Service over back taxes, which he paid. He died peacefully at the age of 67, following surgery for a brain tumor. Even dead, he still attracted money. Publicity-shy mobsters who chose not to attend his funeral expressed their respect by sending emissaries bearing envelopes full of cash for the grieving family. ◆

The Gardener

In Senate testimony in 1963, renegade Mafia soldier Joe Valachi named Ruggiero "Richie the Boot" Boiardo as a power in La Cosa Nostra. Not so, said Boiardo, then in his seventies. He was simply a retired bricklayer who loved gardening.

It was true that Richie the Boot liked gardening. He could be seen on most summer days hobbling about the vegetable patch on his estate in Livingston, New Jersey. It was also true that he had once been a mason—back in 1910, as a young immi-

The Livingston, New Jersey, estate of Ruggiero "Richie the Boot" Boiardo featured statues of the don's own family, dominated by an equestrian statue of the Mafia boss himself.

167

Frail and addled with age, 89-year-old Mafia boss Ruggiero Boiardo leaves Somerset County Courthouse in New Jersey in 1980 after being found unfit to stand trial on charges that included murder and extortion.

grant from Italy. But bootlegging, extortion, racketeering, loan-sharking, and murder were his real vocations, and Boiardo was so good at them that for decades he reigned over the Newark, New Jersey, underworld and served as capo in the 600-member Genovese crime family.

Once he reached eminence in the mob, Boiardo rewarded himself by moving into an imposing stone mansion. A magazine once uncharitably described it as Transylvanian Traditional in style, and it certainly reflected an ego adequate to the famed mobster's station.

Inside a huge gate topped with bronze swans was a group of large painted statues that represented Richie the Boot and various members of his family. The most prominent figure, naturally, was the representation of the patriarch himself, who was depicted on horseback as a Roman general.

Impressive as such fixtures were, the best-known feature of the estate, at least in mob circles, was probably an incinerator located behind the house. Boiardo used it to turn hit victims into ashes, according to an overheard conversation between two New Jersey gangsters in the early 1960s. "Stay away from there," admonished one. "So many guys have been hit there. There's this furnace way up in back. That's where they burned them." The hood then proceeded to name several former colleagues who had gone up in smoke at Boiardo's place, and he went on to say that he had personally dragged one dead man to the incinerator by a chain looped around the corpse's neck.

Despite the reported magnitude of his crimes, Boiardo's career suffered only occasional minor setbacks. He was wounded in one gangland shootout, and he spent 22 months in jail in the 1930s on a concealed weapons charge. But so corrupt was local government in northern New Jersey that the don rarely had to worry about the law. Not until the 1980s was a serious cleanup attempted by the authorities—and by then Boiardo was an old man. Although prosecutors sought to charge him with a long list of major crimes, a judge ruled that he was too infirm to stand trial. Until his death in 1984 at 93, the ancient don puttered feebly in his cherished garden—and, it is said, in his cherished domains of extortion and gambling as well. ◆

Big
Tuna

- - - - - - - - - - - - -

Among Chicago mobsters who knew them both, it was sometimes said of Anthony Joseph Accardo that he had more brains before breakfast than Al Capone had all day long. Certainly Accardo had better survival instincts than Capone, who lasted only four years as boss of the local mob before going to prison for tax evasion. Accardo remained a power in Chicago for more than six decades.

For much of that time Accardo headed the Outfit, as Chicago's branch of the Mafia is called, and lived in a style that he considered suitable for a king of crime. His 22-room stone mansion in exclusive, suburban River Forest had two bowling alleys, an indoor swimming pool, a pipe organ, a roof garden, and, in the master's luxurious bathroom, a tub carved from a single piece of Mexican onyx and filled from gold faucets. At the frequent parties staged in this palatial home, violinists strolled among the guests and an electric fountain gushed champagne.

Along with luxurious accommodations, Accardo favored upscale sports, such as game fishing; the best known of his various nicknames was Big Tuna, for a 400-pound fish he caught. And he enjoyed pheasant hunting, although apparently not in its conventional form. It is said that the don and his cronies once traveled in a caravan of Cadillacs to South Dakota, where they

Subpoenaed in 1984, 78-year-old Chicago boss Anthony "Big Tuna" Accardo, carrying his signature tuna-headed cane, appears before a Senate subcommittee.

blasted at the birds with machine guns.

For all his obvious appreciation of the good life, Tony Accardo had no soft and cultured core. He was a hard man to his center, expert in the violence that had propelled him to the top of his profession. Born in the tough Badlands section of Chicago in 1906, he began making homemade booze for bootleggers in his teens and worked his way up through the ranks to become one of Capone's bodyguards. Accardo was called Tough Tony and Joe Batters in those days for his skill with a Louisville Slugger—not on a baseball diamond, of course, but for the close-quarters destruction of his enemies. He reportedly held one of the guns at the St. Valentine's Day Massacre—the rubout of seven Capone rivals in 1929—then moved into the top ranks of the Outfit when his boss went off to jail three years later.

By 1943 Accardo's various competitors in Chicago had fallen by the wayside: Paul "the Waiter" Ricca was put away for tax evasion, Charles "Cherry Nose" Gioe was the victim of an unsolved gangland hit, and Frank "the Enforcer" Nitti committed suicide rather than face prison. Accardo had the field to himself, and not even World War II could touch him: He was absolved from military service as "morally unfit."

During Tony Accardo's years as king of the Chicago rackets, mobsters cast a predatory net over an ever-growing number of restaurants, hotels, and saloons, and even such businesses as diaper services and funeral parlors. Moreover, the net spread far beyond Chicago: Accardo operated throughout the Great Lakes area, did business in Nevada and California, and signed on with major Eastern dons for a piece of Mafia ventures in Miami and the Bahamas.

Authorities made many attempts to reel in Big Tuna. In 1958 he was called before the U.S. Senate Labor Management Investigating Committee to answer questions about labor rackets. He took the Fifth Amendment 172 times, even for such queries as, "Have you any scruples against killing?" In 1960 he was brought to trial for tax evasion—specifically for deducting $3,994 as operating expenses for his sports car, a red Mercedes-Benz 300SL. Accardo claimed that he used the car in the course of employment as a salesman for a Chicago beer company, but the jury found that explanation hard to believe. He was convicted and sentenced to six years in prison; that verdict, however, was overturned on appeal in 1962.

By that time, Accardo had begun to withdraw from everyday control of the Outfit, opting for the comfortable role of elder statesman in a Palm Springs, California, setting. But true retirement proved an impossibility. In the late 1980s, arrests and mob hits threw the Outfit into such disarray that Accardo was forced to step back in and take over.

Somehow, in a lifetime of racketeering, Big Tuna managed to escape the nets of the law. Old age, not justice, got him in the end. The 86-year-old don died in May 1992 of heart failure, having never spent a single night in jail. ◆

Honor among Thieves?

For sheer viciousness, few Mafia bosses ever equaled Raymond Patriarca, long the maestro of New England crime. Although his remarkable malignity was often directed at fellow hoods, he cunningly managed to reign without serious challenge. In fact, the mob often used him as a mediator in gang wars, knowing that sentiment never clouded his judgment.

Curiously, Patriarca was something of a bungler in his early years. The son of Italian immigrant parents, he was born in Worcester, Massachusetts, in 1908 and began compiling a lengthy arrest record while still a teenager. The police took him in for hijacking, armed robbery, assault, safecracking, auto theft, being an accessory before the fact to murder, and a number of other infractions. He was convicted five times and had spent 10 years in jail by the time he turned 30. After one conviction he broke out of jail, but he was soon recaptured. In 1930 his efforts to free some friends from prison cost four lives in an aborted breakout. The violent spirit behind these deeds, if not the deeds themselves,

captured the notice of New England's Mafia boss, Phil Buccula, and Patriarca was soon given capo status in the local mob.

Buccula's choice proved sound, for Patriarca was more than just a strong arm; he was also a masterful corrupter, without honor even among fellow thieves. During Prohibition, Patriarca arranged to hijack shipments of alcohol that he'd been hired to guard. As a capo, he once forced his own men to restore lost profits to him after a load of stolen cigarettes was seized by the FBI. Convicted of burglary, Patriarca won a full pardon from Massachusetts governor Charles F. Hurley in 1938, even though the FBI had once designated the mobster Public Enemy Number One in his home base of Providence, Rhode Island, and had ordered agents to arrest him on sight. It turned out that the governor had been prompted to his act of mercy by a personal secretary, actu-

ally a mob tool who concocted an emotional plea for clemency from a nonexistent priest.

In 1954 Phil Buccula retired to Sicily, and Patriarca rose to bossdom. He moved smartly to expand mob operations in his sprawling dominion of Rhode Island, Connecticut, Massachusetts, and Maine. Besides gambling, loansharking, hijacking, and other crime staples, the mob extracted profits from an ever-growing list of restaurants, resorts, vending businesses, linen services, and garbage collection companies. Patriarca's power became so complete that he could insist on approving in advance crimes planned by nonmob thugs. Anyone trying to compete on his turf was killed.

Patriarca was uncommonly rough on people who failed to pay their debts to his loan sharks. Rather than suspend interest payments when the debtor was hopelessly broke, Patriarca often preferred to kill the deadbeat and accept the loss of the principal. One expert on organized crime, perhaps overstating Patriarca's clout, estimated that this vengeful impulse lay behind two-thirds of all maimings and murders in New England.

The New England don was not much gentler toward his confederates. Patriarca once ordered an underling to kill his own son to atone for losing money on a soured deal; the man fell to his knees and begged for his boy's life, but Patriarca refused to withdraw the verdict until a trusted adviser intervened. At one period, the steely boss even had his own brother under death sentence for failing to detect an FBI bug.

In 1966 Patriarca's money lust was put to the test when a subordinate, Joseph Barboza, was arrested for a firearms violation and given an unusually high bail of $100,000. Underworld code called for the boss to pay in those circumstances, but Patriarca decided to let Barboza languish. When two friends of the arrested man tried to raise the bail on their own, Patriarca had them murdered for flouting his wishes.

As it happened, Patriarca was being wiretapped at the time. FBI agents visited Barboza in jail and played a tape of the boss saying, "Barboza's a ——— bum. He's expendable." The frightened Barboza began to talk. To silence him, Patriarca tried an indirect form of intimidation: A bomb planted in the car of Barboza's lawyer nearly blew the man's legs off. Amid public outrage, Patriarca was tried and convicted of conspiring to commit murder. He went to prison for six years.

Such was Patriarca's power, however, that he continued to rule his empire from inside the penitentiary in Atlanta. When he told other dons to stay out of New England, they did. But the good old days of being left alone were over; the law had got his scent. After Patriarca emerged from jail in 1975, he found himself hauled back into court time and again. Indicted in 1980 for labor racketeering and in 1981 for ordering the execution of two mobsters, the beleaguered old double-dealer complained bitterly, "I don't care if I die tomorrow, they're going to harass me." Patriarca died three years later, in Providence, at the age of 76. The don's heart—such as it was—had finally betrayed him. ◆

Defiant to the last, New England crime boss Raymond Patriarca flips his cigar at a television cameraman before entering a Cranston, Rhode Island, prison to begin a five-year federal sentence for conspiracy to commit murder.

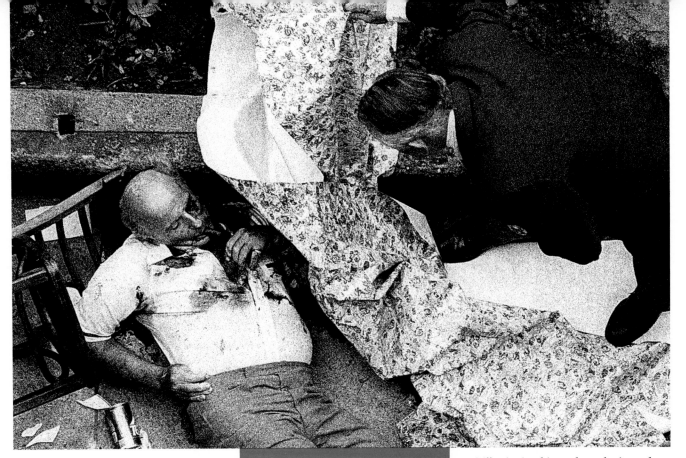

Still gripping his trademark cigar, the late Carmine Galante slumps in a mess of plates and pasta after gunmen sprayed his courtyard table with automatic-weapons fire on July 12, 1979.

The Man Who Would Be King

A fireplug of a man with an ever-present cigar in his grandfatherly face, chunky, five-foot-four Carmine "the Cigar" Galante was a tangle of contradictions. On the one hand, his instincts for money and murder stood out even among his fellow mobsters. On the other, he was soft-spoken, widely read, multilingual, and, in most respects, a pillar of Mafia tradition.

Like the man who'd made him an underboss, Joe Bonanno, Galante professed to be an old-school mafioso, a believer in obedience and discipline. Yet he bent tradition when it suited him. Despite the usual Mafia aversion to the press, Galante courted reporters to achieve greater recognition. Mafia tradition demanded allegiance to wife and children; mistresses were allowed, but they weren't to interfere with family life. But Galante, while married, defied the code by living openly with another wom-

an, Ann Acquavella, for some 20 years. He even had children by her, although—conceding to tradition—he had her marry another man to legitimize her offspring. And Galante abandoned another Mafia canon: He believed, unlike many of his colleagues, that the mob belonged in drugs, despite the heat from federal authorities that such traffic usually brought.

But Galante had never worried much about such things. He was in almost constant trouble as a youth in Harlem, where he was born in 1910. When he was 17 he was convicted of assault and imprisoned at Sing Sing in New York. After two years he got out, but only briefly: An armed robbery conviction sent him back to Sing Sing in 1930. After his 1939 parole, he headed up a gang on the Lower East Side and served as a "button man," or killer, for Vito Genovese. Legend has it that Galante

murdered radical journalist Carlo Tresca in 1943 as a favor to Genovese's good friend, Italian dictator Benito Mussolini. Though a prime suspect in the New York sidewalk shooting, Galante was not tried; but the assassination added luster to his reputation. By the early 1950s he'd become an enforcer and underboss in the Bonanno family. Colleagues boasted that Galante would kill someone in church during High Mass without thinking twice about it.

Such a man seemed an excellent candidate to help the mob in the controversial drug trade. In the ongoing debate within the mob over whether or not to enter the narcotics business in a big way, Joe Bonanno took the public position that selling drugs was unmanly. But with profits from the drug trade so huge, it was only a matter of time before American mafiosi followed the lead of their Sicilian cousins and got

into the game. In 1957 American and Sicilian dons met in Palermo and hatched a scheme in which the Sicilians—who were largely unknown to American law-enforcement agencies—would be given drug import and distribution rights in the United States. Their American brethren would stay safely on the sidelines but would receive a share of the proceeds.

Galante became a key player in this arrangement. Fluent in Italian dialects and French and Spanish as well, he flew around the world arranging million-dollar heroin deals. He helped consolidate the so-called French Connection, which imported drugs from Southeast Asia through the French port of Marseilles, then into Canada and the United States. Galante envisioned a nationwide network that would entirely corner the heroin market.

As antidrug mafiosi had feared, however, the burgeoning narcotics trade soon drew the attention of the American government. In 1958 federal drug enforcement agents won indictments relating to drug trafficking against Galante, among others. After a yearlong worldwide search, agents collared the Cigar near Seaside Heights, New Jersey, within sight of the New York skyline. Convicted in 1962, he began serving a 20-year sentence in the federal penitentiary in Lewisburg, Pennsylvania.

During his years inside, Galante's grand ambitions simmered on. "He used his 12 years in prison as a kind of health farm," one federal agent told reporters, "building up his body with exercising and handball. And when he got out he made some sym-

Police carry a stretcher bearing Carmine Galante's remains out of Joe & Mary's, one of the Mafia chief's favorite dining spots. Galante, his lieutenant, and the restaurant owner were all mowed down in the Brooklyn restaurant's courtyard as they ate lunch.

bolic moves to let people know he was back and a power to be reckoned with."

Galante emerged in 1974 and quickly set to work establishing a new narcotics network, dubbed the Pizza Connection because many of the distributors operated pizza parlors, which also served to launder drug money *(page 32)*. The operators were largely Sicilians, known in the business as zips, for their rapid speech. Over a period of five years, the network imported more than a ton of heroin, worth $1.65 billion. But Galante wanted more.

By then Galante had decided that he could take command of all Mafia operations in New York and become the boss of bosses. His base was the remnants of the Bonanno organization, leaderless since 1964, when Joe Bonnano was exiled to Arizona after plotting to kill fellow New York dons in the so-called Banana War *(page 121)*. The Cigar worked hard to rebuild the old Bonanno enterprises, many of which had been ceded to the family of ailing Carlo Gambino, the undisputed king of Mafia crime in New York. Galante intended to absorb both the Gambino and Genovese families, and hatching the plans he'd incubated in prison, he sent out his gunmen to kill off the opposition. When

Gambino's weak heart failed in 1976, Galante stepped into the line of succession, pitting himself directly against Aniello Dellacroce—the name in Italian means "little lamb of the cross"—who was expected to succeed Gambino. Some 20 Mafia soldiers were killed in the ensuing bloodbath.

Galante fully expected to win. During his stay in Lewisburg, according to some accounts, he'd persuaded a number of bosses outside New York to back him. Busted on a probation violation in 1978, however, the Cigar was briefly returned to jail and perhaps lost some momentum. No one don would stand up to the violent little man, so they all united against him. A reported meeting in Boca Raton, Florida, produced a contract on the Cigar, ratified by the full leadership of the organization—even by semiretired Joe Bonanno.

On July 12, 1979, having impulsively stopped at Joe & Mary's, a favorite restaurant in Brooklyn's Little Italy, Carmine Galante sat down to a fine lunch in the courtyard. He was joined by an underboss, two other trusted colleagues, and the restaurant's owner. As the don finished the main course and lighted his customary cigar, three men in ski masks burst into the courtyard and began blazing away at his table with shotguns and .45-caliber pistols. The restaurant owner and one of Galante's lieutenants were killed. Galante was hurled backward in his chair, shot through the eye and chest. Lying in a litter of salad and pasta, his recently lighted cigar still clamped in his teeth, the 69-year-old boss died, taking his vast ambitions with him. ◆

Bay of Pigs

The low-lying peninsula of Florida has a geography that makes it a smuggler's heaven: miles of ragged, almost submerged mangrove coastline, along with proximity to the drug works of South America. But when Mafia boss Joe Adonis arrived there in 1933, hoping to extend the mob's New York empire, he found that there was somebody in the way: Santo Trafficante, Sr., was already ensconced in Tampa, with a powerful grip on the reins of crime.

The Sicilian-born Trafficante later came out on top after the so-called Era of Blood, a Tampa Bay gang war that lasted from 1937 until 1945. At his side were his six sons, especially his alter ego, Santo junior, whose hard, hook-nosed profile would be stamped like a Roman emperor's on the coin of Florida crime. In 1946 the son took up residence in Cuba, helping build a rich and untroubled empire of gambling, drug running, and prostitution under the benign eye of a greedy and cooperative dictator, Fulgencio Batista.

Those were salad days for the Tampa mob. Santo junior managed the Sans Souci casino in Havana and helped ensure that Cuban gambling and vice stayed within the grasp of the Mafia. His links with Batista guaranteed the mobster's safety as well as his wealth. It is said that four gunmen fielded by competitors to kill young Santo were sent home by Cuban police. If they wanted to kill Trafficante, the police officers reportedly advised them, they would have to do it somewhere else.

In 1954 Santo Trafficante, Sr., died, and junior succeeded his father. The 39-year-old princeling was a good choice: Like his father, he was traditional in his actions and beliefs, observing the rules of humility and austerity, and committed utterly to the code of omertà.

Santo quickly allied himself with Meyer Lansky to expand the Florida rackets and Cuban operations. According to some accounts, Trafficante also acted on Lansky's behalf in arranging the 1957 hit of former Murder, Incorporated, boss Albert Anastasia. Anastasia had reportedly refused to back off from his demands for a larger share of Cuba, which was a Lansky-Trafficante gold mine.

When Cuban revolutionary Fidel Castro swept to power in 1959, Trafficante expected that the casinos would remain open and under Mafia control. After all, he had hedged the mob's political bets by slipping financial aid to the bearded rebel. Castro

was going his own way, however. He not only closed the casinos, but also tossed Trafficante and New Orleans rackets boss Carlos Marcello *(pages 177-178)* into jail. Later released and back in the Tampa Bay area, Trafficante continued to flourish, but he sorely missed the lost fortunes that he'd left behind in Havana. Linked to four gangland killings, he managed to avoid conviction, as he did when charged with labor racketeering. His witness-stand omertà was impeccable. Called to account in 1968, he merely coughed or laughed or took the Fifth Amendment. During his life of crime he never served a long jail term.

But, in 1975, Trafficante was curiously talkative with investigators, testifying that he and some fellow patriots had fallen into bed with the American government. He said that he'd participated in the Central Intelligence Agency's various schemes against Fidel Castro: the now-famous plans for defoliating the dictator's beard, producing strange behavior with LSD-like substances, and outright assassination with poison. Some observers believe that Trafficante's role in the CIA ploys was minor, that he'd merely provided expertise and translation services. Whatever his true involvement, Trafficante's testimony put him at the center of an incredibly complex web of alleged conspiracy.

According to his tangled tale, Trafficante and some of his colleagues had hoped that an April 1961 invasion of Castro's Cuba would restore their lost criminal empire. But the attempt ended in a debacle at the island's Bay of Pigs, partly because the

newly inaugurated president, John F. Kennedy, had curtailed American support. Trafficante alleged that the mob then turned against the young Democrat. In the meantime, the president's brother, Attorney General Robert F. Kennedy, was attacking labor racketeering, bringing the mob's anger against the Democratic administration to critical mass—and causing people to die.

President Kennedy was assassinated in Dallas in 1963, and his Cuba-linked assassin, Lee Harvey Oswald, was fatally shot by one Jack Ruby, a small-time Dallas nightclub operator who had ties to the Santo Trafficante family. Ruby was also evidently linked to Mafia bosses Carlos Marcello in New Orleans and Sam Giancana in Chicago.

Most of these players have since perished, but not the widespread belief in a vast, perfect conspiracy—one of several theories that persist about Kennedy's death. Jack Ruby died of heart disease in jail in 1967, mum to the end. No one knows for certain whether he intended to avenge the Kennedy killing or silence Oswald for the mob. Giancana was murdered in June 1975, not long after he was summoned to testify before Congress on the Castro plot.

And Santo Trafficante, Jr., the man whose brief breaking of the code of silence helped propel the juggernaut of rumor, is also gone. In 1987, the 72-year-old don died of a heart ailment, taking his knowledge of such plots—if, indeed, there were any—to the grave. ◆

CARLOS MARCELLO

Boss in the Bayous

It is said that New York Mafia don Vito Genovese, as safe in most American cities as the great white shark is in the sea, always asked permission before visiting New Orleans. The man he asked: Carlos "Little Man" Marcello. Claiming to make his living from growing tomatoes, the barrel-chested, five-foot-two-inch Mafia don ruled his lazily corrupt kingdom for more than four decades alone: Other mafiosi need not apply.

From his plush office behind the Town and Country Motel in Jefferson Parish, on the west bank of the Mississippi below New Orleans, Marcello monitored a web of narcotics, labor racketeering, bribery, prostitution, gambling, and a host of other questionable practices, mixed in with scores of legitimate businesses; his versatile shrimp boats also hauled in drugs from Mexico and Central America. The Marcello empire ranged from the Mississippi Delta to Dallas, the Ozark foothills, and the Florida Panhandle, where Little Man's grip slackened in favor of Tampa Bay boss

Santo Trafficante, a favorite associate of the New Orleans don.

But Marcello's billion-dollar-a-year operation was never the usual Mafia domain. It has possessed a distinctly Louisianan flavor, born of a longstanding, cozy relationship between the family and its political friends. Associations that would destroy public careers elsewhere are tolerated as a fact of life in Louisiana. As one mob-breaking attorney has described it, most people straddle the fence between honesty and crookedness—except in Louisiana, where there's no fence.

Marcello came to the bayou country as eight-month-old Calorso Minicari, the Tunis-born son of Sicilian parents. As a boy he worked in his father's prospering grocery business, taking produce to the rough downtown markets, where he drifted toward crime. By the age of 19, he'd been charged, along with his father and one of his six brothers, in a bold $7,000 bank robbery. He drew nine to 12 years in Angola state prison but served only four before being pardoned by Governor O. K. Allen in 1934. Older and wiser, Marcello returned to a budding career as a young Mafia thug, avoiding jail except for a 10-month hitch in 1938 for selling 23 pounds of marijuana. He became a protégé of powerful New York mobster Frank Costello, who was equipping Louisiana with illegal slot machines. To no one's surprise, when the New Orleans throne became vacant in 1947, Marcello was anointed by the northern dons to fill it. His rule unfolded virtually unchallenged by the law.

Because nothing in Louisiana's legal apparatus threatened Marcello, the federal government aimed at his one soft spot: He was a resident alien, traveling with a dubious Guatemalan passport issued against a forged birth certificate. The U.S. Immigration and Naturalization Service began trying to deport Marcello in 1953, but attempts to ship him to Italy failed. Although born of Sicilian parents, noted the Italian government, Marcello did not claim citizenship or even carry an Italian passport; Sicily wasn't his home. Italy's reluctance to accept him reportedly cost Marcello $10,000 per official in bribes.

Finally, at the behest of Mafia-baiting attorney general Robert F. Kennedy, the Immigration Service seized the bull by the horns. On April 4, 1961, Marcello was manacled when he arrived to make his required periodic alien's report and hustled off to Guatemala. That small nation quickly sent him to neighboring El Salvador, where soldiers held and questioned him for six days before shuttling him to Honduras. There, incredibly, Marcello and his lawyer simply boarded a commercial flight and returned illegally to New Orleans—and to business as usual.

This experience caused Marcello's already vocal hatred of the Kennedys to rise several octaves, feeding speculation that he played a key role in the 1963 assassination of President John Kennedy, and even in the 1968 murder of Robert. Conspiracy mongers point to other signs, among them Marcello's close association with Santo Trafficante, another player in the alleged plot, and the Louisiana don's supposed involvement in CIA efforts to destroy Fidel Castro. There are also claims that Marcello knew both Lee Harvey Oswald, the president's assassin, and Jack Ruby, the Dallas nightclub owner who killed Oswald.

After managing to stay free and [clear of] charge for some 43 years, in 1980 Marcell[o] was finally swept up in a federal investiga[-] tive net called Brilab, named for two thing[s] close to his heart: bribery and labor. Brila[b] was a sting operation aimed mainly at fe[r-] reting out corrupt public officials, an[d] Marcello, who could corrupt with the bes[t] of them, found himself facing charges i[n] both Louisiana and California. In April [of] 1983 the little don entered a federal pen[i-] tentiary in Texarkana, Texas, to begi[n] serving a 10-year sentence for conspiring t[o] bribe a federal judge who was about to pr[e-] side over a racketeering and extortion cas[e] involving some of Marcello's friends. (Th[e] don had been convicted in a separate tria[l] in Louisiana of bribing a state commission[-] er and a New Orleans lawyer, but the ver[-] dict was overturned on appeal in 1989[.])

Marcello served almost six years in Tex[-] arkana. In March 1989, after suffering [a] series of mild strokes, he was transferred t[o] a federal prison hospital in Rochester, Min[-] nesota. That October, the diminutive do[n] finished his prison time and was freed.

Since the aging boss's release, Louisian[a] has become even more of a mecca for or[-] ganized crime. Passage of its 1991 casin[o] law legalized a state lottery and vide[o] poker in saloons, and paved the way fo[r] gambling on riverboats and in casinos. Bu[t] as of 1992, the 82-year-old Carlos Ma[r-] cello might have been too old and ill t[o] play. "I'm retired," he told reporters afte[r] his release. "I'm happy. Everybody's bee[n] nice to me."

As for the standing deportation orde[r] against him, it may never be executed. Al[-] though the government wants him to g[o,] no other country will take him.◆

Brotherly Love

A man with the gentle air of Angelo Bruno, Philadelphia's so-called Docile Don, would not find prison much to his taste no matter what the circumstances. But when the revered 63-year-old boss was sent to New Jersey's midstate Yardville pen in 1970 for refusing to talk to the New Jersey Crime Commission, he discovered that his punishment had a cruel and unusual twist: The widely despised Nicodemo "Little Nicky" Scarfo was at his side. When fellow prisoners from the powerful New York Mafia families came by, courtesy compelled Bruno to introduce Scarfo as "a friend of ours"—Mafia code for a fellow member. A decade later, this unfortunate endorsement would turn the City of Brotherly Love into a killing field—Little Nicky's natural habitat.

Philadelphia's Mafia family had been founded by Salvatore Sabella, who arrived from Sicily in 1911 and began the usual suite of rackets: extortion, loansharking, gambling, and the like. Most of Sabella's activities were contained within the city's Little Italy until 1926, when a vicious gang war began that racked Philadelphia for a year. In 1927 Sabella was arrested after killing two rival mobsters in a gunfight. Although charges were eventually dropped, the glare of publicity revealed his high Mafia rank, and the federal government deported him to Sicily.

His successor, John Nazone Avena, crucially modified the Philadelphia Mafia by grafting it more closely to New York's powerful Cosa Nostra families after the Castellammarese War of 1930 and 1931 (*pages 73-75*). When Avena was gunned down in August 1936, one Joseph Bruno—also known as Giuseppe Dovi, and no relation to Angelo—took over for a decade before dying of natural causes. The next boss, Joe Idda, fled to Italy in 1957 after being identified as a participant in the notorious Apalachin, New York, Mafia summit meeting. He was succeeded by Antonio Pollina and a staff of lieutenants that included Angelo Bruno.

Bruno had been born in Villalba, Sicily, in 1911, and he evidently began his career of genteel criminality sometime in the 1920s. By the late 1950s, chafing under Antonio Pollina's leadership, Bruno journeyed to New York, where he received permission to kill Pollina and take his place at the top. Rather than murder the don, however, Bruno decided to topple him very gently: He merely demoted Pollina, thus ensuring a nonviolent transition of power as he took over the City of Brotherly Love and the family's modest outpost in nearby Atlantic City.

Bruno swiftly broadened the Philadelphia family's operational base, shuffling a number of legal enterprises into his illegal ones and branching out. He was good friends with New York City's Carlo Gambino, the boss of bosses, who'd helped Bruno oust Pollina. Nevertheless, while Gambino was shooting Harlem full of heroin, the Philadelphia don shunned the nasty business himself. He looked the other way—but exacted tribute—when drug traffickers sold narcotics to Philadelphia's poor. He also closed the books on further family membership, sealing the Philadelphia Mafia around a tight, traditional, and mostly Sicilian core.

Undeniably a gangster, Bruno nevertheless possessed an aura of gentility that endeared him to fellow mobsters and to Philadelphians generally. The press called him the Docile Don for his resistance to casual murder. As a youth he was trim, dapper, and charming, evoking, as one writer put it, film mobster George Raft. He was also a wonderfully musical man with a pleasing tenor, who lived with his wife and two children in a small row house in South Philadelphia. "All we do," he told reporters in 1972, fourteen years into his 22-year-reign as boss, "is let people gamble."

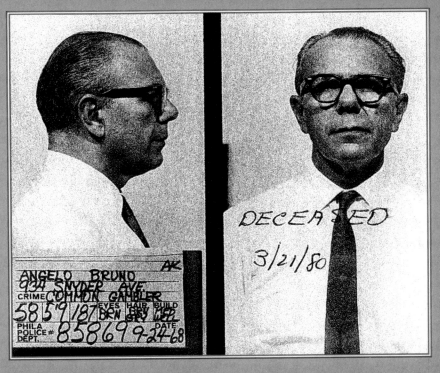

A 1968 Philadelphia police mug shot of Angelo "Docile Don" Bruno bears a final notation—the date of Bruno's assassination in March 1980.

When, in 1963, a cocky little 34-year-old hood named Nicodemo Scarfo knifed a longshoreman named Dugan in an urban eatery, Bruno bit his lip. On the one hand, he hated that kind of hotheaded instability, and he'd always detested the lowlife Scarfo. But, averse to murder in general and not wanting to risk peace by having Scarfo killed, Bruno exiled him to Atlantic City. The banishment carried with it a promotion to capo, but the territory the new boss acquired wasn't very promising: Atlantic City in those days was a quiet, shabby seaside resort, aging badly after an era of elegance in the 1920s and 1930s. It wasn't much, but Scarfo sat tight and waited for his luck to change.

Eventually, it did. With the 1977 passage of New Jersey's Casino Act, which brought immensely lucrative legal gambling to Atlantic City, Scarfo held sway over a prospective gold mine.

Predictably, the gold mine didn't escape the notice of New York's potent Gambinos and Genoveses. Bruno wisely proclaimed Atlantic City open to all comers; there was enough for everyone. But some of the younger men among his followers—including his non-Sicilian consigliere, Antonio Rocco Caponigro—thought he'd given up too much, betraying Philadelphian interests. Caponigro appealed to the Mafia's Commission in New York for permission to erase his boss, and he thought he'd received it. On March 1, 1980, the Docile Don was killed by shotgun blasts as he sat in front of his home in the passenger seat of a colleague's car. If the Commission had indeed sanctioned the hit, however, it now denied it. Caponigro and a co-conspirator, his brother-in-law Alfred Salerno, were summoned to New York and made to answer for Bruno's assassination. The two mobsters were tortured viciously before being killed.

When Philip Testa moved in as the new boss, he quickly opened the local mob to new members, most of them in their twen-

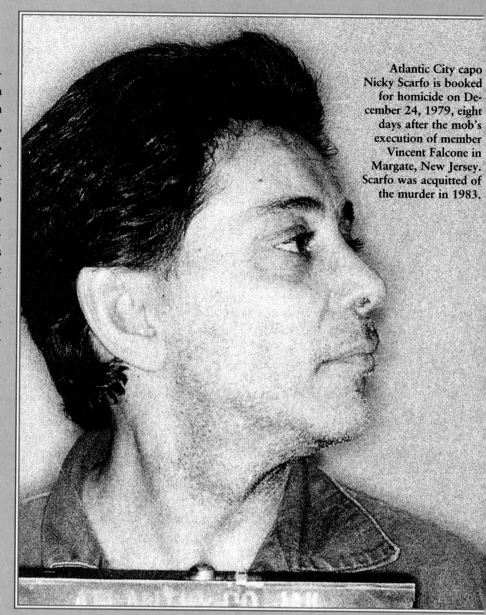

Atlantic City capo Nicky Scarfo is booked for homicide on December 24, 1979, eight days after the mob's execution of member Vincent Falcone in Margate, New Jersey. Scarfo was acquitted of the murder in 1983.

ties and thirties—inexperienced street hoods with no understanding of the venerable strands of Old World behavior with which Bruno had kept Philadelphia peaceful for more than two decades. Testa chose as underboss a favorite protégé: Little Nicky Scarfo. But Testa's reign was a short one. On March 18, 1981, he was blown up by a bomb hidden under the porch of his South Philadelphia home at the behest of two disgruntled underlings. Then the murderers were themselves quickly caught and executed, Mafia-style, and Little Nicky, faced with a power vacuum, was suddenly Philadelphia's king of crime.

Like Antonio Caponigro, Scarfo was not Sicilian but Calabrian, and his rise to pow-

er was partly the ascension of mafiosi whose roots lay in the violent toe of the Italian Boot. As Nicky Scarfo once put it, "The Calabrese are the real people. We're the real ones, we're the real gangsters, and we do our stuff."

No one ever questioned Scarfo's claim to being a real gangster. Named boss in 1981, he added to the mob rackets a shakedown called the Elbow, a tax exacted from all criminals operating on family territory, with half the proceeds funneled directly to Scarfo. Little Nicky's other innovation was more a matter of personal style: Where Bruno had tried conciliation first, Scarfo went straight to violence; murder was his preferred solution to any problem. He is

said to have been personally involved in at least 26 killings and to have ordered many more. He also has the distinction of having triggered a near fatality closer to home; in 1988 his 16-year-old son Mark hanged himself out of shame for his father. The boy suffered irreparable brain damage before being cut down.

From the outset Scarfo concentrated on eradicating survivors from Bruno's day, especially such independent-minded men as Harry "the Hunchback" Riccobene, one of the oldest mafiosi in the United States. His four-foot-eleven-inch frame tilted slightly forward by a humpback, Riccobene was 72 when Nicky Scarfo turned on him in 1982. Like Angelo Bruno, the Hunchback

had nothing but contempt for the Scarfos of the world. He told mob-busting Philadelphia detective Frank Friel that Scarfo was "a brash, violent dope. This new breed, they're not like us old guys who know what we're doin'; we took our lickin's and kept on tickin'."

Little Harry, though wounded five times, nevertheless kept on tickin' through two attempts on his life by Scarfo's killers. But the law took Riccobene out of Scarfo's range, first to serve a nine-year prison term for gambling, then, in 1984, a life sentence for the murder of Nicky's underboss, Frank Monte. Although Riccobene survived, Scarfo managed to kill many of the old men who had been with Bruno, includ-

ing the courtly Frank D'Alfonso—Frankie Flowers—gunned down in July 1985 while walking his dog.

The murderous Scarfo now began to have legal troubles of his own, beginning with prosecutorial assaults on some of his satellites. Michael Matthews, the mob-run mayor of Atlantic City, went to jail in 1984 after accepting an extortion payment from an FBI undercover agent. In January 1985, Frank Lentino, organizer of the Atlantic City local of the bartenders' union, got a 10-year sentence for his part in the conspiracy. Finally, in June 1986, the Scarfo family made its crucial misstep. When it attempted to extort a million dollars from Philadelphia developer Willard G. Rouse, the intended victim went straight to the FBI, which assigned an undercover agent to act as Rouse's representative in subsequent dealings. Scarfo's man became a government witness.

At the same time, Scarfo evidently developed some mental problems. Blinded by rabid suspicions and imagined injuries, he became unable to distinguish loyal followers from turncoats. He began killing the loyalists. Men who'd made their living frightening others now found themselves terrified of their homicidal boss, and they sought the only available safety: They became informers for the police.

The combined effects of Scarfo's paranoia and incursions by the law were devastating to the mob. Two years after the attempt to shake down Willard Rouse, Little Nicky and 16 family members were convicted on federal racketeering charges under the RICO statute. Scarfo drew 15 years. He was then tried for killing Frank D'Alfonso.

Just 10 years earlier, peering into the bloody face of a murdered rival, Scarfo had confided to his comrades, "I love this. I love it." In April 1989 Little Nicky went to prison for life for that pleasure, becoming the first Mafia boss ever jailed for first-degree murder. ◆

MICHAEL FRANZESE

Upward Mobility

When he signed on with New York's Colombo crime family in 1975, Michael Franzese saw himself as something different, perhaps even as a model for the Mafia's future. He had three years of college, was deft in financial matters, and relied on charm rather than force to get deals done. He claimed that for him, the traditional Mafia entrance requirement—committing a murder—had been waived. It wasn't that he disdained the older ways: Michael was very fond of his stepfather, Sonny Franzese, a Colombo-family enforcer linked by police to scores of killings, and admired the way Sonny's power persisted even during prison stints. (The body of a man who began seeing Sonny's wife after the enforcer went to jail was discovered with its severed genitals stuffed into its mouth.) While this violent legacy didn't revolt Michael, white-collar crime seemed to him a field more suited to his particular gifts.

The personable young capo was good at this gentler brand of theft. In one exemplary venture, he paid construction-union bosses $400,000 to stay away from a condominium project. This saved the developers about $8 million in labor costs—and young Franzese received a $2 million fee for "general contracting." In another illegal deal, he and the president of a union for security guards siphoned $500,000 from the members' health-and-welfare fund.

Franzese's most ambitious operation was designed to help service stations in the New York City area escape the payment of gasoline taxes. The scheme relied on a multilayered edifice of dummy companies that supposedly sold gasoline wholesale, and it worked beautifully for a while. By the time he turned 33, Franzese was one of the Mafia's biggest moneymakers, bringing in millions of dollars each week. Although most of it went to the Colombo family, his personal share may have reached $25 million.

Yuppie mafioso Michael Franzese cuddles future bride Camille Garcia *(below)* during a break in shooting his B-movie *Knights of the City* in 1984. Two years later, Franzese *(opposite)* operates from a bleak interview room in a Los Angeles federal prison, where he was serving a 10-year sentence for racketeering.

He spent some of it making B-grade movies in Los Angeles and Miami.

Unfortunately for the smooth young entrepreneur, federal investigators managed to unravel the secrets of the gasoline game. In 1985 Franzese was charged with racketeering; he pleaded guilty and received a sentence of 10 years. As part of his plea bargain, he agreed to make restitution of $15 million, presumably from his investments in movies and real estate. After only three years in prison, he won early release, having agreed to help the authorities in their investigation of other crime figures. He even wrote a book, *Quitting the Mob:*

How the Yuppie Don Quit the Mob and Lived to Tell All, a confessional work laced with regrets for his past life. In 1989 he was baptized as a born-again Christian.

Observers of the reformed don soon had reason to doubt the depth of his spiritual rebirth. Although he testified against two former confederates, neither was in the mob; what he told investigators in private was unknown, but it probably wasn't much, since he was still alive. Nor did he pay any of the promised $15 million in restitution, even though authorities suspected that he had millions stashed away. As for going straight, it became clear that the new

Michael Franzese differed little, if at all, from the old one. In late 1991 he was arrested in Los Angeles for fraud: He'd used faked collateral to obtain bank loans, and he'd also bilked landlords on properties that he had rented. As one prosecutor observed wryly, the likes of Michael Franzese are incapable of going through a day without committing a crime.

Admitting to two probation violations—writing a bad check and failing to file income tax returns for two of his prison years—the Yuppie Don was returned to prison in 1991 to serve four more years of his 10-year term. ◆

Acknowledgments

The editors thank the following individuals and institutions for their valuable assistance in the preparation of this volume:

Letizia Battaglia, Palermo, Italy; Daniele Billitteri, Palermo, Italy; G. Robert Blakey, Notre Dame Law School, Notre Dame, Ind.; Elisabetta Brai, Palermo, Italy; Alessandro Fucarini, Palermo, Italy; Judith Harris, Rome; Karen Kinney, U.S. Attorney's Office, Eastern District, Office of Organized Crime and Racketeering, Brooklyn, N.Y.; Nino Labruzzo, Palermo, Italy; Frederick T. Martens, Executive Director, Pennsylvania Crime Commission, Conshohocken; Giorgio Mulé, Palermo, Italy; Joseph O'Brien, New York, N.Y.; Paulo Pignatelli, Litchfield, Conn.; Isabelle Sauvé-Astruc, Musée des Collections Historiques de la Préfecture de Police, Paris, France; Nicola Scafidi, Palermo, Italy; Ernest Volkman, Danbury, Conn.; Franco Zecchin, Palermo, Italy.

Bibliography

Books:

Abadinsky, Howard, *Organized Crime.* Chicago: Nelson-Hall, 1985.

Albanese, Jay, *Organized Crime in America.* Cincinnati: Anderson, 1985.

Arlacchi, Pino, *Mafia Business: The Mafia Ethic and the Spirit of Capitalism.* Transl. by Martin Ryle. London: Verso, 1987.

Baiamonte, John V., Jr., *Spirit of Vengeance: Nativism and Louisiana Justice, 1921-1924.* Baton Rouge: Louisiana State University Press, 1986.

Balsamo, William, and George Carpozi, Jr., *Under the Clock: The Inside Story of the Mafia's First Hundred Years.* Far Hills, N.J.: New Horizon Press, 1988.

Blok, Anton, *The Mafia of a Sicilian Village, 1860-1960.* New York: Harper & Row, 1975.

Bonanno, Joseph, with Sergio Lalli, *A Man of Honor: The Autobiography of Joseph Bonanno.* New York: Simon and Schuster, 1983.

Brashler, William, *The Don: The Life and Death of Sam Giancana.* New York: Harper & Row, 1977.

Cantalupo, Joseph, and Thomas C. Renner, *Body Mike: An Unsparing Exposé by the Mafia Insider Who Turned on the Mob.* New York: Villard Books, 1990.

Chandler, David Leon, *Brothers in Blood: The Rise of the Criminal Brotherhoods.* New York: E. P. Dutton, 1975.

Cressey, Donald R., *Theft of the Nation: The Structure and Operations of Organized Crime in America.* New York: Harper & Row, 1969.

Cummings, John, and Ernest Volkman, *Goombata: The Improbable Rise and Fall of John Gotti and His Gang.* Boston: Little, Brown, 1990.

Davis, John H., *Mafia Kingfish: Carlos Marcello and the Assassination of John F. Kennedy.* New York: McGraw-Hill, 1989.

Dolci, Danilo, *Waste: An Eye-Witness Report on Some Aspects of Waste in Western Sicily.* Transl. by R. Munroe. New York: Monthly Review Press, 1964.

Fox, Stephen, *Blood and Power: Organized Crime in Twentieth-Century America.* New York: William Morrow, 1989.

Friel, Frank, and John Guinther, *Breaking the Mob.* New York: Warner Books, 1992.

Gage, Nicholas, *The Mafia Is Not an Equal Opportunity Employer.* New York: McGraw-Hill, 1971.

Gage, Nicholas, ed., *Mafia, U.S.A.* New York: Dell, 1972.

Gentry, Curt, *J. Edgar Hoover: The Man and the Secrets.* New York: W. W. Norton, 1991.

Giancana, Antoinette, and Thomas C. Renner, *Mafia Princess: Growing Up in Sam Giancana's Family.* New York: William Morrow, 1984.

Giancana, Sam, and Chuck Giancana, *Double Cross: The Explosive, Inside Story of the Mobster Who Controlled America.* New York: Warner Books, 1992.

Goode, James, *Wiretap.* New York: Simon & Schuster, 1988.

Gosch, Martin A., and Richard Hammer, *The Last Testament of Lucky Luciano.* Boston: Little, Brown, 1975.

Hess, Henner, *Mafia and Mafiosi: The Structure of Power.* Transl. by Ewald Osers. Lexington, Mass.: Lexington Books, 1973.

Hobsbawm, E. J., *Primitive Rebels: Studies in Archaic Forms of Social Movement in the 19th and 20th Centuries.* New York: Frederick A. Praeger, 1959.

Ianni, Francis A. J., with Elizabeth Reuss-Ianni, *A Family Business: Kinship and Social Control in Organized Crime.* New York: Russell Sage, 1972.

Lacey, Robert, *Little Man: Meyer Lansky and the Gangster Life.* Boston: Little, Brown, 1991.

Landesco, John, *The Illinois Crime Survey.* Part 3 of *Organized Crime in Chicago.* Chicago: The University of Chicago Press, 1929.

Lewis, Norman, *The Honored Society: A Searching Look at the Mafia.* New York: G. P. Putnam's Sons, 1964.

Maas, Peter, *The Valachi Papers.* New York: Bantam Books, 1968.

McClellan, John L., *Crime without Punishment.* New York: Duell, Sloan & Pearce, 1962.

Moldea, Dan, *The Hoffa Wars.* New York: Paddington Press, 1978.

Moore, William Howard, *The Kefauver Committee and the Politics of Crime, 1950-1952.* Columbia: University of Missouri Press, 1974.

Mustain, Gene, and Jerry Capeci, *Mob Star: The Story of John Gotti.* New York: Dell, 1988.

Nelli, Humbert S., *The Business of Crime.* New York: Oxford University Press, 1976.

O'Brien, Joseph F., and Andris Kurins, *Boss of Bosses: The Fall of the Godfather—The FBI and Paul Castellano.* London: Simon & Schuster, 1991.

O'Neill, Gerard, and Dick Lehr, *The Underboss: The Rise and Fall of a Mafia Family.* New York: St. Martin's Press, 1989.

Pantaleone, Michele, *Mafia e Politica.* Turin, Italy: Einaudi, 1972.

Petacco, Arrigo, *Joe Petrosino.* Transl.

by Charles Lam Markmann. New York: Macmillan, 1974.

Peterson, Virgil W., *The Mob: 200 Years of Organized Crime in New York*. Ottawa, Ill.: Green Hill, 1983.

Pitkin, Thomas Monroe, and Francesco Cordasco, *The Black Hand: A Chapter in Ethnic Crime*. Totowa, N.J.: Littlefield, Adams, 1977.

Reid, Ed, *The Grim Reapers*. Chicago: Henry Regnery, 1969.

Roemer, William F., Jr.:
Roemer: Man against the Mob. New York: Ballantine Books, 1989.
War of the Godfathers: The Bloody Confrontation between the Chicago and New York Families for Control of Las Vegas. New York: Donald I. Fine, 1990.

Salerno, Ralph, and John S. Tompkins, *The Crime Confederation*. Garden City, N.Y.: Doubleday, 1969.

Schlesinger, Arthur M., Jr., *Robert Kennedy and His Times*. Boston: Houghton Mifflin, 1978.

Schneider, Jane, and Peter Schneider, *Culture and Political Economy in Western Sicily*. New York: Academic Press, 1976.

Selvaggi, Giuseppe, *The Rise of the Mafia in New York from 1896 through World War II*. Transl. and ed. by William A. Packer. Indianapolis: Bobbs-Merrill, 1978.

Servadio, Gaia, *Mafioso: A History of the Mafia from Its Origins to the Present Day*. New York: Stein and Day, 1976.

Sifakis, Carl, *The Mafia Encyclopedia*. New York: Facts on File, 1987.

Sondern, Frederic, Jr., *Brotherhood of Evil: The Mafia*. New York: Farrar, Straus and Cudahy, 1959.

Sterling, Claire, *Octopus: The Long Reach of the International Sicilian Mafia*. New York: Simon & Schuster, 1990.

Talese, Gay, *Honor Thy Father*. New York: World, 1971.

Teresa, Vincent, with Thomas C. Renner, *Vinnie Teresa's Mafia*. Garden City, N.Y.: Doubleday, 1975.

Thernston, Stephan, ed., *Harvard Encyclopedia of American Ethnic Groups*. Cambridge, Mass.: Harvard University Press, 1981.

Thompson, Craig, and Allen Raymond, *Gang Rule in New York*. New York: Dial Press, 1940.

Wolf, George, with Joseph DiMona, *Frank Costello: Prime Minister of the Underworld*. New York: William Morrow, 1974.

Periodicals:
"Abscam." *Time*, Feb. 25, 1980.

"Al Capone." *Murder Casebook*, Vol. 4, Part 51.

"America's King of Crime." *Murder Casebook*, Vol. 2, Part 22.

Barnes, Edward, and William Shebar, "Quitting the Mafia." *Life*, Dec. 1987.

Beck, Melinda, and Dan Shapiro, "Death of a Godfather." *Newsweek*, July 23, 1979.

Behar, Richard:
"A Gang That Still Can't Shoot Straight." *Time*, Jan. 20, 1992.
"An Offer They Can't Refuse." *Time*, Sept. 25, 1991.
"The Underworld Is Their Oyster." *Time*, Sept. 3, 1990.

Berger, Joseph, "Raymond Patriarca, 76, Dies; New England Crime Figure." *New York Times*, July 12, 1984.

"Boiardo Cut from Trial." *Daily News*, Feb. 12, 1980.

Bowles, Pete, "A Quiet Gotti Sentenced to Life in Prison." *Newsday*, June 24, 1992.

Brennan, Ray, "Hole in the Ground Gives Accardo Security on a Cash Basis." *Chicago Sun-Times*, July 12, 1958.

"The Brilab Sting Hits a Mafia Don." *Newsweek*, June 30, 1980.

Cannizaro, Steve:
"Marcello Attends Meeting with U.S. Probation Officials." *New Orleans Times Picayune*, Oct. 24, 1989.
"Marcello Prepares for New Life Outside as Prison Term Ends." *New Orleans Times Picayune*, Oct. 15, 1989.
"Marcello Suffers Strokes in Prison." *New Orleans Times Picayune*, Mar. 14, 1989.

Cannizaro, Steve, and Ed Anderson, "Brilab Convictions Overturned." *New Orleans Times Picayune*, June 24, 1989.

Capeci, Jerry, "Still All in the Family." *Daily News*, June 24, 1992.

"Capone Heir Held as Tax Gyp." *New York Mirror*, Apr. 27, 1960.

Carillo, Charles, Karen Phillips, and Mike Hurewitz, "What a Wild and Crazy Way to Start a Sentence." *New York Post*, June 24, 1992.

"Carlos Marcello: King Thug of Louisiana." *Life*, Sept. 8, 1967.

Carpenter, Teresa, book review of *The Pizza Connection* by Shana Alexander. *New York Times*, Sept. 11, 1988.

"The Conglomerate of Crime." *Time*, Aug. 22, 1969.

Cook, Fred J., "The People v. the Mob; Or, Who Rules New Jersey?" *New York Times Magazine*, Feb. 1, 1970.

Cortesi, Arnaldo:
"Bandit Guiliano Is Slain in Sicily; Killer of 100 Falls with Gun Ablaze." *New York Times*, July 6, 1950.
"Italy Gives Bonus in Fight on Bandit." *New York Times*, Sept. 7, 1949.

"A Courtroom Battle of Wits." *New York Times*, Dec. 3, 1989.

Cowell, Alan, "Anti-Mafia Dragnet Catches 75 in Italy." *International Herald Tribune*, Nov. 18, 1992.

Coxe, John E., "The New Orleans Mafia Incident." *Louisiana Historical Quarterly*, Oct. 1937.

"Death in the Afternoon." *Time*, July 23, 1979.

DeMott, John S., "The 'Dapper Don' Beats a Rap." *Time*, Mar. 23, 1987.

"Died: Joseph Zerilli." *Time*, Nov. 14, 1977.

"Died: Raymond Patriarca." *Time*, July 23, 1984.

Donovan, Jeffrey, "Mafia." *Catholic World Report*, Mar. 1992.

Doty, Robert C., "Sicilian Mafia Moving from Crime into Business and Politics." *New York Times*, Apr. 25, 1967.

"Eight-Horse Salute for Lucky Luciano." *Life*, Feb. 9, 1962.

Endean, Chris, "The Mafia 'Winning the War.'" *The European*, May 31, 1992.

Farrell, Nicholas, " 'The Mafia Must Die. . .' " *Sunday Telegraph*, May 31, 1992.

Faso, Frank, and Henry Lee, "Tapes Begin to Unravel the Strollo Mystery." *Daily News*, Jan. 10, 1970.

Ford, Andrea, "Ex-Captain for Mob

Seized in L.A. on Fraud Charges."
Los Angeles Times, Nov. 15, 1991.

Fox, Robert, "Dishonoured Society:
The Assassination of the Scourge of the
Mafia, Judge Giovanni Falcone, Was a
Telling Blow Against Law and Order—
and the Very Stability of Italy." *Sunday
Telegraph,* May 31, 1992.

Franks, Lucinda, "An Obscure Gangster Is Emerging as the Mafia Chieftain in New York." *New York Times,*
Feb. 20, 1977.

Franzese, Michael, and Dary Matera,
"Quitting the Mob: How the 'Yuppie
Don' Left the Mafia and Lived to Tell
All." *Publishers Weekly,* Dec. 6,
1991.

Frost, Ed, "The Life and Crimes of
'Sammy Bull' Gravano." *Crime Beat,*
June 1992.

Gage, Nicholas, "Key Theory in Hoffa
Case Is Still Lacking Evidence." *New
York Times,* Nov. 26, 1975.

"Giuseppe Genco Russo, 80, Dies: One
of Last Sicily Mafia Chiefs." *New
York Times,* Mar. 19, 1976.

"A Godfather's Fall: Mob under Fire."
Newsweek, Dec. 30, 1985.

"The Gotti Papers." *New York Post,*
May 19, 1986.

"The Great Mafia Roundup." *U.S.
News and World Report,* Apr. 16,
1990.

Greene, Robert W., ed., "The Mob on
Trial." *Newsday,* 1989.

Gross, Ken, "Cold-Blooded King of a
Hill under Siege." *People,* Mar. 27,
1989.

Harris, Leonard, "Cop Who Battled
Mafia." *New York World-Telegram,*
May 27, 1960.

Hinckle, Pia, "The Grip of the Octopus: Will the Assassination of a Revered Anti-Mafia Crusader Inspire
Italy to Stand Up to the Mob?"
Newsweek, June 8, 1992.

"Hitting the Mafia." *Time,* Sept. 29,
1986.

Holland, Beth, and Patricia Hurtado,
"Crowd Storms Courthouse." *Newsday,* June 24, 1992.

"Hoodlum of Distinction: Anthony Joseph Accardo." *New York Times,*
July 12, 1958.

"How the Mafia Began and the Current Battle to Destroy It." *Life,*
Mar. 1985.

"Italy's Mafia Roundup Rips Cosa
Nostra." *New York Daily News,*
Aug. 3, 1965.

"Joseph Zerilli, 79; Detroit Mafia
Boss." *New York Times,* Nov. 1,
1977.

Kahn, Toby, "Passages." *People,* June
15, 1992.

Kaufman, Michael J., "Boiardo's
Daughter Killed while Cleaning a
Window." *New York Times,* Oct. 19,
1973.

Kelley, Kitty, "The Dark Side of Cam-
elot: John Kennedy's Former Lover
Judith Campbell Exner Tells at Last
of Being the President's Courier to the
Mob." *People,* Feb. 29, 1988.

Kempton, Murray, "Friends until the
Final Act." *Newsday,* June 24, 1992.

Kendall, John S., "Who Killa de
Chief?" *Louisiana Historical Quarterly,* Apr. 1939.

Kim, Rose, " 'It Was Unjust': Gotti
Neighbors Rap Verdict, Sentence."
Newsday, June 24, 1992.

Lacayo, Richard, "Why Is 'Sammy the
Bull' Singing?" *Time,* Mar. 16, 1992.

"Law Enforcement's Attack on Organized Crime." *Newsday,* Sept. 12,
1986.

"Life." *New York Post,* June 24, 1992.

"The Life and Times of John Gotti."
Daily News, June 24, 1992.

Lister, Walter, Jr., "Accardo, 'Heir' to
Capone, Arrested in Tax Evasion."
New York Herald Tribune, Apr. 27,
1960.

"The Little Fellow." *New York Post,*
Mar. 28, 1939.

Lubasch, Arnold H.:
"Agent Tells about Tension in Bo-
nanno Group." *New York Times,*
Feb. 9, 1986.
"Defendant Takes Stand in 'Pizza
Connection' Trial." *New York Times,*
Oct. 15, 1986.
"Ex-Mafia Chief Focus of Tapes at
'Pizza' Trial." *New York Times,* July
18, 1986.
"Informer Is Questioned on Key 'Piz-
za' Defendant." *New York Times,*
Nov. 14, 1985.
"Key Defendant in 'Pizza' Trial Is
Tied to Mob." *New York Times,* Jan.
29, 1986.
"Mafia Member Testifies on Sicily
'Commission.' " *New York Times,*

Nov. 1, 1985.
"Major U.S. Narcotics Trial Involving
the Mafia to Open at Foley Sq." *New
York Times,* Sept. 29, 1985.
"Mobster Sentenced in Probation Violation." *New York Times,* Dec. 28,
1991.
"U.S. Says Mob Gained Grip of Window Trade." *New York Times,* Apr.
21, 1991.

"Lucky Luciano: America's King of
Crime." *Murder Casebook,* Vol. 2,
Part 22.

McAlary, Mike, "Mobster Is America's
Own Citizen Bane." *New York Post,*
June 24, 1992.

McClellan, George B., "The Terror of
the Camorra." *Cosmopolitan,* Aug.
1911.

McNamara, Joseph, "The Finest of the
Finest." *New York Daily News,* July
22, 1984.

"The Mafia: Back to the Bad Old
Days?" *Time,* July 12, 1971.

"Mafia—Chicago Style." *New York
Daily News,* June 26, 1960.

"Mafia on Trial." *Time,* Sept. 29,
1986.

Magnuson, Ed:
"The Assassination: Did the Mob Kill
J.F.K?" *Time,* Nov. 28, 1988.
"Hitting the Mafia." *Time,* Sept. 29,
1986.
"The Mafia's Murderous Code."
Time, Nov. 11, 1985.

"Manners & Morals: 'I Never Sold
Any Bibles.' " *Time,* Nov. 28, 1949.

Marzulli, John, "Gotti's Blowout Still
on for 4th." *Daily News,* June 24,
1992.

Meskil, Paul, "Mobster Galente Seized
in N.J. Trap." *New York World-
Telegram,* June 3, 1959.

Michelini, Alex, "Shelve N.J. Chief in
Mobster Payoff." *New York Daily
News,* Feb. 28, 1970.

"The Mob: Empire of Organized
Crime, Its Power Structure, Tactics,"
with reports by Sandy Smith. *Life,*
Part I, Sept. 1, 1967; Part II, Sept. 8,
1967.

Moody, John, "Getting Away with
Murder." *Time,* Aug. 3, 1992.

Mustain, Gene, and Jerry Capeci:
"Gets Life; Pals Riot Outside." *Daily
News,* June 24, 1992.
"Themes, Schemes on Judgment

Day." *Daily News,* June 24, 1992.

Newton, Jim, "Fate of a Jailed Mobster: Films, Fortune or a Bullet?" *Los Angeles Times,* Apr. 6, 1992.

"A Night for Colombo." *Time,* Apr. 5, 1971.

"N. O. Gaming Opens Door, Police Say." *New Orleans Times Picayune,* June 11, 1992.

Pelleck, Carl J., Cy Egan, and Anne E. Murray, "Mob Rivals OKd Hit on 'Big Paul.'" *New York Post,* Dec. 18, 1985.

Persico, Joseph E., "Vendetta in New Orleans." *American Heritage,* June 1973.

Phillips, Karen, with Don Broderick and Marvin Smilon, "Joking Don Finally Shuts Up but 'Mob' Outside Court Gets Violent." *New York Post,* June 24, 1992.

Pileggi, Nicholas, "The Decline and Fall of the Mafia." *Life,* Mar. 3, 1972.

"Pizza Penance: A Jury Convicts 18 Mobsters." *Time,* Mar. 16, 1987.

"Police Indicted in Bribe." *New York Times,* Mar. 18, 1970.

"Public Relations: A Night for Colombo." *Time,* Apr. 5, 1971.

Quinn, Marvin, "Old Man in a Chair: Johnny Torrio, Founder of Capone Dynasty, Dead." *Chicago Sun-Times,* May 8, 1957.

Raab, Selwyn:

"A Battered and Ailing Mafia Is Losing Its Grip on America." *New York Times,* Oct. 22, 1990.

"Experts Assess Mental Fitness of a Defendant." *New York Times,* Mar. 12, 1991.

"Galante's Image Belied Role He Played in Life." *New York Times,* July 13, 1979.

"Gotti Not Guilty on All 6 Assault Charges in Assault Trial." *New York Times,* Feb. 10, 1990.

"How Gotti's No. 2 Gangster Turned His Coat." *New York Times,* Nov. 15, 1991.

"Running the Mob." *New York Times Magazine,* Apr. 2, 1989.

"Strange Old Man on Sullivan St.: A New Mob Power." *New York Times,* Feb. 3, 1988.

"What's Ahead in '87: Family Quarrels." *New York Times,* Dec. 29, 1986.

Raab, Selwyn, with Joseph A. Cincotti, "With Growing Reputation, Gotti's Swagger Is Bolder." *New York Times,* Oct. 27, 1987.

"Respectability and Crime: Private Life and Violent Death of Paul Castellano." *New York Times,* Dec. 18, 1985.

Reston, James, Jr., "The Assassination: Was Connally the Real Target?" *Time,* Nov. 28, 1988.

Rhoden, Robert, and Steve Cannizaro, "Marcello Freed, Welcomed Home." *New Orleans Times Picayune,* Oct. 21, 1989.

Richards, Charles:

"He Was Single Greatest Threat to Cosa Nostra." *The Independent,* May 25, 1992.

"Mafia Adds to Italy's Despair." *The Independent,* May 25, 1992.

"Murder Concentrates Political Minds." *The Independent,* May 25, 1992.

"Palermo Mourns as Mafia Kills Its Bravest Son." *The Independent,* May 25, 1992.

Riesel, Victor, "Mob Played It Cool Down in Hot Springs." *New York Mirror,* Mar. 7, 1961.

"Rivals Ordered Big Paul's Death." *New York Post,* Dec. 18, 1985.

Rowan, Roy, "The Biggest Mafia Bosses." *Fortune,* Nov. 30, 1986.

Rudy, William H., *New York Post,* Nov. 13, 1960.

"Santo Trafficante, Reputed Mafia Chief, Dies at 72." *New York Times,* Mar. 19, 1987.

Saunders, D. J., and Frank Lombardi, "Courts Will Be Mobbed." *Daily News,* Sept. 29, 1985.

Secchia, Peter, "The Assassination of Giovanni Falcone." *Washington Post,* July 7, 1992.

Serao, Ernesto, "The Truth about the Camorra." *Outlook,* July 29-Aug. 5, 1911.

"Shot by Shot, an Ex-Aide to Gotti Describes the Killing of Castellano." *New York Times,* Mar. 4, 1992.

"Sicily's Favorite Outlaw." *Life,* Mar. 1985.

Simons, Mary, and Daniele Billitteri, "A Wounded Mafia: The Latest Chapter in a Long and Bloody History." *Life,* Mar. 1985.

Smith, Sandy, "The Fix." *Life,* Sept. 1, 1967.

Stasi, Linda, "Gotti Tells His Family: 'Don't Worry.'" *Newsday,* June 24, 1992.

Steele, Jack, "Tax Laws Help Trap Top Hoods." *New York World-Telegram,* May 22, 1961.

Stone, Michael, "After Gotti." *New York,* Feb. 3, 1992.

Thomas, Jo, "Simple Funeral Marks End of a Detroit Crime Boss." *New York Times,* Nov. 4, 1977.

"Tony Accardo Arrested by U.S. on 3-Year Income-Tax Charge." *New York Times,* Apr. 26, 1960.

"Trial and Terror: A Victim's Memory Is Mugged." *Time,* Apr. 7, 1986.

"Unlucky at Last." *Newsweek,* Feb. 5, 1962.

"The U.S. Gets a Close Look at Crime." *Life,* Mar. 26, 1951.

Weiss, Murray, "It's Gonna Be a Donnybrook." *New York Post,* June 24, 1992.

"Who's a Liar?" *Life,* Apr. 2, 1951.

"Why Lillo Is Lying Low." *Time,* Nov. 13, 1978.

Woodsworth, Charles J. "Sicily's Mythical Robin Hood." *Evening Citizen,* Sept. 7, 1950.

Other Sources:

Carroll, Ralph Edward, Jr., *The Mafia in New Orleans, 1900-1907.* New Orleans: Notre Dame Seminary, June 1956.

Carroll, Richard Louis, *The Impact of David C. Hennessey on New Orleans Society and the Consequences of the Assassination of Hennessey.* New Orleans: Notre Dame Seminary, June 1957.

Duggan, Christopher, *The Sicilian Origins of the Mafia.* London: The Centre for Security and Conflict Studies, Sept. 1987.

Organized Crime: 25 Years After Valachi. Hearings before the Permanent Subcommittee on Investigations of the Committee on Governmental Affairs United States Senate. Washington, D.C.: U.S. Government Printing Office, Apr. 11, 15, 22, 29, 1988.

Organized Crime in America. Hearings before the Committee on the Judiciary, United States Senate. Washington, D.C.: U.S. Government Printing Office, Jan. 27, Feb. 16, Mar. 2 and 3, 1983.

Organized Crime in Pennsylvania: A Decade of Change, 1990 Report. Pennsylvania Crime Commission. Conshohocken: Printed in the Commonwealth of Pennsylvania, 1990.

Series of 16 reports written by Daniele Billitteri for *Life* magazine when the magazine was preparing a story on the Mafia in 1984-1985. The reports date from Nov. 19, 1984-Jan. 17, 1985.

U.S. Department of Justice, Federal Bureau of Investigation, "Arrest of Phillip Rizzuto" (news release). New Orleans, Aug. 5, 1981.

"Wanted by the FBI: The Mob." FBI Organized Crime Report—25 Years After Valachi, U.S. Department of Justice, Federal Bureau of Investigation.

Television/Video:

Assignment. BBC-TV (London), July 7, 1992.

JFK, Hoffa and the Mob. A Stuart Television Production for *Frontline*, Nov. 1992.

"The Last Godfather: The Rise and Fall of John Gotti." Fox News Special, STF Productions, 1992.

Mob Wars. A BBC TV Production in Association with CBS Broadcast International. Lionheart Television.

"The Rise & Fall of a Godfather." Thames Television Production for ITV, 1992.

Index

Numerals in italics indicate an illustration of the subject.

Picture Credits

The sources for the illustrations that appear in this book are listed below. Credits from left to right are separated by semicolons, from top to bottom by dashes.

Cover: AP/Wide World Photos, New York. **4, 5:** Publifoto, Palermo. **6:** Franco Zecchin, Palermo. **8:** Mapping Specialists, Ltd., Madison, Wis. **10:** Enzo Brai, Publifoto, Palermo. **13:** Publifoto, Palermo. **15:** Archivio Storico Nicola Scafidi, Palermo. **16:** Publifoto, Palermo. **19:** Archivio Storico Nicola Scafidi, Palermo. **21:** Italy's News Photo's, Rome; Labruzzo, Palermo. **23:** Labruzzo, Palermo. **25:** Archivio Storico Nicola Scafidi, Palermo. **26, 27:** AP/Wide World Photos, New York; Labruzzo, Palermo. **30, 31:** Franco Zecchin, Palermo. **33:** Labruzzo, Palermo. **34:** Roberto Koch/Contrasto, Rome. **36, 37:** Publifoto, Palermo, insets, Augusto Casasoli/Team, Rome; Antonio Scatolon/Team, Rome; Labruzzo, Palermo. **38:** AP/Wide World Photos, New York. **40, 41:** Mulberry Bend, circa 1888, The Jacob A. Riis Collection, #114, Museum of the City of New York; The Bettmann Archive, New York. **42:** Archivio Storico Nicola Scafidi, Palermo. **45:** Culver Pictures, New York. **46-48:** Library of Congress LC300130. **49:** Frank Wood's Picture Bank, Alexandria, Va. **50, 51:** Frank Wood's Picture Bank, Alexandria, Va.; Library of Congress. **52, 53:** The Bettmann Archive, New York. **54, 55:** UPI/Bettmann, New York. **56:** Publifoto, Palermo. **57-59:** Archivio Storico Nicola Scafidi, Palermo. **60:** Popperfoto, Overstone, Northamptonshire, England. **64, 65:** Collections of the Municipal Archives of the City of New York (3)—bottom left, *The Miami Herald,* Miami. **66:** The Bettmann Archive, New York. **67-70:** AP/Wide World Photos, New York. **71:** UPI/Bettmann, New York. **72, 73:** The Bettmann Archive, New York. **74-81:** UPI/Bettmann, New York. **82, 83:** UPI/Bettmann, New York (2); AP/Wide World Photos, New York. **85:** Private Collection. **86-89:** UPI/Bettmann, New York. **90:** UPI/Bettmann, New York—National Archives # 306-NT-889E. **92-96:** AP/Wide World Photos, New York. **98, 99:** Michael Rougier for LIFE. **100:** AP/Wide World Photos, New York. **101:** New York City Municipal Archives, New York. **102, 103:** UPI/Bettmann, New York. **104-107:** AP/Wide World Photos, New York. **108, 109:** UPI/Bettmann, New York, insets, AP/Wide World Photos, New York (2); Ralph Morse. **110:** Photo. No. 443 in the John F. Kennedy Library, Boston. **111, 112:** AP/Wide World Photos, New York. **113:** Courtesy Time Magazines Picture Collection. **114:** AP/Wide World Photos, New York. **116, 117:** UPI/Bettmann, New York. **119:** AP/Wide World Photos, New York. **120:** Bill Bridges for LIFE. **122, 123:** AP/Wide World Photos, New York. **125:** UPI/Bettmann, New York. **126:** AP/Wide World Photos, New York. **128, 129:** Tom Monaster/New York *Daily News,* New York, insets, Henry Groskinsky, courtesy Private Collection, EDNY. **131:** Tom Monaster/New York *Daily News* Photo, New York. **132, 133:** Henry Groskinsky, courtesy Private Collection, EDNY; courtesy Joe O'Brien and Andris Kurins, authors of *Boss of Bosses.* **135:** Henry Groskinsky, courtesy Private Collection, EDNY. **137:** Photocopy by Yvonne Hemsey/Gamma-Liaison, New York. **138, 139:** Henry Groskinsky, courtesy Private Collection, EDNY. **140:** New York *Daily News,* New York. **141:** Carmine Donofrio/New York *Daily News* Photo, New York. **142:** AP/Wide World Photos, New York. **145:** Private collection. **146, 147:** Marina Garnier, insets, Pennsylvania Crime Commission, Conshohocken, Pa.—Mary McLoughlin/*New York Post,* New York. **148:** New York *Daily News* Photo, New York. **149:** UPI/Bettmann, New York. **151:** UPI/Bettmann, New York, inset, AP/Wide World Photos, New York. **152-155:** Henry Groskinsky, courtesy Private Collection, EDNY. **157:** AP/Wide World Photos, New York. **159:** Enrico Ferorelli, **161, 162:** UPI/Bettmann, New York. **163:** AP/Wide World Photos, New York. **164, 165:** UPI/Bettmann, New York. **167:** Bob Gomel for LIFE. **168:** UPI/Bettmann, New York. **169:** AP/Wide World Photos, New York. **170:** UPI/Bettmann, New York. **171:** AP/Wide World Photos, New York. **172, 173:** UPI/Bettmann, New York. **174-177:** AP/Wide World Photos, New York. **179-181:** Pennsylvania Crime Commission, Conshohocken, Pa. **182:** Alex Webb/Magnum, New York. **183:** Courtesy Time Magazines Picture Collection.

Time-Life Books

EDITOR-IN-CHIEF: Thomas H. Flaherty

Director of Editorial Resources:
Elise D. Ritter-Clough
Executive Art Director: Ellen Robling
Director of Photography and Research:
John Conrad Weiser
Editorial Board: Dale M. Brown, Janet Cave,
Roberta Conlan, Robert Doyle, Laura Foreman,
Jim Hicks, Rita Thievon Mullin, Henry
Woodhead
Assistant Director of Editorial Resources:
Norma E. Shaw

PRESIDENT: John D. Hall

Vice President and Director of Marketing:
Nancy K. Jones
Editorial Director: Russell B. Adams, Jr.
Director of Production Services: Robert N. Carr
Production Manager: Prudence G. Harris
Director of Technology: Eileen Bradley
Supervisor of Quality Control: James King

Editorial Operations
Production: Celia Beattie
Library: Louise D. Forstall
Computer Composition: Deborah G. Tait
(Manager), Monika D. Thayer, Janet Barnes
Syring, Lillian Daniels
Interactive Media Specialist: Patti H. Cass

Time-Life Books is a division of Time Life
Incorporated

PRESIDENT AND CEO: John M. Fahey, Jr.

Library of Congress Cataloging in Publication Data
Mafia/by the editors of Time-Life Books.
    p.   cm. — (True crime)
Includes bibliographical references and index.
ISBN 0-7835-0008-4
1. Mafia — History. I. Time-Life Books. II. Series.
HV6441.M332 1993
364.1'06 — dc20   92-42181
                                              CIP
ISBN 0-7835-0009-2 (lib. bdg.)

TRUE CRIME

SERIES EDITOR: Laura Foreman
Administrative Editor: Jane A. Martin
Art Director: Christopher Register
Picture Editors: Jane Jordan, Jane A. Martin

Editorial Staff for *Mafia*
Text Editors: Robert A. Doyle (principal),
Carl Posey
Associate Editors/Research: Susan Arritt, Mark G.
Lazen, Vicki Warren
Assistant Art Director: Brook Mowrey
Senior Copyeditors: Elizabeth Graham (principal),
Colette Stockum
Picture Coordinator: Jennifer Iker
Editorial Assistant: Donna Fountain

Special Contributors: Jyl Cecilia Benson, Katherine
Hackett, Paige Henke, Sheila K. Jordan, Elizabeth
L'Hommedieu King, Patricia A. Paterno, Kathy Wis-
mar (research); George Constable, George Daniels,
Gene Ely, Ellen Galford, Jack McClintock, David
Nevin, Roxie France-Nuriddin, Anthony K. Pordes,
George Russell, Daniel Stashower (text); John
Drummond (design); Mel Ingber (index).

Correspondents: Elisabeth Kraemer-Singh (Bonn);
Christine Hinze (London); Christina Lieberman
(New York); Maria Vincenza Aloisi (Paris); Ann
Natanson (Rome). Valuable assistance was also pro-
vided by Liz Corcoran, Caroline Wood (London);
Elizabeth Brown, Katheryn White (New York); Ann
Wise, Lenora Dodsworth (Rome).

Consultants:
Award-winning journalist Daniele Billitteri is a Palermo native who specialized in crime reporting at the
Giornal di Sicilia before becoming assistant editor of
the newspaper. Mr. Billitteri is also a professor of
publishing technology at journalism schools in Palermo and Urbino. Winner of the prestigious Top Italian Reporter of the Year in 1982 for Mafia-related
articles, Mr. Billitteri has collaborated with several
leading authors of books on the Mafia, among them
Claire Sterling and Pino Arlacchi, and he has helped
prepare Mafia stories for *Time* and *Life* magazines
and *The New York Times.*

Betty B. Bosarge, an expert on the American criminal justice system, has served as a consultant in
that capacity to the International Association of
Chiefs of Police, the National Sheriffs' Association,
the National Institute of Corrections, the International Academy of Security Educators and Trainers,
and numerous other clients. Ms. Bosarge is also a
writer on the subject of criminal justice, the author
of several textbooks on the subject, and the managing editor of the Washington Crime News Services
Newsletters.

Other Publications:
THE WEIGHT WATCHERS SMART CHOICE
    RECIPE COLLECTION
THE AMERICAN INDIANS
THE ART OF WOODWORKING
LOST CIVILIZATIONS
ECHOES OF GLORY
THE NEW FACE OF WAR
HOW THINGS WORK
WINGS OF WAR
CREATIVE EVERYDAY COOKING
COLLECTOR'S LIBRARY OF THE UNKNOWN
CLASSICS OF WORLD WAR II
TIME-LIFE LIBRARY OF CURIOUS AND
    UNUSUAL FACTS
AMERICAN COUNTRY
VOYAGE THROUGH THE UNIVERSE
THE THIRD REICH
THE TIME-LIFE GARDENER'S GUIDE
MYSTERIES OF THE UNKNOWN
TIME FRAME
FIX IT YOURSELF
FITNESS, HEALTH & NUTRITION
SUCCESSFUL PARENTING
HEALTHY HOME COOKING
UNDERSTANDING COMPUTERS
LIBRARY OF NATIONS
THE ENCHANTED WORLD
THE KODAK LIBRARY OF CREATIVE
    PHOTOGRAPHY
GREAT MEALS IN MINUTES
THE CIVIL WAR
PLANET EARTH
COLLECTOR'S LIBRARY OF THE CIVIL WAR
THE EPIC OF FLIGHT
THE GOOD COOK
WORLD WAR II
HOME REPAIR AND IMPROVEMENT
THE OLD WEST

*For information on and a full description of any of
the Time-Life Books series listed above, please call
1-800-621-7026 or write:*
Reader Information
Time-Life Customer Service
P.O. Box C-32068
Richmond, Virginia 23261-2068

This volume is one of a series that examines
the phenomenon of crime. Other books in the
series include:
Serial Killers
Mass Murderers